The Translator of Desir

The Lockert Library of Poetry in Translation

For other titles in the Lockert Library, see the list at the end of this volume.

The Translator of Desires

POEMS BY

MUHYIDDIN IBN 'ARABI

TRANSLATED BY

Michael Sells

PRINCETON UNIVERSITY PRESS

PRINCETON AND OXFORD

Published by Princeton University Press
41 William Street, Princeton, New Jersey 08540
6 Oxford Street, Woodstock, Oxfordshire OX20 1TR

press.princeton.edu

Library of Congress Cataloging-in-Publication Data

Names: Ibn al-ʻArabī, 1165–1240, author. | Sells, Michael Anthony, editor.
Title: The translator of desires / Muhyiddin Ibn ʻArabi ; translated by
Michael Sells.
Other titles: Turjumān al-ashwāq. English
Description: Princeton : Princeton University Press, [2021] | Series: The
Lockert library of poetry in translation | Originally published in
Arabic as Turjumān al-ashwāq.
Identifiers: LCCN 2020036857 (print) | LCCN 2020036858 (ebook) | ISBN
9780691181349 (trade paperback ; acid-free paper) | ISBN 9780691181332
(hardback ; acid-free paper) | ISBN 9780691212548 (epub)
Subjects: LCSH: Sufi poetry, Arabic—Translations into English. | Love
poetry, Arabic—Translations into English. | LCGFT: Poetry.
Classification: LCC PJ7755.I175 T813 2021 (print) | LCC PJ7755.I175
(ebook) | DDC 892.7/134—dc23
LC record available at https://lccn.loc.gov/2020036857
LC ebook record available at https://lccn.loc.gov/2020036858

British Library Cataloging-in-Publication Data is available

Editorial: Anne Savarese and Jenny Tan
Production Editorial: Ellen Foos
Text Design: Pamela Schnitter
Jacket/Cover Design: Pamela Schnitter
Production: Erin Suydam
Publicity: Alyssa Sanford and Amy Stewart
Copyeditor: Daniel Simon

Cover art: (front) Fragments of a carpet with lattice and blossom pattern, ca. 1650.
Made in India or present-day Pakistan, Kashmir, or Lahore. Bequest of Benjamin Altman,
1913 / The Metropolitan Museum of Art. (spine) "A Prince Sitting on a Terrace." Illustration
from Ardashir Album, Mughal, 17th century / Museum of Islamic Art, Doha

The Lockert Library of Poetry in Translation is supported by a bequest from Charles Lacy
Lockert (1999–1974)

This book has been composed in Adobe Text Pro and Minon Pro

Printed on acid-free paper. ∞

Printed in the United States of America

10 9 8 7 6 5 4 3 2 1

To Janet, Ariela, and Maya

CONTENTS

ILLUSTRATIONS

TRANSLATOR'S INTRODUCTION

Muḥyī al-Dīn Ibn ʿArabī tells us that he compiled his famous volume of love poems, *Tarjumān al-ashwāq* ("The Translator of Desires"), in 1214 CE during a visit to the Kaʿba shrine in Mecca.[1]

Born in 1165 to a prosperous and politically connected family in al-Andalus, Ibn ʿArabī benefited from an immersive education in religious, literary, and philosophical studies. At a young age, however, he chose to separate himself from court circles in favor of a life of itinerant learning. For the next two decades, he was constantly on the move through networks of Sufi mystics, religious scholars, and poets, with weeks- or monthslong stays in such Andalusian and North African cities as Seville, Fez, Marrakesh, and Tunis. After two decades of travel, study, and contemplation, he set out for Mecca—only to be marooned in Cairo because of a plague that left the city under quarantine.

After finally reaching Mecca in 1202, he began to experience visions that, by his own account, would inspire much of his vast literary production over the next four decades. It was while circling the Kaʿba that he encountered the mystical youth (young man or boy, *fatā*) who inspired his monumental masterwork, *The Meccan Openings*, which he would compose over the next three decades. On another occasion, his encounter with the Kaʿba, personified, prompted him to compose a series of love letters addressed to the shrine itself, titled *Diadem of Epistles*, in an intricate and elegant rhymed prose (*sajʿ*).[2] And it was at the Kaʿba in 1202 that he encountered a young woman who fiercely critiqued each of the four verses of a love poem he was reciting—an experience that led him to compose sixty more poems during a subsequent stay in Mecca and, eventually, to publish all sixty-one under the title *Tarjumān al-Ashwāq*.

After his first stay in Mecca (from 1202 to 1204), he resumed his peripatetic life. His journeys would now take him through cultural centers within the Islamic East: Mosul, Baghdad, Damascus, Aleppo, and the Anatolian cities of Konya and Malatya (Melitene). These journeys formed elliptical orbits around the Ka'ba, to which he returned time and again. His itinerancy notwithstanding, and despite the lack of formal institutional support, Ibn 'Arabī was prolific, and during the four decades following his first arrival in Mecca he produced dozens of books, treatises, and collections of poetry—the latter composed in a variety of genres and styles.

In the second and third decades of the thirteenth century, Ibn 'Arabī compiled a belletristic work, *Sessions of the Righteous*, into which he placed hundreds of love poems composed by himself and by earlier poets as well as remarks on the occasions during which he recited such verses in the company of other scholars and poets. *Sessions of the Righteous* includes most of the *Tarjumān* but places the poems in different sequences, and within different thematic, hermeneutical, and autobiographical settings.[3]

By the time he settled in Damascus in 1223, Ibn 'Arabī was surrounded by scholars and followers who were reading, editing, and disseminating his works. There he completed the second edition of the *Meccan Openings* as well as his classic work of mystical philosophy, *Ringstones of Wisdom*.[4] During the same period, he produced what is known as his "Great Dīwān," which brought together some 3,500 of his poetic compositions.[5] At the time of his death in 1240 (638 of the Islamic calendar), he was well on the way to being known as *al-shaykh al-akbar* or "the grand master" of Islamic mystical thought.[6]

Ibn ʿArabī's notoriety throughout premodern Islamic civilizations ensured that many of his works—including the *Tarjumān*—would be preserved, disseminated, argued over, and passed on through the centuries. But that same notoriety at times overshadowed the writing itself with its various controversies over—for instance—his alleged monism or pantheism, the attacks on his character and his orthodoxy leveled by the fourteenth-century Damascene preacher and jurist Ibn Taymiyya, and more recent contentions relating to Sufism, colonialism, and modernity.

Ibn ʿArabī himself offered contrasting accounts of the genesis and intent of the *Tarjumān* poems in the course of his own autobiographical and prefatory writings, and those accounts have been passed on by subsequent generations down to the present. We might call that metaliterature "The Tale of the *Tarjumān*," with three interrelated aspects: "The Romance of the *Tarjumān*," "The Trial of the *Tarjumān*," and the "Allegory of the *Tarjumān*."

Tarjumān al-ashwāq

The first word of the title, which can be vocalized as either *Tarjumān* or *Turjumān*, might be rendered as translator, translation, interpreter, interpretation, discloser, disclosure, guide, or guidebook. The word is also closely related to the word for biography, *tarjama*.[7] For whom, we might ask, do these poems translate, and what might they disclose?

Arabic poetry employs more than two dozen words that in the lexicons are rendered as love, desire, passion, or longing. One of those words is *shawq* (plural *ashwāq* [*ash* as in "hush" + *wāq* as in English "walk"]). Ibn ʿArabī's *shawq* is analogous to classical Greek *eros* insofar as it was taken as a fundamental driving force within human life, art, and thought. In relationship to the finite human subject, *shawq* is infinite; and the poet-lover within the poems is presented at once as the subject, victim, champion, and voice of *shawq*-conditioned human existence. The paradoxes of this condition—that love is both disease and cure, for example, or that the lover longs to be near the beloved, even though nearness only intensifies the longing—pervade love lyrics across many traditions. But within the broader context of Arabic poetry and song, and within the *Tarjumān* in particular, these paradoxes play on particularly acute and culturally specific associations.

In pre-Islamic and very early Islamic Arabic poetry of the sixth and seventh centuries CE, erotic themes were primarily expressed in the first movement of the classical Arabic ode (*qaṣīda*), a metrically rigorous, end-rhymed poem that began with the *nasib*, a movement centered on remembrance of a lost beloved. In the tripartite ode common in the pre-Islamic period, the nasib could then lead into a journey-quest and culminate in a galvanizing battle boast, praise of the tribe, or panegyric to a king. Later poets tended to compose bipartite odes consisting largely of nasib and journey or nasib and panegyric.[8]

By the end of the first century of Islam, a freestanding love poem, known as *ghazal*, was emerging. Early Arabian ghazals drew upon and intensified the nasib. The Arabic ghazal tradition could take on various voices, including the tragic mode known as ʿUdhrī (after the Arabian tribe that produced some of its famous poets) and associated most famously with the figures of Majnūn and Laylā. The poet, Qays, goes mad through his love of Laylā, a madness that gives him his nickname of Majnūn Laylā (mad or "jinned" for Laylā). In the legendary biographies of Majnūn, his mad love is both a cause and a result of his inability to be with her, and he ultimately perishes after love has emaciated him. He and other ghazal poet-lovers become "martyrs" to love, and early Sufi writings present them as models for the adepts who perish and, by passing away from themselves, become one with the divine beloved.

The other major style of early ghazal takes on a more urbane voice. In this style or mode, known as ʿUmarite after its most important early master, ʿUmar bin abī Rabiʿa (who died ca. 700), the poet-lover not only mourns the loss of his beloved(s) but also boasts of his amatory adventures or turns his language into a form of flirtation. Yet even as the styles and subgenres of Arabic ghazal continued to evolve, one core nasib motif remained, explicitly or implicitly, at the heart of any love lyric: the poet's encounter with the *aṭlāl*—the ruins or traces of the beloved's abandoned campsite.

The act of *poesis* emerges from the poet's decoding of the *aṭlāl* and his realization that these are not the traces of just any camp, but of the camp struck by the beloved in her journey away from him. With that moment of recognition, the poetic voice surges. Through contagion, other sites and features can take on the power of the *aṭlāl*: the mere mention of one of the stations of the beloved's journey away from the poet; a scent of the Eastwind that carries news of the beloved's location; the sight and scent of the moringa, a desert tree associated with the beauty and grace of the beloved; the verse of an earlier poet in memory of his lost beloved, a verse that might contain a fragment of a verse of a still earlier poet. The contagion extends across space through messengers like the Eastwind and its analogues, and across time through the resonance of a verse or phrase through poems of the past.

By the tenth century CE, court circles in urban centers like Baghdad were compiling collections of ghazal lyrics and the romantic legends associated with the early Arabian poet-lovers and their beloveds, collections that culminated with the *Great Book of Songs*, a massive collection of poetry and romance narratives. The author-compiler, Abū al-Faraj al-Isfahānī (d. 967), provided descriptions of the musical modes employed in the performance of the verses he quoted. Even though his descriptive notation does not allow a modern reconstruction of the modes and melodies indicated, it offers clear indication of the mutual permeation of poetic verses and musical performance in high Abbasid culture.

This urban literature of ghazal poetry, song, and Bedouin romance emerged parallel with the development of a variety of odes and ghazals in which the ruins of a great city, palace, or civilization took the place of the Bedouin campsite as the site and source of longing (see appendix 4 for an example).[9] The various voices of love (tragic, triumphant, sorrowful, provocative, pious, and ribald in turn) continued to inflect the ghazal tradition. A stanzaic form known as the garland poem (*muwashshaḥa*), which flourished especially in the eleventh to the thirteenth centuries, offered yet another mold for ghazal.[10] By the time of Ibn ʿArabī, a Persian ghazal tradition was also ascendant, and later epochs would see the emergence of ghazal traditions in Ottoman, Urdu, Punjabi, and other languages. Each of these traditions shared major themes of the Arabic ghazal, but they were also bound more specifically to a particular poetic genre.[11]

The poetic imaginary embraced a correspondence between love and religion. Love poetry had its own version of *ḥalāl* and *ḥarām* (allowable and prohibited, in the vocabulary of religious observance) and its own *sunna* and *sharīʿa* (sacred path and law, in the same). Love and fate served as judges and muftis (authors of legal religious opinions). The poets also performed a theology of love: just as the divine reality in its infinite depth exceeds all naming and description, so does the beloved or love itself.

No aspect of religious teachings and practice is more central to the *Tarjumān* than the hajj pilgrimage, which for those who are able to perform it marks the culmination of devotional life. At the center of the hajj experience are three rituals that carry the pilgrim back in time to the origins of Islam and of the world itself and forward to meeting the creator on the day of judgment. Pilgrims ritually circle the Ka'ba shrine that, according to Islamic tradition, was constructed by Abraham. At 'Arafa, a plain and adjacent mount about twelve miles from Mecca from which the prophet Muḥammad delivered his farewell address, pilgrims stand throughout the day and chant the words "here I am for you" that all souls will recite as they meet their creator. At Minā, pilgrims cast pebbles at three stone pillars and, on the holiest day of the Muslim year, reenact Abraham's sacrifice.[12] The *Tarjumān* returns time and again to these rites as it articulates the experiential dimensions of *shawq*. At the same time, it mixes the stations of the hajj and the stations of the beloved's journey, tying together the poetic and religious solemnities of place, and establishing an implicit homology between the poet's wandering from site to site in pursuit of the beloved and a pilgrim's station-by-station movement during the pilgrimage.

Just as ritual reenactment can collapse time, bringing the pilgrim back to the origins of the faith and bringing those sacred origins into the present, so too does the practice of *ḥadīth* transmission, which becomes a core element within the *Tarjumān*'s poetics. A hadith consists of a report of the words or actions of the prophet Muḥammad or his companions, along with the transmission genealogy (*isnād*): the chain of transmitters who passed the report, generation to generation, from the birth of Islam down to the time of the final individual in the chain. Islamic culture in the thirteenth century was both literate and oral, and hadith transmission linked the two modes. Although the written hadith compilations were considered authoritative by most Sunni Muslims, the pious still traveled widely to hear oral hadiths from a living transmitter who himself had heard them orally from a predecessor back to the time of Muḥammad. Such a practice emphasized the vast temporal distance between the Prophet and the present but also, through nested levels of embedded quotation, collapsed it: at the moment of hearing a hadith transmitted, the hearer was hearing the words of the Prophet as if they were in a certain sense being spoken live. Early on, the *ḥadīth-isnād* model was appropriated by other literary (and not necessarily religious) genres. Poetry anthologists, historians, and storytellers would provide *isnād*s for the verses and stories they recounted. In the *Tarjumān*, the poet presents the words of the beloved or her companions as transmitted through a chain of natural phenomena or interior emotive states stretching back to the primordial moments of early Islam, or back further to the garden of Eden, or even to before the creation of the world.

Of the lyric mode of expression, literary theorist Northrop Frye wrote that the poet normally pretends to be talking to himself or to someone else: "a spirit of Nature, a muse, a personal friend, a lover, a god, a personified abstraction or a natural object."[13] In the case of the *Tarjumān*, we might add to that list the critic or scold (*al-ʿādhil*) and note that in defending himself against the critic, the poet is also addressing himself, the critic within. Here Ibn ʿArabī animates the conventional image of the scold in medieval Arabic poetry and brings us into its heart. The poems of the *Tarjumān* destabilize the notion of a single addressee, shifting from the beloved, to muse, to the personification of beauty, to friend, to critic, to the interiorized critic within the poet, to an element of nature, to all lovers everywhere, and through all of the above in either singular or plural, masculine or feminine. Both the Qur'an and classical Arabic poetry (each in its own distinct way) contain radical shifts in voice, constantly engaging the reader in adjusting to apostrophic changes in addresser and addressee. Indeed, classical Arabic rhetoricians considered this feature, called *iltifāt* (turning, shifting, wrapping), a distinctive and audacious aspect of Arabic expression. In the *Tarjumān*, the persona of the poet-lover also shifts. It presents itself conventionally as male but may speak in the first-person singular (I) or plural (we), even as it speaks *to* various personae, including itself (within self-address), or *of* various personae (including itself).

Take, for example, the first verses of the *Tarjumān* where the poet ponders where "they are," what "they know," and whether "they are safe." Readers familiar with the Arabic tradition will easily infer that the verse evokes the beloved and the other women of her tribe traveling away from the poet, but will also understand that the plural serves as a metonym for the beloved. At the same time, an echo can be heard of the same question as addressed by poets of other beloveds and, more widely, within the world of *shawq* conjured by the poet, by other past and present star-crossed lovers.

In other poems the poet shifts from the singular to the plural in referring to himself. From early in the tradition, the singular/plural shifting was more than a movement between two synonyms. The "we" assumes a specific tonality that contrasts with the "I," often taking on the possibility of speaking as lovers generally or the possibility of mutuality between lover and beloved ("we" were in love, "we" were separated against our will), though the poet's effort to express or create such mutuality can be ironized or undermined by the poem itself. The "we" can also include the wider group of which the poet was, and poetically purports to still be, a part: family, tribe, nation, and civilization—that is, the group to which the poet once belonged, longs to still belong to, and poetically strives to belong to again.[14] Similarly, the stations of the beloved in her journey away from the poet can spur longing for those sites of earlier happiness, for a homeland, a sense of belonging, and a lost youth.

The beloved can be male or female, pubescent or postpubescent, married or unmarried, slave or free, divine or human.

In the *Tarjumān*, the beloved is primarily imagined as female, but there are significant appearances of the beloved as male as well, and sometimes the gender switch can take place within a single poem. The *Tarjumān* consists of ever-repeated acts of reenchantment as the beloved is brought back to the present and the withered world is revived. But the poems are also fevered with the knowledge that such a rebirth can only last an instant and must be constantly repeated.

The Tale of the *Tarjumān*

In what most scholars believe to be his first preface to the *Tarjumān*, Ibn ʿArabī tells us that the poems were inspired by a young woman named Niẓām, who was the daughter and niece, respectively, of two Persian scholars, a brother and sister, who had settled in Mecca. I've rendered the word *niẓām*—which in Arabic means "ordered arrangement"—as "harmony" to reflect the wordplay within the poem and the ambiguity between its possible meanings as a common noun or a female name. Niẓām's reputed role in the inspiration of Ibn ʿArabī's poetry has drawn comparisons to the role of Beatrice in Dante's poetry and thought.[15]

The poems of the *Tarjumān* do indeed contain erotic dialectic between the Arab poet-lover persona, a "son of Yemen" as he refers to himself, and a beloved who represents for him the quintessential non-Arab (*ʿajamī*) civilization of Persia. In addition to the personal affection Ibn ʿArabī may have had for Niẓām, the *Tarjumān*'s Arabic-Persian dynamic may reflect the wider cultural symbiosis within thirteenth-century Islamic civilization. Although Ibn ʿArabī never acknowledges knowing Persian or listening to Persian poetry, he was a man of profound linguistic gifts, someone who had

Persian poets and scholars among his companions and who spent considerable time in Anatolia where Persian flourished as an administrative and literary language. He would not have been impervious to contemporary developments in Persian ghazal and Persian-language Sufi literature.

In his other preface, Ibn 'Arabī relates that while he was circumambulating the temple of the Ka'ba, some poetry came to his mind. He left the paved central area around the Ka'ba to avoid disturbing other pilgrims and recited the verses on the sandy periphery. Although they have been included as poem 1 in the *Tarjumān,* Ibn 'Arabī does not claim authorship of them, leaving their author indeterminate.

No sooner had he begun reciting, Ibn 'Arabī tells us, than he felt a jolt between his shoulders "from a hand softer than undyed silk." When he turned around he found there before him a maiden (*jāriya*, an unmarried woman, usually a young female slave or freed slave). He tells us that she was from among the Rūm, meaning that she was from areas of Anatolia, which were or had been under the control of the Byzantine Roman Empire. At the time, the word could designate Christians specifically or (as was the case with the poet Jalāl al-Dīn Rūmī who settled in Anatolia in the early thirteenth century) Muslims living in the former Christian territory. The *jāriya* fiercely criticizes each of the four verses, refuting each part of them and rebuking Ibn 'Arabī for reciting verses unbecoming of a personage of his stature. When Ibn 'Arabī asks her name, she responds that he could call her by the nickname Qurrat al-'Ayn, an endearment that means "comfort for the eye."

Interpreters and translators have commonly viewed Qurrat al-'Ayn as being identical with Niẓām. Indeed, Ibn 'Arabī's suggestion at the end of his Qurrat al-'Ayn account that he would come to know the young woman well seems to support that reading, as does the similarity in language in his homages to the young woman's beauty, artistry, and wisdom in both the Niẓām and Qurrat al-ʿAyn prefaces. However, Ibn ʿArabī defines Niẓām emphatically as being of the finest Persian heritage but describes Qurrat al-ʿAyn as of Christian or Muslim Anatolian background. Ibn ʿArabī's fascination with Christian cultic practices and theology runs throughout his writings, and allusions to Christian ritual and Trinitarian debate can be found in several poems of the *Tarjumān*, allusions that are expanded upon in his commentary. Qurrat al-ʿAyn, though a *jāriya* of possible Christian background, might well have converted to Islam, and thus it would not be surprising to find her visiting the Kaʿba.[16]

Was Niẓām a historical personage either as a cherished acquaintance or wife of the poet, or was she a personification of beauty? She may have been both. The social detail of her family of illustrious scholars was quite specific, and had Ibn ʿArabī invented the story, it would have been easily refuted by his contemporaries. Yet the depiction of her in the preface and the allusions to a Niẓām figure in the poems place her within a visionary imaginary as beauty, eloquence, and grace par excellence. Similarly, was Qurrat al-ʿAyn a historical personage, and if so, was she Niẓām? Was she a visionary apparition? Or was she a development of a long literary history of *jāriya*-savants at the Kaʿba, a literary motif that makes a strong appearance in Ibn ʿArabī's own *Sessions of the Righteous*?[17] These choices may not be mutually exclusive. The romance of the *Tarjumān* is powerfully told, and because Ibn ʿArabī's writings about the *Tarjumān* are, like everything he wrote, brilliantly associative, elusive, and tied into everything else he has written, these questions are not likely to be resolved at the level of historical biography, any more than the accounts of Qays and Laylā and other famous lovers and poets gathered in the *Great Book of Songs* are amenable to distinctions between historicity and legend. However, while the compiler of the *Great Book of Songs* wove together traditions regarding the poets and lovers of the past to form romances, in the case of the *Tarjumān*, Ibn al-ʿArabī served as his own romancier.[18]

No sooner had it begun to circulate than the *Tarjumān* was confronted with controversy. A jurist in Aleppo had rebuked Ibn ʿArabī's claim made in the Niẓām preface that the erotic homages to her reflected a realm of spiritual love and refined and intimate mystical knowledge or *connaissance* (*maʿrifa*). The critic suggested that Ibn ʿArabī, who was known as a man of religion, was attempting to hide the true nature of the poems behind an allegorical façade. Two of Ibn ʿArabī's companions appealed to Ibn ʿArabī to respond to the criticism, and he did so in the form of a short, versified apologia, followed by a lengthy verse-by-verse commentary on the poems that he titled *Priceless Treasures*.[19] An assembly of religious and literary notables convened to adjudicate the controversy over the poems, during which Ibn ʿAdīm (d. 1262)—another jurist, who would become one of the most important historical chroniclers of medieval Syria—recited a large part of the commentary in the presence of both the poet and his critic. Ibn ʿArabī adds that after the event concluded, the critic declared himself persuaded that the poems were indeed allegorical expressions for the Sufi's love for and journey toward the divine beloved.[20]

Priceless Treasures inaugurated a new tradition of extensive mystical commentaries on Arabic love poetry. That tradition bears similarities to Song of Songs commentaries in medieval Judaism and Christianity, and remarkable structural similarities to the Spanish poet John of the Cross's commentary on his erotic poem "Canticle of the Soul," which was modeled on the biblical Song of Songs (although there is little chance that John would have had access to

Ibn ʿArabī's work in either the original or translation).[21] Yet there is a twist, as there always seems to be in Ibn ʿArabī's accounts of the *Tarjumān*. While the Aleppan jurist criticized Ibn ʿArabī for disavowing the erotic nature of his poems, the maiden at the Kaʿba rebuked the first poem for not being extravagant enough in its expression of desire, that is, for not culminating in the complete passing away of the poet-lover in love for the beloved.

Ibn ʿArabī may be best known for his mystical philosophy, which took shape around the notion of *waḥdat al-wujūd* ("the unity of existence"), although he nowhere employed that phrase. The ontological and metaphysical aspects of such thought are not addressed explicitly in the *Tarjumān*. However, several of the poems do contain intimations of the Sufi notion of "mystical union." In Sufi thought, God cannot be known as an object: the infinite existence of the divine reality exceeds the knower-known duality and cannot be described or even referenced in human language. The goal of the religious and mystical path is the annihilation or passing away (*fanāʾ*) of the ego-self in union with the divine beloved. For Ibn ʿArabī, the key sacred source expounding such a union comes in the form of a "divine saying" (a hadith that, instead of reporting words or actions *of* Muḥammad, reports words of God addressed *to* Muḥammad). In this saying, the divine speaker states that nothing is dearer to him than his servant drawing near through devotions above and beyond those required of the believer. When the servant draws near, "I [the divine speaker] am the hearing with which he hears, the seeing with which he sees, the hands with which he holds, and the feet with which he walks."[22]

In a famous opening passage from *Ringstones of Wisdom,* Ibn ʿArabī presents the human being in its archetypal state, represented by the prelapsarian Adam, as the "polishing of the mirror" that is the world. Insofar as that mirror is polished, it reflects the image of

God, and in that image the divine and the human are one. For the human being in space and time, such polishing occurs at the moment of *fanā'*, when a person passes away from the ego-self. At that point the divine persona manifests itself in the polished mirror of the heart. Because God or "the Real" is infinite, beyond space and time, its manifestation in space and time lasts only for a moment. In every new moment the manifestation changes. Whoever attempts to hold onto the image locks himself into the dead husk of that manifestation and precludes himself from receiving new manifestations of the divine. The goal is to let go of the previous image in order to be receptive to the divine appearance the next moment within the polished mirror of the heart. A bittersweet dynamism haunts the *Tarjumān*: the beloved(s) or personified embodiments of beauty can never be possessed. The beloved appears to the poet and in her apparition he passes away, only to find himself cast back into the world of time and loss.[23]

* * *

Was Ibn ʿArabī a Sufi poet? He was certainly a contemplative mystic (*muʿtabir*, "one who observes and ponders") and Sufi. He also composed a large number of Sufi poems, that is, poems that are imbued with the vocabulary of Sufi psychology, cosmology, and metaphysics. Yet the poems of the *Tarjumān* do not fit neatly into that category. Had Ibn ʿArabī not been known as their author, they might not have been classified as Sufi poems, although they would have been appreciated by Sufis, who were steeped in the tradition of ghazal and nasib. Many cherished poems within the Islamic tradition—including the *Tarjumān* as well as poems by Ibn ʿArabī's younger contemporaries, al-Fāriḍ and al-Shushtarī, not to mention a treasury of Persian, Ottoman, and Urdu ghazals—tread a fine line between sacred and profane.[24] That phenomenon makes perfect sense from the perspective of Ibn ʿArabī's conception of *shawq*. *Shawq*, eros, is infinite. It cannot be confined into mutually exclusive categories of human and divine. At the most basic level, the *shawq* at the heart of pre-Islamic and Islamic love poetry may carry within it an inherently mystical dimension. In *shawq*, the normal rules of logic are suspended, and the human being opens onto the unlimited, a force that cannot be contained in space or time. Like the divine reality, *shawq* kills and brings to life, exists without and within, is both beyond the world and deep in the heart of the lover.

Much of the reception to the *Tarjumān* has been driven by Ibn ʿArabī's commentary, which is focused on tying the poetry to Sufi psychology and cosmology and which distracts attention from the poems as poetry.[25] Yet the mystical thought touched upon in the commentary emerged in fully developed form decades later with such works as the *Meccan Openings* and *Ringstones of Wisdom*. It may be more accurate to view that poetry as foreshadowing the later teachings. Far from being versified philosophy or attractive illustrations of his philosophical ideas arrived at independently, the poems of the *Tarjumān* were in a very real sense generative of Ibn ʿArabī's vision of existence as a *shawq*-driven process born of the tension between a creator's longing to create and the paradoxical longing of the nonexistent creature to be and, once existent, to return to its source.

Translating the *Tarjumān*

In 1911 the British scholar Reynold Nicholson published what was both the first translation of the *Tarjumān* as well as the first printed edition of it; a pioneering work that has been read and appreciated over the decades. The more recent history of *Tarjumān* translations began with the 1977 Spanish rendition of Vicente Cantarino, and since that time the *Tarjumān* has received generous attention from Spanish, French, and German translators. (An account and appreciation of this translation history is found in appendix 7.) This volume constitutes the first edition and first complete English translation of the *Tarjumān* since Nicholson.

To translate classical Arabic poetry entails finding a balance between conservation and compensation. Each poem of the *Tarjumān*, as is the case with most classical Arabic poetry, follows one of about a dozen standard meters, and the poetry's pulse is quickened by the tension between the meter and the syntax.[26] When the syntactical pause falls in the middle of a metrical foot, it creates a tension; when it falls at the end of a foot it provides a release. Arabic meters, like those of classical Greek and Latin, are quantitative instead of accentual. (A syllable is long if it includes a long vowel or a short vowel followed by two consonants.) Arabic meters can employ metrical feet of two, three, four, or five syllables.[27] To offer one example, I present below the opening verse of poem 11 from the *Tarjumān*. It is in the meter known as *ṭawīl,* which is based on alternating three- and four-syllable feet. The three-syllable foot can follow one of two patterns: ˘¯¯ or ˘¯˘. The four-syllable foot can also follow one of two patterns: ˘¯¯¯ or ˘¯˘¯; and as with other meters, a line can end with a full foot or a shortened (catalectic) one.

The first verse of poem 11 reads as follows in my translation:

Gentle now, doves
  of the sprigberry and
moringa, don't add your
  sighs to my heart-ache

Here below is a scansion, transliteration, and word-by-word gloss of the verse:

˘ - -/ ˘ - - -/ ˘- ˘/˘ - - -

alā yā ḥamāmāti l-arākati *wa l-bānī*

oh! O doves of the sprigberry and moringa

˘ - -/ ˘- ˘ -/ ˘ - -/ ˘ - --

taraffaqna lā tuḍiʿfna bi-sh-shajwi *ashjānī*

be gentle don't increase by your lament my sorrows

In addition, the classical Arabic poem, however long, follows a single end rhyme from beginning to end, another feature that is not amenable to modern English poetry. Equally impervious to direct translation is *jinās*, the combination of etymological play, punning, and repetitions of consonants that marked what was called the "new style" of poetry in ninth-century Baghdad and that recurs in several of the *Tarjumān* poems.[28]

Classical Arabic poetics is also based on the independent line of verse; enjambment is rare, and end rhymes provide a strong sense of closure to each verse. That verse-by-verse independence engages the reader in bridging the semantic and rhetorical gap between verses, a gap intensified by the *Tarjumān*'s frequent if not incessant apostrophic turning. I employ punctuation sparingly to preserve this critical aspect of Ibn ʿArabī's poetic voice. I have eschewed end-stops altogether, with line breaks, capitalization, and spacing serving as guides where needed.

I have used stanzas of two, three, or four lines, depending on the poem, to correspond to an Arabic verse. I have numbered the Arabic verses and their parallel English stanzas at intervals of 5, 10, 15, 20, 25, and 30. On rare occasions I have found it necessary to condense the translation of two Arabic verses into one stanza or to expand the translation of one verse into two stanzas. In those cases the design of the facing-page text has been adjusted to make these adjustments transparent. The verse numbers in the English correspond to their numbered Arabic counterparts in those cases as well, in order to clarify the relationship between the two pages.

The poems of the *Tarjumān* redound with place-names and the names of various trees, bushes, and herbs that have no direct equivalent in anglophone lands. Each specific place and plant is embedded in a web of literary, cultural, and religious associations that reflect topography and botany but extend them mythopoetically. For the Bedouin, or for the pilgrim traveling through the arid regions of central and northern Arabia, the herbs, shrubs, flowers, and trees they encountered took on a sensual impact that those of us from moderate climes can scarcely imagine.[29] To approach an oasis, even an oasis consisting of little more than a few trees and shrubs, is to be overcome with the intense fragrance of wet earth and of the flora that grow there. I have resisted simplifying matters by removing the specific plant names, a simplification that would strip the poetry of a core element. However, in order to fit those names naturally within the English cadence of the translation, I employ an adapted and flexible transliteration that allows the Arabic words to fit within an English accentual rhythm and acoustics, without making the name in question unrecognizable to Arabic speakers. In some cases, I translate place-names on the basis of their root meanings (Sand Hill), and plant names where there is an appropriate English equivalent (tamarisk, lote, and artemisia).

A similar rationale guides the approach to prophets mentioned in the Qur'an, many of whom have biblical analogues. I employ the Arabic, Qur'anic names rather than the common English versions of the biblical names. Mūsā rather than Moses, Sulaymān rather than Solomon, 'Īsā rather than Jesus, and Idrīs, the Qur'anic prophet who was associated with the biblical Enoch by Islamic tradition. Preserving the Arabic allows those names to fit into a translation that includes many names of Arabic lovers and beloveds as well (such as Qays, Laylā, Mayya, and Ghaylān), and, in the natural flow of the verse, it gives readers a palpable sense of the power these words hold for readers, or listeners, in Arabic. It also serves to mark the distinctiveness of Qur'anic prophetic figures vis-à-vis their biblical counterparts. While the Qur'anic and biblical accounts can overlap in substance, they can also diverge, sometimes starkly. The Qur'anic 'Īsā, like the biblical Jesus, is the messiah (*masīḥ*) and, according to hadith accounts, will return at the end of times. Like his biblical counterpart, he was born of a virgin mother and raised the dead to life. In contrast to his biblical counterpart, however, he is not considered the Son of God.

* * *

In a short introductory remark to a poem that he presents in *Sessions of the Righteous*, Ibn 'Arabī provides a key to his own understanding of himself as a translator of desires. Eros (*shawq*, *ashwāq*) comes in two forms or "languages": longing for what is in the past, or distant; and longing for what is near, or at hand, or for what one already has, which Ibn 'Arabī calls *ishtiyāq*. The introduction presents the poem as, in fact, authored by the fully personified Ashwāq: "Among the poems that the Ashwāq composed (*naẓamat*) in the language of *ishtiyāq* are what I said regarding Niẓām. . . ."[30] Niẓām emerges here not only as the subject of the poem that follows but as the very act of composing it. In theological terms, she transcends the poem that is about her, but she is also immanent within it. As a muse, Niẓām is not only the beloved who inspires the poet's verses but the creative spark within them.

Meaning in *Tarjumān al-ashwāq* is in constant movement—like beings, like the longings that "come upon" us as voices, apparitions, and emotions; like the beloved in her journey from station to station; like the mystic's heart being transformed each moment; like the ever-changing manifestations of the beloved in the mirror of a human heart. To be is to be moved from site to site, from word to word, from self to self, ever lost and ever regained—always in translation. Poet, lover, and beauty itself are in a state of constant bewilderment, which forms the subject of the first poem of the *Tarjumān*, recurs throughout it, and culminates in the final poem of the collection.

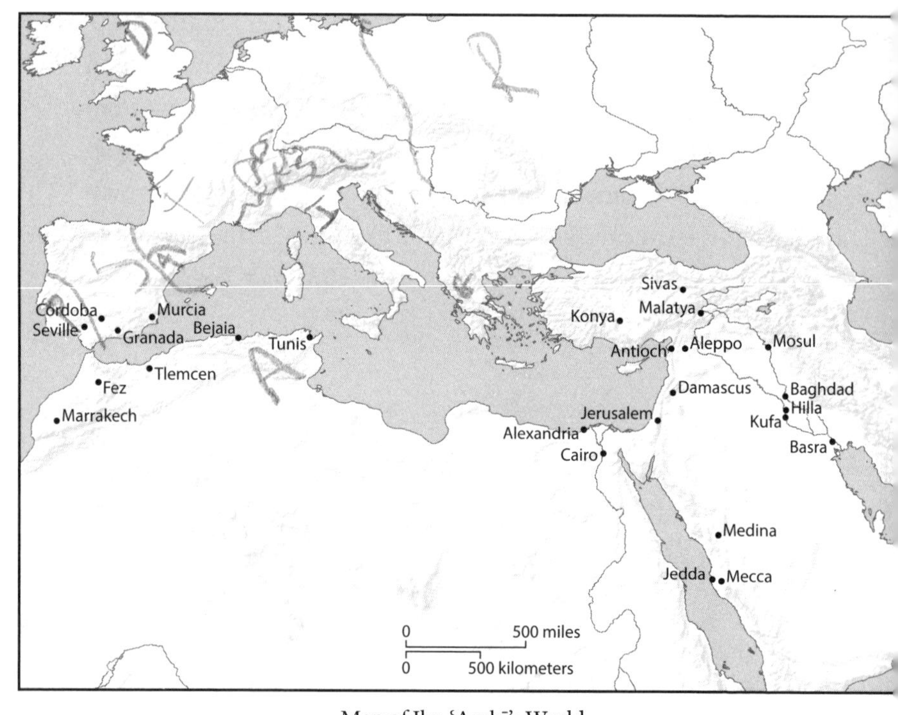

Map of Ibn ʿArabī's World

ACKNOWLEDGMENTS

My deepest gratitude to the many who have contributed their voices, insight, and encouragement to this project over the years.

And to Wayel Azmeh, along with Sara Aziz, Clay Lemar, Nick Lorenz, and Hilmi Okur, who offered invaluable assistance with the collation of manuscripts for this Arabic edition. To Izzet Coban for his proofreading of the penultimate draft of the Arabic edition. To Wayel again and Ahmad Arafat for their valuable perspectives on key passages from *Dīwān al-Maʿārif* and *Sessions of the Righteous*.

To the Muhyiddin Ibn Arabi Society, which has established an international forum, a journal, annual symposia, a digital manuscript collection, and library, all devoted to Ibn ʿArabī's writings and heritage. To society members and organizers, including Pablo Beneito, Aaron Cass, Grenville Collins, Stephen Hirtenstein, David Hornsby, Cecilia Twinch, Richard Twinch, Jane Carroll, Jane Clark, Bob Towns, Caroline Notcutt, Martin Notcutt, Maren Gleason, Johnny Mercer, Christopher Ryan O'Hawick, Frances Ryan, Alison Yiangou, and Nick Yiangou, for arranging and hosting the society's symposia; and to Jane Clark for helping me with access to the *Tarjumān* manuscripts consulted for this edition.

To *La Corónica*, *Poetry*, CDL Press, Gorgias Press, the *Journal of Arabic Literature*, and the *Journal of the Muhyiddin Ibn Arabi Society* for publishing earlier versions of some of my *Tarjumān* translations; with special appreciation to Stephen Hirtenstein and

Michael Tiernan at the *Journal of the Muhyiddin Ibn Arabi Society*, to Simone Fattal at Post-Apollo Press, and to Peter Cole at Ibis Editions.

To Etel Adnan, Erin Atwell, William Chittick, Francesca Chubb-Confer, Ahmed Ghani, Elizabeth Kendick, Rachel Krauser, Susan Lee, Lauren Osborne, Jawad Qureshi, Elizabeth Sartell, John Seybold, Jaroslav Stetkevych, Suzanne Pinckney Stetkevych, Bernard McGinn, James Morris, Louay Safi, Ruth Ost, Fazlur Rahman, and Nasrin Qadr. To Lourdes María Alvarez, Walter Feldman, Seemi Bushra Ghazi, Emil Homerin, Lenny Lewison, Paul Losensky, and Scott Kugle for our times spent immersed in the translations of Islamicate love poetry. To my students at Haverford College and the University of Chicago, whose questions, insights, and engagement have been a continual source of inspiration. To dear friends in Morocco, Tunisia, and Syria who offered me their hospitality, wit, wisdom, and passion for poetry over many stays and visits. Special appreciation to Lori Holland for her design of the Arabic text and the facing-page Arabic-English alignment.

Most immediately, and immeasurably, to Peter Cole, Richard Sieburth, and Rosanna Warren for the care, graciousness, sensitivity, and rigor of their readings and comments on successive drafts of the translation; and to Peter again for his meticulous readings of the entire manuscript.

Chicago
May 5, 2020

NOTE ON ARABIC NAMES

In order to facilitate focus and flow, Arabic terms and names within the translation in this volume follow a modified and flexible transliteration system. Outside of the translation, the standardized transliteration protocol is employed. In the glossary, both the poetically modified and the standard transliteration are provided.

The following signs are employed in the translation:

* An acute accent indicates the stress accent of a syllable, as in Khawárnaq, the name of an ancient monument in the area between Arabia and Iraq.
* The vocable *â* takes a stress accent within the English rendition of the poetry and is pronounced like the "a" in "llama"; as in Râma, the name of a relay station in Arabia associated by Arabic poets with the lost beloved.
* The vocable *ā* takes a stress accent within the English rendition of the poetry and is pronounced like the "a" in "badger"; as in Hājir, a relay station on the pilgrimage route from Iraq to Medina and Mecca.
* The vocable *ū* takes a stress accent within the English rendition of the poetry and is pronounced like the "oo" in "mood"; as with Zarūd, a way station south of the Nefūd desert in north-central Arabia.
* The vocable *ī* takes a stress accent within the English rendition of the poetry and is pronounced like the "ee" in

"free"; as with Hadītha, a city on the Euphrates River in Iraq.

* The markers ' for the letter *'ayn* and ' for the letter *hamza* indicate two sounds that to the non-Arabic speaker are indistinguishable and can best be thought of a short catch in the breath, as in Shi'ite and Qur'an. For Arabic speakers the *'ayn* is a deep guttural and the *hamza* a glottal stop.

The Translator of Desires

1

لَيْتَ شِعْرِي هَلْ دَرَوْا
أَيَّ قَلْبٍ مَلَكُوا

وَفُؤَادِي لَوْ دَرَى
أَيَّ شِعْبٍ سَلَكُوا

أَتُرَاهُمْ سَلِمُوا
أَمْ تُرَاهُمْ هَلَكُوا

حَارَ أَرْبَابُ ٱلْهَوَى
فِي ٱلْهَوَى وَٱرْتَبَكُوا

Bewildered

I wish I knew if they knew
    whose heart they've taken

Or my heart knew which
    high-ridge track they follow

Do you see them safe
    or perishing?

The lords of love are in love
    ensnared, bewildered

2

مَا رَحَّلُوا يَوْمَ بَانُوا ٱلْبُزَّلَ ٱلْعِيسَا
إِلَّا وَقَدْ حَمَلُوا فِيها ٱلطَّوَاوِيسَا

مِنْ كُلِّ فَاتِكَةِ ٱلْأَلْحَاظِ مَالِكَةٍ
تَخَالُهَا فَوْقَ عَرْشِ ٱلدُّرِّ بِلْقِيسَا

إِذَا تَمَشَّتْ عَلَى صَرْحِ ٱلزُّجَاجِ تَرَى
شَمْسًا عَلَى فَلَكٍ فِي حِجْرِ إِدْرِيسَا

يُحْيِي إِذَا قَتَلَتْ بِٱللَّحْظِ مَنْطِقُهَا
كَأَنَّهَا عِنْدَمَا تُحْيِي بِهِ عِيسَى

تَوْرَاتُهَا لَوْحُ سَاقَيْهَا سَنًا وَأَنَا [5]
أَتْلُو وَأَدْرُسُهَا كَأَنَّنِي مُوسَى

Release

They led the red-roans
    away the day
of departure, with peacocks
    high in howdahs

Who take possession
    with glances that kill
like Bilqīs of Sheba
    on her throne of pearl

She crosses the polished
    glass and you see
the sun circling
    in Idrīs's sphere

What her glance kills
    her speech revives,
bringing the dead
    to life, like ʿĪsā

Like Torah's tablets [5]
    her legs in splendor
I follow, learn
    and recite like Mūsā

أُسْقُفَّةٌ مِنْ بَنَاتِ ٱلرُّومِ عَاطِلَةٌ
تَرَى عَلَيْهَا مِنَ ٱلْأَنْوَارِ نَامُوسَا

وَحْشِيَّةٌ مَا بِهَا أُنْسٌ قَدِ ٱتَّخَذَتْ
فِي بَيْتِ خَلْوَتِهَا لِلذِّكْرِ نَاوُوسَا

قَدْ أَعْجَزَتْ كُلَّ عَلَّامٍ بِمِلَّتِنَا
وَدَاوُدِيًّا وَحَبْرًا ثُمَّ قِسِّيسَا

إِنْ أَوْمَأَتْ تَطْلُبُ ٱلْإِنْجِيلَ تَحْسَبُنَا
أَقِسَّةً أَوْ بَطَارِيقًا شَمَامِيسَا

[10] نَادَيْتُ إِذْ رَحَّلَتْ لِلْبَيْنِ نَاقَتَهَا
يَا حَادِيَ ٱلْعِيسِ لَا تَحْدُو بِهَا ٱلْعِيسَا

عَبَّيْتُ أَجْنَادَ صَبْرِي يَوْمَ بَيْنِهِمُ
عَلَى ٱلطَّرِيقِ كَرَادِيسًا كَرَادِيسَا

A bishop, she is,
    Byzantium's child
bathed in the light
    of the Holy Ghost

Wild, lone,
    she takes a tomb
as her retreat
    to remember and pray

She has baffled
    all our sages
as well as psalmists,
    rabbis and priests

Were she to beckon
    toward the gospel
you'd see us as vicars,
    deacons or priests

Driver, I cried, [10]
    as she saddled to leave,
don't carry her
    away in your train!

The day she left me
    I set loose squadrons
along the path,
    armies of patience

سَأَلْتُ إِذْ بَلَغَتْ نَفْسِي تَرَاقِيَهَا
ذَاكَ ٱلْجَمَالَ وَذَاكَ ٱللُّطْفَ تَنْفِيسَا

فَأَسْلَمَتْ وَوَقَانَا ٱللَّهُ شِرَّتَهَا
وَزَحْزَحَ ٱلْمَلِكُ ٱلْمَنْصُورُ إِبْلِيسَا

With soul in throat

    slipping away

I implored that gracious

    beauty for release

She yielded   God

    spared us her fury

May salvation's king

    steal Iblīs away

3

خَلِيلَيَّ عُوجَا بِٱلْكَثِيبِ وَعَرِّجَا
عَلَى لَعْلَعٍ وَٱطْلُبْ مِيَاهَ يَلَمْلَمِ

فَإِنَّ بِهَا مَنْ قَدْ عَلِمْتَ وَمَنْ هُمُ
صِيَامِي وَحَجِّي وَٱعْتِمَارِي وَمَوْسِمِي

فَلَا أَنْسَ يَوْمًا بِٱلْمُحَصَّبِ مِنْ مِنًى
وَبِٱلْمَنْحَرِ ٱلْأَعْلَى أُمُورًا وَزَمْزَمِي

مُحَصَّبُهُمْ قَلْبِي لِرَمْيِ جِمَارِهِمْ
وَمَنْحَرُهُمْ نَفْسِي وَمَشْرَبُهُمْ دَمِي

[5] فَيَا حَادِيَ ٱلْأَجْمَالِ إِنْ جِئْتَ حَاجِرًا
فَقِفْ بِٱلْمَطَايَا سَاعَةً ثُمَّ سَلِّمِ

The Offering

Turn at al-Kathīb,
    friends, then pass
by Lá'la'i, in search
    of Yalámlam's waters

There you'll find
    those you'd known
My hajj is for them,
    my fast and feast

I'll never forget
    Muhássab near Mína,
the field of sacrifice,
    or Zámzam's spring

As if they cast
    live coals from my heart,
offered my soul,
    drank my blood!

When you come to Hājir, [5]
    driver, halt
the camels there,
    shout forth a greeting

وَنَادِ ٱلْقِبَابَ ٱلْحُمْرَ مِنْ جَانِبِ ٱلْحِمَى
تَحِيَّةَ مُشْتَاقٍ إِلَيْكُمْ مُتَيَّمِ

فَإِنْ سَلَّمُوا فَٱهْدِ ٱلسَّلامَ مَعَ ٱلصَّبَا
وَإِنْ سَكَتُوا فَٱرْحَلْ بِهَا وَتَقَدَّمِ

إِلَى نَهْرِ عِيسَى حَيْثُ حَلَّتْ رِكَابُهُمْ
وَحَيْثُ ٱلْخِيَامُ ٱلْبِيضُ مِنْ جَانِبِ ٱلْفَمِ

وَنَادِ بِدَعْدٍ وَٱلرَّبَابِ وَزَيْنَبٍ
وَهِنْدٍ وَلُبْنَى ثُمَّ سَلْمَى وَزَمْزَمِ

وَسَلْهُنَّ هَلْ بِٱلْحَلْبَةِ ٱلْغَادَةُ ٱلَّتِي [10]
تُرِيكَ سَنَا ٱلْبَيْضَاءِ عِنْدَ ٱلتَّبَسُّمِ

And call toward the red
    pavilions of Híma,
call out a greeting
    of longing and loss

If you hear back
    bear them blessings
and fond regards
    If not, journey on

To the river of ʿĪsā
    where their camels graze
and white tents nestle
    by the stream

Ring forth the names
    of Daʿd and Rabáb,
Záynab and Hind,
    Lúbna then Sálma

Then ask if there's [10]
    a girl at Hálba
who shows the sun
    in her smile

4

سَلَامٌ عَلَى سَلْمَى وَمَنْ حَلَّ بِٱلْحِمَى
وَحُقَّ لِمِثْلِي رِقَّةً أَنْ يُسَلِّمَا

وَمَاذَا عَلَيْهَا أَنْ تَرُدَّ تَحِيَّةً
عَلَيْنَا وَلٰكِنْ لَا ٱحْتِكَامَ عَلَى ٱلدُّمَى

سَرَوْا وَظَلَامُ ٱللَّيْلِ أَرْخَى سُدُولَهُ
فَقُلْتُ لَهَا صَبًّا غَرِيبًا مُتَيَّمَا

أَحَاطَتْ بِهِ ٱلْأَشْوَاقُ شَوْقًا وَأُرْصِدَتْ
لَهُ رَاشِقَاتُ ٱلنَّبْلِ أَيَّانَ يَمَّمَا

فَأَبْدَتْ ثَنَايَاهَا وَأَوْمَضَ بَارِقٌ [5]
فَلَمْ أَدْرِ مَنْ شَقَّ ٱلْحَنَادِسَ مِنْهُمَا

As Night Let Down Its Curtain

Peace, Sálma
    and peace to those
who halt at al-Híma
    It's right I greet you

Would it have hurt
    to return the greeting?
A lady of stone
    never responds

They left as night
    let down its curtain
Pity a lad, I said,
    dazed and forsaken

Hemmed in by longings,
    pierced by their arrows
on target always
    wherever he goes

She smiled, lightning [5]
    flashed, and I couldn't
tell what it was
    that split the night

وَقَـالَـتْ أَمَـا يَـكْفِـيـهِ أَنِّي بِقَـلْبِـهِ
يُشَـاهِـدُنِي فِي كُـلِّ وَقْـتٍ أَمَـا أَمَـا

Each moment he

beholds me anew

in his heart, she said

What more can he ask?

5

أَنْجَدَ ٱلشَّوْقُ وَأَتْهَمَ ٱلْعَزَا
فَأَنَا مَا بَيْنَ نَجْدٍ وَتِهَامْ

وَهُمَا ضِدَّانِ لَنْ يَجْتَمِعَا
فَشَتَاتِي مَا لَهُ ٱلدَّهْرَ نِظَامْ

مَا صَنِيعِي مَا ٱحْتِيَالِي دُلَّنِي
يَا عَذُولِي لَا تَرُعْنِي بِٱلْمَلَامْ

زَفَرَاتٌ قَدْ تَعَالَتْ صُعُدًا
وَدُمُوعٌ فَوْقَ خَدَّيَّ سِجَامْ

حَنَّتِ ٱلْعِيسُ إِلَى أَوْطَانِهَا [5]
مِنْ وَجَى ٱلسَّيْرِ حَنِينَ ٱلْمُسْتَهَامْ

Harmony Gone

Yearning sought the highlands,
    consolation the plain
and here I'm stranded
    between Najd and Tihām

Opposites never
    to be joined—
Undone, unstrung
    Harmony gone

Where is my craft?
    What can I do?
Guide me, scold—don't
    crush me with blame

Sighs ascend
    to the highest heavens,
tears streaming
    from my eyes

The red-roans yearned [5]
    for the meadows of home,
on cracked hooves racing
    like a crazed lover

مَا حَيَاتِي بَعْدَهُمْ إِلَّا ٱلْفَنَا
فَعَلَيْهَا وَعَلَى ٱلصَّبْرِ ٱلسَّلَامْ

I live on and

    in living die

Farewell to her, then,

    and to patience, farewell

6

بَانَ ٱلْعَزَاءُ وَبَانَ ٱلصَّبْرُ إِذْ بَانُوا
بَانُوا وَهُمْ فِي سَوَادِ ٱلْقَلْبِ سُكَّانُ

سَأَلْتُهُمْ عَنْ مَقِيلِ ٱلرَّكْبِ قِيلَ لَنَا
مَقِيلُهُمْ حَيْثُ فَاحَ ٱلشِّيحُ وَٱلْبَانُ

فَقُلْتُ لِلرِّيحِ سِيرِي وَٱلْحَقِي بِهِمِ
فَإِنَّهُمْ عِنْدَ ظِلِّ ٱلْأَيْكِ قُطَّانُ

وَبَلِّغِيهِمْ سَلَامًا مِنْ أَخِي شَجَنٍ
فِي قَلْبِهِ مِنْ فِرَاقِ ٱلْقَوْمِ أَشْجَانُ

Artemisia and Moringa

Patience and solace are gone—

gone with those

who live within

my heart's dark core

I asked where they'd kneel

their camels at noon

By the artemisia,

I heard, and moringa

I asked the wind

to track them to

the thicket's shade

where their tent wings spread

To bring them greetings

from the slave of grief

His heart was torn

when the tribe dispersed

7

وَزَاحَمَنِي عِنْدَ ٱسْتِلَامِي أَوَانِسٌ
أَتَيْنَ إِلَى ٱلتَّطْوَافِ مُعْتَجِرَاتِ

حَسَرْنَ عَنَ ٱنْوَارِ ٱلشُّمُوسِ وَقُلْنَ لِي
تَوَرَّعْ فمَوْتُ ٱلنَّفْسِ فِي ٱللَّحَظَاتِ

فَكَمْ قَدْ قَتَلْنَا بِٱلْمُحَصَّبِ مِنْ مِنىً
نُفُوسًا أَبِيَّاتٍ لَدَى ٱلْجَمَرَاتِ

وَفِي سَرْحَةِ ٱلْوَادِي وَأَعْلَامِ رَامَةٍ
وَجَمْعٍ وَعِنْدَ ٱلنَّفْرِ مِنْ عَرَفَاتِ

[5] أَلَمْ تَدرِ أَنَّ ٱلْحُسْنَ يَسْلُبُ مَنْ لَهُ
عَفَافٌ فَيُدْعَى سَالِبَ ٱلْحَسَنَاتِ

Gowns of Dark

I touched the stone

    through a whirl of young women

circling the Ká‘ba,

    faces veiled

They lowered their veils,

    revealing the sun

Death stalks the

    gaze, they warned

Many’s the proud

    soul we’ve taken

questing at the threshold

    of Mína’s cairns

In the wádi courts,

    near the heights of Râm

and Jem, through the throngs

    on ‘Árafa plain

See how beauty [5]

    plunders the chaste

“Spoiler of virtue”—

    so aptly named

فَمَوْعِدُنَا بَعْدَ ٱلطَّوَافِ بِزَمْزَمٍ
لَدَى ٱلْقُبَّةِ ٱلْوُسْطَى لَدَى ٱلصَّخَرَاتِ

هُنَالِكَ مَنْ قَدْ شَفَّهُ ٱلْوَجْدُ يَشْتَفِي
بِمَا شَاقَهُ مِنْ نِسْوَةٍ عَطِرَاتِ

إِذَا خِفْنَ أَسْدَلْنَ ٱلشُّعُورَ فَهُنَّ مِنْ
غَدَائِرِهَا فِي أَلْحُفِ ٱلظُّلُمَاتِ

We'll meet at Zámzam

after the circling,

by the middle tent,

near the boulders

There a man starved

by love's fever

is cured by the scent

of those who lured him

Roused, they loosen

their hair and let it

fall, enfolding them-

selves in dark

8

دَرَسَتْ رُبُوعُهُمُ وَأَنَّ هَوَاهُمُ
أَبَدًا جَدِيدٌ بِٱلْحَشَا مَا يَدْرُسُ

هٰذِي طُلُولُهُمُ وَهٰذِي ٱلْأَدْمُعُ
وَلِذِكْرِها أَبَدًا تَذُوبُ ٱلْأَنْفُسُ

نَادَيْتُ خَلْفَ رِكَابِهِمْ مِنْ حُبِّهِمْ
يَا مَنْ غِنَاهُ ٱلْحُسْنُ هَا أَنَا مُفْلِسُ

مَرَّغْتُ خَدِّي رِقَّةً وَصَبَابَةً
فَبِحَقِّ حَقِّ هَوَاكُمُ لَا تُوْيِسُوُا

مَنْ ظَلَّ فِي عَبَرَاتِهِ غَرِقًا وَفِي [5]
نَارِ ٱلْأَسَى حَرِقًا وَلَا مُتَنَفَّسُ

Who Forever

Their spring meadows
    are desolate now
but desire for them
    lives on in the heart

        These are their ruins
            tears in memory
        of those who melt
            the soul forever

I called out, following,
    love-dazed, after
You so full with
    beauty—I've nothing

        With desire maddened,
            I rubbed my face
        in the dust   By the
            right of true love

Don't crush a man [5]
    drowned in tears
yet aflame
    with ceaseless sorrow

يَا مُوقِدَ ٱلنَّارِ ٱلرُّوَيْدَا هٰذِهِ
نَارُ ٱلصَّبَابَةِ شَأْنَكُمْ فَلْتَقْبِسُوُا

Put down your flint,

fire-striker

Here is passion's fire

Take an ember

9

لَمَعَتْ لَنَا بِٱلْأَبْرَقَيْنِ بُرُوقُ
قَصَفَتْ لَهَا بَيْنَ ٱلضُّلُوعِ رُعُودُ

وَهَمَتْ سَحَائِبُهَا بِكُلِّ خَمِيلَةٍ
وَبِكُلِّ مَيَّادٍ عَلَيْكَ يَمِيدُ

فَجَرَتْ مَذَانِبُهَا وَفَاحَ نَسِيمُهَا
وَهَفَتْ مُطَوَّقَةٌ وَأَوْرَقَ عُودُ

نَصَبُوا ٱلْقِبَابَ ٱلْحُمْرَ بَيْنَ جَدَاوِلٍ
مِثْلِ ٱلْأَسَاوِدِ بَيْنَهُنَّ قُعُودُ

بِيضٌ أَوَانِسُ كَٱلشُّمُوسِ طَوَالِعٌ
عِينٌ كَرِيمَاتٌ عَقَائِلُ غِيدُ [5]

Soft-Eyed Graces

Lightning flashed
        in Abraqáyn
Thunder roared
        within our ribs

A fine rain fell
        on sand-slipped hills,
quivering branches
        bending toward you

Streams gushing,
        soft winds fragrant,
doves in the boughs,
        tender new sprigs

They pitched their red
        tents between rivers
winding like snakes—
        and there they stood

Splendid as rising [5]
        suns, they were
Soft-eyed graces
        Beyond compare

10

قَالَتْ عَجِبْتُ لِصَبٍّ مِنْ مَحَاسِنِهِ
يَخْتَالُ مَا بَيْنَ أَزْهَارٍ بِبُسْتَانِ

فَقُلْتُ لَا تَعْجَبِي مِمَّا تَرَيْنَ فَقَدْ
أَبْصَرْتِ نَفْسَكِ فِي مِرْآةِ إِنْسَانِ

Mirror

I wonder at a love
    that flaunts its glory
among the garden
    flowers, she said

Don't, I said
    You're seeing yourself
in the mirror
    of humankind

11

أَلَا يَا حَمَامَاتِ ٱلْأَرَاكَةِ وَٱلْبَانِ
تَرَفَّقْنَ لَا تُضْعِفْنَ بِٱلشَّجْوِ أَشْجَانِي

تَرَفَّقْنَ لَا تُظْهِرْنَ بِٱلنَّوْحِ وَٱلْبُكَا
خَفِيَّ صَبَابَاتِي وَمَكْنُونَ أَحْزَانِي

أُطَارِحُهَا عِنْدَ ٱلْأَصِيلِ وَبِٱلضُّحَى
بِحَنَّةِ مُشْتَاقٍ وَأَنَّةِ هَيْمَانِ

تَنَاوَحَتِ ٱلْأَرْوَاحُ فِي غَيْضَةِ ٱلْغَضَى
فَمَالَتْ بِأَفْنَانٍ عَلَيَّ فَأَفْنَانِي

وَجاءَتْ مِنَ ٱلشَّوْقِ ٱلْمُبرِّحِ وَٱلْجَوَى [5]
وَمِنْ طُرَفِ ٱلْبَلْوَى إِلَيَّ بِأَفْنَانِ

Gentle Now, Doves

Gentle now, doves
    of the sprigberry and
moringa, don't add your
    sighs to my heart-ache

Gentle now, lest
    your sad cooing show
the love I hide,
    the sorrow I seal

In the evening I echo
    back, in the morning
echo the longing
    of the lovesick and lost

Spirits moan
    in the Ghâda trees
bending branches over me
    as I pass away

Bringing yearning, [5]
    heartbreak and ever
new twists of pain
    to try me

فَمَنْ لِي بِجَمْعٍ وَٱلْمُحَصَّبِ مِنْ مِنىً
وَمَنْ لِي بِذَاتِ ٱلْأَثْلِ مَنْ لِي بِنَعْمَانِ

تَطُوفُ بِقَلْبِي سَاعَةً بَعْدَ سَاعَةٍ
لِوَجْدٍ وَتَبْرِيحٍ وَتَلْثِمُ أَرْكَانِي

وَكَمْ عَهِدَتْ أَنْ لَا تَحُولَ وَأَقسَمَتْ
وَلَيْسَ لِمَخْضُوبٍ وَفَاءٌ بِأَيْمَانِ

وَمِنْ أَعْجَبِ ٱلْأَشْيَاءِ ظَبْيٌ مُبَرْقَعٌ
يُشِيرُ بِعُنَّابٍ وَيُومِي بِأَجْفَانِ

[10] وَمَرْعَاهُ مَا بَيْنَ ٱلتَّرَائِبِ وَٱلْحَشَى
وَيَا عَجَبًا مِنْ رَوْضَةٍ وَسْطَ نِيرَانِ

لَقَدْ صَارَ قَلْبِي قَابِلاً كُلَّ صُورَةٍ
فَمَرْعَى لِغِزْلَانٍ وَدَيْرٌ لِرُهْبَانِ

Who's here for me
    in Jem and Muhássab,
at Tamarisk and
    camp Na'mān?

Hour by hour they
    circle my heart
in rapture and graze
    its corners with a kiss

They swore they'd never
    change and vowed
Who dyes herself
    with henna's unfaithful

A veiled gazelle's
    an amazing sight,
her henna hinting,
    eyelids signaling

A pasture between [10]
    breastbone and spine
Marvel, a garden
    among the flames!

My heart can take on
    any form
For gazelles a meadow
    A cloister for monks

وَبَـيْـتٌ لِأَوْثَـــانٍ وَكَـعْـبَـةُ طَـائِـفٍ
وَأَلْـــوَاحُ تَـــوْرَاةٍ وَمُـصْـحَـفُ قُـرْآنِ

أَدِيـنُ بِـدِيـنِ ٱلْحُـبِّ أَنَّى تَـوَجَّـهَـتْ
رَكَـائِـبُـهُ فَـٱلـدِّيـنُ دِيـنِـي وَإِيمَـــانِي

لَـنَـا أُسْــوَةٌ فِي بِـشْـرِ هِـنْـدٍ وَأُخْـتِـهَـا
وَقَـيْـسٍ وَلَـيْـلَـى ثُمَّ مَـيٍّ وَغَـيْـلَانِ

A temple for idols,
    pilgrim's Ka`ba,
tablets of Torah,
    scrolls of the Qur'ân

I profess the religion
    of love   Wherever
its camels turn, there
    lives my faith

Like Bishr and Hind,
    love-mad Qays
and his lost Láyla
    Máyya and stricken Ghaylān

12

بِذِي سَلَمٍ وَٱلدَّيْرِ مِنْ حَاضِرِ ٱلْحِمَى
ظِبَاءٌ تُرِيكَ ٱلشَّمْسَ فِي صُوَرِ ٱلدُّمَى

فَأَرْقُبُ أَفْلَاكًا وَأَخْدُمُ بَيْعَةً
وَأَحْرُسُ رَوْضاً بِٱلرَّبِيعِ مُنَمْنَمَا

فَوَقْتًا أُسَمَّى رَاعِيَ ٱلظَّبْيِ بِٱلْفَلَى
وَوَقْتًا أُسَمَّى رَاهِبًا وَمُنَجِّمَا

تَثَلَّثَ مَحْبُوبِي وَقَدْ كَانَ وَاحِدًا
كَمَا صَيَّرُوا ٱلْأُقْنُومَ بِٱلذَّاتِ أَقْنُمَا

[5] فَلَا تُنْكِرَنْ يَا صَاحِ قَوْلِي غَزَالَةً
تُضِيءُ لِغِزْلَانٍ يَطُفْنَ عَلَى ٱلدُّمَى

Sunblaze

At Sálam and Híma's
    cloister, gazelles
reveal the sun
    as marble statues

I observe the spheres,
    serve a basilica,
guard a garden
    jeweled with spring

Gazelle-minder
    of the empty quarter,
astrologer, monk—
    is what they call me

The one I love is
    three though one
like the three they call
    a single being

Believe what I tell you, [5]
    friend, about Sunblaze
guiding gazelles
    circling the statues

فلِلظَّبْيِ أَجْيَادًا وَلِلشَّمْسِ أَوْجُهًا
وَلِلدُّمْيَةِ ٱلْبَيْضَاءِ صَدْرًا وَمِعْصَمَا

كَمَا قَدْ أَعَرْنَا لِلْغُصُونِ مَلَابِسًا
وَلِلرَّوْضِ أَخْلَاقًا وَلِلبَرْقِ مَبْسِمَا

A gazelle with a neck

 a sun with a face

a blood-marbled statue

 with wrist and breast

As we lend raiment

 to branches, virtues

to a garden and

 to lightning—a smile

13

نَـاحَـتْ مُـطَـوَّقَـةٌ فَـحَـنَّ حَـزِيـنُ
وَشَـجَـاهُ تَـرْجِـيـعٌ لَهَـا وَحَـنِـينُ

جَرَتِ ٱلدُّمُوعُ مِنَ ٱلْعُيُونِ تَفَجُّعًا
لِحَنِينِـهَـا فَـكَـأَنَّـهُـنَّ عُـيُـونُ

طَارَحْتُهَا ثَكْلَى بِفَقْدِ وَحِيدِهَا
وَٱلثُّكْلُ مِنْ فَقْدِ ٱلْوَحِيدِ يَكُونُ

طَارَحْتُهَا وَٱلشَّجْوُ يَمْشِي بَيْنَنَا
مَـا إِنْ تَـبِـينُ وَإِنَّـــنِي لَأُبِـــينُ

[5] بِي لَاعِـجٌ مِنْ حُـبِّ رَمْلَةِ عَـالِجٍ
حَيْثُ ٱلْخِيَامُ بِهَا وَحَيْثُ ٱلْعِينُ

Grief Between

A ringdove cooed
    A sad man yearned,
stirred by the echoing
    yearning and grief

At the sound of her cry,
    his eyes welled
like pools filling
    above a spring

She mourns her one
    and only: how deep
the loss of the only!
    I called

Back, as grief
    passed between us
I, revealed,
    she still hidden

At the sands of Ālij [5]
    I felt love's sting—
white tents on slopes
    Eyes wide open

مِنْ كُلِّ فَاتِكَةِ ٱللِّحَاظِ مَرِيضَةٍ
أَجْفَانُهَا لِظُبَى ٱللِّحَاظِ جُفُونُ

مَا زِلْتُ أَجْرَعُ دَمْعَتِي مِنْ عِلَّتِي
أُخْفِي ٱلْهَوَى عَنْ عَاذِلٍ وَأَصُونُ

حَتَّى إِذَا صَاحَ ٱلْغُرَابُ بِبَيْنِهِمْ
فَضَحَ ٱلْفِرَاقُ صَبَابَةَ ٱلْمَحْزُونِ

وَصَلُوا السُّرَى قَطَعُوا ٱلْبُرَى فَلِعِيسِهِمْ
تَحْتَ ٱلْمَحَامِلِ رَنَّةٌ وَأَنِينُ

[10] عَايَنْتُ أَسْبَابَ ٱلْمَنِيَّةِ عِنْدَمَا
أَرْخَوْا أَزِمَّتَهَا وَشُدَّ وَضِينُ

إِنَّ ٱلْفِرَاقَ مَعَ ٱلْغَرَامِ لَقَاتِلٌ
صَعْبُ ٱلْغَرَامِ مَعَ ٱللِّقَاءِ يَهُونُ

Gazes languid
    glances fatal
eyelids sheaths
    of glistening swords

I held back tears
    at the ache within,
hiding love from
    blame, acting

Till the crow cawed
    gone! exposing
the wild love of a
    man in sorrow

The riders pressed,
    spurring the camels,
red-roans beneath
    the howdahs, groaning

As they cinched [10]
    the saddles and loosened
the reins, I beheld
    death's cords before me

In love's fever
    distance is mortal
Finding her would
    ease the pain

مَا لِي عَذُولٌ فِي هَوَاهَا إِنَّهَا
مَعْشُوقَةٌ حَسْنَاءُ حَيْثُ تَكُونُ

What do I care if

they blame my loving?

She is loved where-

ever she turns

14

رَأَى ٱلْبَرْقَ شَرْقِيًّا فَحَنَّ إِلَى ٱلشَّرْقِ
وَلَوْ لاَحَ غَرْبِيًّا لَحَنَّ إِلَى ٱلْغَرْبِ

فَإِنَّ غَرَامِي بِٱلْبَرِيقِ وَلَمْحِهِ
وَلَيْسَ غَرَامِي بِٱلْأَمَاكِنِ وَٱلتُّرْبِ

رَوَتْ لِي ٱلصَّبَا عَنْهُمْ حَدِيثًا مُعَنْعَنًا
عَنِ ٱلْبَثِّ عَنْ وَجْدِي عَنِ ٱلْحُزْنِ عنْ كَرْبِي

عَنِ ٱلسُّكْرِ عَنْ عَقْلِي عَنِ الشَّوْقِ عَنْ جَوًى
عَنِ الدَّمْعِ عَنْ جَفْنِي عَنِ ٱلنَّارِ عَنْ قَلْبِي

[5] بِأَنَّ ٱلَّذِي تَهْوَاهُ بَيْنَ ضُلُوعِكُمْ
تُقَلِّبُهُ ٱلْأَنْفَاسُ جَنْبًا إِلَى جَنْبِ

Hadith of Love

Lightning flashed
    and he yearned for the East
Had it flashed from the West
    there he'd have turned

I burn for the lightning,
    the flash, not for this
or for some other
    piece of ground

The Eastwind brought us
    the word—from distraction
from rapture and sorrow
    from my disarray

From drunkenness, reason,
    longing and grief,
from the fire
    from my heart

The one you seek [5]
    is within your ribs
turned in each breath
    from side to side

فقُلْتُ لَهَا بَلِّغْ إِلَيْهِ بِأَنَّهُ
هُوَ ٱلْمُوقِدُ النَّارَ ٱلَّتِي دَاخِلَ ٱلْقَلْبِ

فَإِنْ كَانَ إِطْفَاءٌ فَوَصْلٌ مُخَلَّدٌ
وَإِنْ كَانَ إِحْرَاقٌ فَلَا ذَنْبَ لَلصَّبِّ

Tell him (I told them)
    he's the one
who lit the fire
    within my heart

To be with you now
    alone would quench it
If it rages, why
    blame my love?

15

غَـادَرُونِي بِـٱلْأُثَـيْـلِ وَٱلـنَّـقَـا
أَسْكُبُ ٱلدَّمْعِ وَأَشْكُو ٱلْحُرَقَا

بِـأَبِي مَـنْ ذُبْـتُ فِـيـهِ كَـمَـدًا
بِـأَبِي مَـنْ مِـتُّ مِـنْـهُ فَـرَقَـا

حُمْـرَةُ ٱلْخَـجْـلَـةِ فِي وَجْـنَـتِـهِ
وَضَحُ ٱلصُّبْحِ يُنَاغِي الشَّفَقَا

قَوَّضَ الصَّبْرُ وَطَنَّبَ ٱلْأَسَى
وَأَنَـا مَـا بَـيْـنَ هٰـذَيْـنِ لِـقَـا

[5] مَنْ لِبَثِّي مَنْ لِوَجْدِي دُلَّنِي
مَنْ لِحُزْنِي مَنْ لِصَبٍّ عَشِقَا

Just a Flash

They left me between
　Utháyl and White Dune,
scattering tears
　and shouting *fire!*

My father's life
　for the one I mourn,
in whom I disap-
　peared parting

On his cheek a tinge
　of shyness, dawn
light whispering
　into dusk

Patience decamps,
　sorrow pitches
its tent and I am
　frozen in place

Who will guide me [5]
　through the thrall
and throes of this
　unending love?

كُلَّمَا صُنْتُ تَبَارِيحَ ٱلْهَوَى
فَضَحَ ٱلدَّمْعُ ٱلْجَوَى وَٱلْأَرَقَا

فَإِذَا قُلْتُ هَبُوا لِي نَظْرَةً
قِيلَ مَا تُمْنَعُ إِلَّا شَفَقَا

مَا عَسَى تُغْنِيكَ مِنْهُمْ نَظْرَةٌ
هِيَ إِلَّا لَمْحُ بَرْقٍ بَرَقَا

لَسْتُ أَنْسَى إِذْ حَدَا ٱلْحَادِي بِهِمْ
يَطْلُبُ ٱلْبَيْنَ ويَبْغِي ٱلْأَبْرَقَا

[10] نَعَقَتْ أَغْرِبَةُ ٱلْبَيْنِ بِهِمْ
لَا رَعَى ٱللَّهُ غُرَابًا نَعَقَا

مَا غُرَابُ ٱلْبَيْنِ إِلَّا جَمَلٌ
سَارَ بِٱلْأَحْبَابِ نَصًّا عَنَقَا

I'd 've concealed
    the anguish but tears
and bleary eyes
    gave me away

Just a glance?
    I ask but they say,
we hold back only
    out of compassion

Never will
    a glance release you
It's only a flash
    crackling the night

I'll never forget
    how they left for Ábraq
to the chants of guides
    chanting them on their way

Gone! cawed [10]
    the crows of departure
God curse every
    crow that caws!

Parting's crow
    is but a camel
bearing your love
    swiftly away

16

حَمَلْنَ عَلَى ٱلْيَعْمَلَاتِ ٱلْخُدُورَا
وَأَوْدَعْنَ فِيهَا ٱلدُّمَى وَٱلْبُدُورَا

وَوَاعَــدْنَ قَـلْـبِيَ أَنْ يَـرْجِـعُوا
وَهَـلْ تَعِدُ ٱلْخُـودُ إِلَّا غُـرُورَا

وَحَـيَّـتْ بِعُـنَّـابِهَـا لِـلْـوَدَاعِ
فَأَذْرَتْ دُمُوعًا تُهِيجُ ٱلسَّعِيرَا

فَلَـمَّا تَـوَلَّـتْ وَقَـدْ يَمَّـمَتْ
تُـرِيـدُ ٱلْخَـوَرْنَـقَ ثُمَّ ٱلـسَّـدِيـرَا

[5] دَعَـوْتُ ثُـبُورًا عَـلَـى إِثْـرِهِـمْ
فَـرَدَّتْ وَقَـالَـتْ أَتَـدْعُـوا ثُبُورَا

Star Shepherd

They placed the howdahs
    on long-stride camels,
full moons within curtains,
    statues of stone

O they'd return!
    or so they vowed
Beauty's promise,
    delusion

They bid farewell
    with henna-tipped fingers,
unloosed their tears
    yet stoked a fire

They set off for Yemen
    then turned toward
Khawárnaq then
    toward Sadīr

Damn it! I cried [5]
    as they departed
If you want to cry
    damn it, they said

فَلَا تَدْعُوَنَّ بِهَا وَاحِدًا
وَلٰكِنَّمَا ٱدْعُ ثُبُورًا كَثِيرَا

أَلَا يَا حَمَامَ ٱلْأَرَاكِ قَلِيلاً
فَمَا زَادَكَ ٱلْبَيْنُ إِلَّا هَدِيرَا

وَنَوْحُكَ يَا أَيُّهَا ذَا ٱلْحَمَامُ
يُثِيرُ ٱلْمَشُوقَ يُهِيجُ ٱلْغَيُورَا

يُذِيبُ ٱلْفُؤَادَ يَذُودُ الرُّقَادَ
يُضَاعِفُ أَشْوَاقَنَا وَٱلزَّفِيرَا

[10] يَحُومُ ٱلْحِمَامُ لِنَوْحِ ٱلْحَمَامِ
فَنَسْأَلُ مِنْهُ ٱلْبَقَاءَ يَسِيرَا

عَسَى نَفْحَةٌ مِنْ صَبَا حَاجِرٍ
تَسُوقُ إِلَيْنَا سَحَابًا مَطِيرَا

Why this single
    cry of damnation?
Damn it, damn it,
    damn it again!

Easy now, dove
    of the persica
thicket, departure
    has sharpened your cry

Your cooing stirs
    this lover,
inflaming a man
    already afire

It melts the heart,
    drives off sleep,
whets our longing,
    compounds our sighs

Death hovers [10]
    in a dove's cry
I ask remission
    if just for a time

May the Eastwind
    as it hails from Hājir
soothe us with
    a cooling rain

تُـرَوِّي بِهَا أَنْفُسًا قَدْ ظَمِئْنَ
فَمَا ٱزْدَادَ سُحْبُكَ إِلَّا نُفُورَا

فَيَا رَاعِيَ النَّجْمِ كُنْ لِي نَدِيمًا
وَيَا سَاهِرَ ٱلْبَرْقِ كُنْ لِي سَمِيرَا

وَيَـا رَاقِـدَ اللَّـيْـلِ هُنِّئْتَهُ
فَقَبْلَ ٱلْمَمَاتِ عَمَرْتَ ٱلْقُبُورَا

فَلَوْ كُنْتَ تَهْوَى ٱلْفَتَاةَ ٱلْعَرُوبَا [15]
لَنِلْتَ ٱلنَّعِيمَ بِهَا وَٱلسُّرُورَا

تُعَاطِي ٱلْحِسَانَ خُمُورَ ٱلْخُمَارِ
تُنَاجِي ٱلشُّمُوسَ تُنَاغِي ٱلْبُدُورَا

And quench each
    parched soul
Yet your rain clouds
    fly further away

You, star shepherd,
    let's drink by night
and you, lightning-gazer,
    be my companion

And you, who
    sleep the night away
self-entombed
    before you die

If only you'd loved [15]
    a brave beauty
you'd have found
    what you desired

You'd be sharing wine
    with the ladies,
confiding in the sun,
    whispering with the moon

17

يَا حَادِيَ ٱلْعِيسِ لَا تَعْجَلْ بِهَا وَقِفَا
فَـإِنَّـنِي زَمِــنٌ فِي إِثْـرِهَـا غَـادِ

قِفْ بِٱلْمَطَايَا وَشَمِّرْ مِنْ أَزِمَّتِهَا
بِٱللهِ بِٱلْوَجْدِ بِٱلتَّبْرِيحِ يَا حَادِي

نَفْسِي تُرِيدُ وَلٰكِنْ لَا تُسَاعِدُهَا
رِجْلِي فَمَنْ لِي بِإِشْفَاقٍ وَإِسْعَادِ

مَا يَفْعَلُ ٱلصَّنَعُ ٱلنِّحْرِيرُ فِي شُغُلٍ
آلَاتُــهُ آذَنَــتْ فِـيـهِ بِـإِفْـسَـادِ

[5] عَرِّجْ فَفِي أَيْمَنِ ٱلْـوَادِي خِيَامُهُمُ
لِلّٰهِ دَرُّكَ مَا تَحْوِيهِ يَا وَادِي

God Curse My Love

Slow down, red-roan
    drivers, stop—
I'm worn out, broken,
    fallen behind

Whoa, stop,
    pull in the reins,
by God and by the
    pain and passion!

My spirit is willing
    but my legs are weak
Who's here for me now
    with help and cheer?

When the skilled craftsman
    finds his tools
of no avail—
    what can he do?

Look! Their tents [5]
    are on the right
God bless you, wádi,
    for what you hold

جَمَعْتَ قَوْمًا هُمُ نَفْسِي وَهُمْ نَفَسِي
وَهُمْ سَوَادُ سُوَيْدَا خِلْبِ أَكْبَادِي

لَا دَرَّ دَرُّ ٱلْهَوَى إِنْ لَمْ أَمُتْ كَمَدًا
بِحَاجِرٍ أَوْ بِسَلْعٍ أَوْ بِأَجْيَادِ

You hold a people

who are my soul,

my breath and the dark

of my liver's caul

God curse my love

if grief doesn't take me

at Hājir, at Salʿ

or in Ajyâdī

18

قِفْ بِٱلْمَنَازِلِ وَٱنْدُبِ ٱلْأَطْلَالَا
وَسَلِ ٱلرُّبُوعَ ٱلدَّارِسَاتِ سُؤَالَا

أَيْنَ ٱلْأَحِبَّةُ أَيْنَ سَارَتْ عِيسُهُمْ
هَاتِيكَ تَقْطَعُ فِي ٱلْيَبَابِ ٱلآلَا

مِثْلُ ٱلْحَدَائِقِ فِي السَّرَابِ تَرَاهُمُ
أَلْآلُ يُعْظِمُ فِي ٱلْعُيُونِ ٱلآلَا

سَارُوا يُرِيدونَ ٱلْعُذَيْبَ لِيَشْرَبُوا
مَاءً بِهِ مِثْلَ ٱلْحَيَاةِ زُلَالَا

[5] فَقَفَوْتُ أَسْأَلُ عَنْهُمُ رِيحَ ٱلصَّبَا
هَلْ خَيَّمُوا أَوِ ٱسْتَظَلُّوا الضَّالَا

As Cool as Life

Halt at the stations,
    grieve at the ruins,
then ask the meadows
    so desolate now

Where are those
    we loved and their roans?
Over there, cutting
    through the desert haze

They loom before you
    like a garden mirage—
large silhouettes
    in the mist

They've gone in search
    of al-'Udháyb
to drink at its waters
    cool as life

I tracked after them, [5]
    asking the Eastwind
Did they pitch their tents
    or find lote's shade?

قَالَتْ تَرَكْتُ عَلَى زَرُودَ قِبَابَهُمْ
وَٱلْعِيسُ تَشْكُو مِنْ سُرَاهُ كَلَالَا

قَدْ أَسْدَلُوا فَوْقَ ٱلْقِبَابِ مَصَاوِنًا
يَسْتُرْنَ مِنْ حَرِّ ٱلْهَجِيرِ جَمَالَا

فَٱنْهَضْ إِلَيْهِمْ طَالِبًا آثَارَهُمْ
وَٱرْقِلْ بِعِيسِكَ نَحْوَهُمْ إِرْقَالَا

فَإِذَا وَقَفْتَ عَلَى مَعَالِمِ حَاجِرٍ
وَقَطَعْتَ أَغْوَارًا بِهَا وَجِبَالَا

[10] قَرُبَتْ مَنَازِلُهُمْ وَلَاحَتْ نَارُهُمْ
نَارٌ قَدْ أَشْعَلَتِ ٱلْهَوَى إِشْعَالَا

فَأَنِخْ بِهَا لَا يُرْهِبَنَّكَ أُسْدُهَا
فَٱلْإِشْتِيَاقُ يُرِيكَهَا أَشْبَالَا

She said she left them
  at Drifting Sands,
their camels groaning
  through the night journey

They lowered a curtain
  over the flaps
of their tents, sheltering
  beauty from the sun

So set off, friends,
  in their tracks
on amber camels
  pacing in pursuit

Halt near the waymarks
  of Hājir, then
cross its canyons
  and ascend its ridge

As you near them [10]
  a fire will flare
before you and
  ignite your longing

Kneel your camels
  Don't fear their lions
In desire's fire
  they'll look like cubs

19

يَا طَلَلاً عِنْدَ ٱلْأُثَيْلِ دَارِسَا
لَاعَبْتُ فِيهِ خُرَّدًا أَوَانِسَا

بِٱلْأَمْسِ كَانَ مُؤْنِسًا وَضَاحِكًا
وَٱلْيَوْمَ أَضْحَى مُوحِشاً وَعَابِسَا

نَأَوْا وَلَمْ أَشْعُرْهُمُ فَمَا دَرَوْا
أَنَّ عَلَيْهِمْ مِنْ ضَمِيرِي حَارِسَا

يَتْبَعُهُمْ حَيْثُ نَأَوْا وَخَيَّمُوا
وَقَدْ يَكُونُ لِلْمَطَايَا سَائِسَا

حَتَّى إِذَا حَلُّوا بِقَفْرٍ بَلْقَعٍ [5]
وَخَيَّمُوا وَٱفْتَرَشُوا ٱلطَّنَافِسَا

The Tombs of Those Who Loved Them

O windswept ruin at Utháyl
        where I would play
                with lissome girls
who knew discretion

Yesterday, it embraced us
        laughing   Today
                it frowns
in desolation

They left as if
        I'd no clue
                Little did they know
my eye within

Could see and follow them
        to their encampment—
                it might've been me
leading their camels—

Until they halted [5]
        in the Barrenlands
                spread their tents
and unfurled their carpets

عَادَ بِهِمْ رَوْضاً أَغَنَّ يَانِعًا
مِنْ بَعْدِ مَا قَدْ كَانَ قَفْرًا يَابِسَا

مَا نَزَلُوا مِنْ مَنْزِلٍ إِلَّا حَوَى
مِنَ ٱلْحِسَانِ رَوْضُهُ طَوَاوِسَا

وَلَا نَأَوْا عَنْ مَنْزِلٍ إِلَّا حَوَتْ
مِنْ عَاشِقِيهِمْ أَرْضُهُ نَوَاوِسَا

Brought back to a garden

moist colors

singing

on drought-cracked ground

Wherever they stopped

for midday rest

blossomed into

peacock splendor

When they struck camp

they left a land

bearing the tombs

of those who loved them

20

مَرَضِي مِنْ مَرِيضَةِ ٱلْأَجْفانِ
عَلِّلانِي بِذِكْرِهَا عَلِّلانِي

هَفَتِ ٱلْوُرْقُ بِالرِّيَاضِ وَنَاحَتْ
شَجْوُ هٰذَا ٱلْحَمَامِ مِمَّا شَجَانِي

بِأَبِي طَفْلَةٌ لَعُوبٌ تَهَادَى
مِنْ بَنَاتِ ٱلْخُدُورِ بَيْنَ ٱلْغَوَانِي

طَلَعَتْ فِي ٱلْعِيَانِ شَمْسًا فَلَمَّا
أَفَلَتْ أشْرَقَتْ بِأُفْقِ جَنَانِي

In a Bad Way

I'm in a bad
    way, lost
in the languor
    of her eyes

Say her name
    and heal me—
Recalling her's
    my only cure

Doves rustled
    in the green, cooing,
sad with the same
    sadness that's mine

My father's life!
    His life for a girl
walking proud
    among the wives

In my eyes she
    rose like the sun
then set aglow
    on my heart's horizon

يَا طُلُولاً بِرَامَةٍ دَارِسَاتٍ [5]
كَمْ رَأَتْ مِنْ كَوَاعِبٍ وَحِسَانِ

بِأَبِي ثُمَّ بِي غَزَالٌ رَبِيبٌ
يَرْتَعِي بَيْنَ أَضْلُعِي فِي أَمَانِ

مَا عَلَيْهِ مِنْ نَارِهَا فَهْوَ نُورٌ
هٰكَذَا النُّورُ مُخْمِدُ ٱلنِّيرَانِ

يَا خَلِيلَيَّ عَرِّجَا بِعِنَانِي
لِأَرَى رَسْمَ دَارِهَا بِعِيَانِي

فَإِذَا مَا بَلَغْتُمَا الدَّارَ حُطَّا
وَبِهَا صَاحِبَيَّ فَلْتَبْكِيَانِي

وَقِفَا بِي عَلَى ٱلطُّلُولِ قَلِيلاً [10]
نَتَبَاكَى بَلْ أَبْكِ مِمَّا دَهَانِي

O ruins in Râma, [5]
wasted now—
what splendor
you once beheld!

My father's life
my own! for
a gazelle browsing
within my ribs

What burns for her
there is light
and only light
can quell this fire

Take the reins,
friends, as traces
of her camp emerge
before my eyes

When we arrive
at that place
dismount and weep
for me there

Support me then [10]
or try, even
as I face mis-
fortune alone

أَهْـوَى رَاشِـقِـي بِـغَـيْرِ سِـهَـامٍ
أَهْـوَى قَـاتِـلِـي بِـغَـيْرِ سِـنَـانِ

عَـرِّفَـانِي إِذَا بَـكَـيْـتُ لَـدَيْـهَـا
تُسْعِدَانِي عَلَى ٱلْبُكَا تُسْعِدَانِي

وَٱذْكُـرَا لِي حَدِيثَ هِنْدٍ وَلُبْنَى
وَسُلَـيْـمَـى وَزَيْـنَـبٍ وَعِـنَـانِ

ثُمَّ زِيـدَا مِـنْ حَـاجِـرٍ وَزَرُودٍ
خَـبَـرًا عَـنْ مَـرَاتِـعِ ٱلْـغِـزْلَانِ

[15] وَٱنْـدُبَـانِي بِشِعْرِ قَـيْسٍ وَلَـيْلَى
وَبِمَـيٍّ وَٱلْـمُـبْـتَـلَـى غَـيْـلَانِ

طَـالَ شَوْقِي لِطِفْلَةٍ ذَاتِ نَثْرٍ
وَنِـظَـامٍ وَمِـنْـبَرٍ وَبَـيَـانِ

Love struck—
    without an arrow,
without a spear
    she put me away

Tell me again
    as I stand there weeping
will you stay
    by my side?

Remind me of Hind
    and of Lúbna,
Suláyma, Záynab
    and 'Inān

And what transpired
    at Zarūd and Hājir
and out in the wilds
    among gazelles

Then sing my loss [15]
    with the verse of Qays
and Láyla, Máyya
    and stricken Ghaylān

Long is my longing
    for a young girl—
harmony in verse,
    in prose, in oration

مِنْ بَنَاتِ ٱلْمُلُوكِ مِنْ دَارِ فُرْسٍ
مِنْ أَجَلِّ ٱلْبِلَادِ مِنْ إِصْبَهَانِ

هِيَ بِنْتُ ٱلْعِرَاقِ بِنْتُ إِمَامِي
وَأَنَــا ضِــدُّهَــا سَلِيــلُ يَمَــانِ

هَلْ رَأَيْتُمْ يَا سَادَتِي أَوْ سَمِعْتُمْ
أَنَّ ضِــدَّيْــنِ قَــطُّ يَجْتَمِعَانِ

[20] لَــوْ تَــرَانَــا بِــرَامَــةٍ نَــتَــعَــاطَ
أَكْؤُسًا لِلْهَوَى بِغَيْرِ بَنَانِ

وَٱلْهَـوَى بَيْنَنَا يَسُوقُ حَدِيثًا
طَيِّبًا مُطْرِبًا بِغَيْرِ لِسَانِ

لَرَأَيْتُمْ مَا يَذْهَبُ ٱلْعَقْلُ فِيهِ
يَمَــنٌ وَٱلْــعِــرَاقُ مُعْتَنِقَانِ

For the daughter of kings,
    of Persian shahs,
of the city of cities,
    Isfahân

For a daughter of Irâq,
    my master's child
and I, of Yemen,
    her foil

Did you know, my lords,
    have you heard
that contraries could
    ever be joined?

Had you only seen us [20]
    in Râma trading
passion's chalice—
    not moving a hand

As love sang
    a rapture song
between us
    without a sound

You'd have seen
    what melts the mind—
Irâq and Yemen
    intertwined!

كَذَبَ ٱلشَّاعِرُ ٱلَّذِي قَالَ قَبْلِي
وَبِأَحْجَارِ عَقْلِهِ قَدْ رَمَانِي

أَيُّهَا ٱلْمُنْكِحُ ٱلثُّرَيَّا سُهَيْلاً
عَمْرَكَ ٱللَّهُ كَيْفَ يَلْتَقِيَانِ

هِيَ شَامِيَّةٌ إِذَا مَا ٱسْتَقَلَّتْ [25]
وَسُهَيْلٌ إِذَا ٱسْتَقَلَّ يَمَانِ

The poet who
    coined these verses
lied, pelting me
    with logic's stones

O you who'd match
    Suháyl with the Pleiades
God grant you life,
    how can they meet?

As the Pleiades ascend [25]
    in the Syrian East
Suháyl rises south
    southwest, in Yemen

21

أَيَا رَوْضَةَ ٱلْوَادِي أَجِبْ رَبَّةَ ٱلْحِمَى
وَذَاتَ ٱلثَّنَايَا ٱلْغُرِّيَا رَوْضَةَ ٱلْوَادِي

وَظَلِّلْ عَلَيْهَا مِنْ ظِلَالِكَ سَاعَةً
قَلِيلاً إِلَى أَنْ يَسْتَقِرَّ بِهَا النَّادِي

وَتُنْصَبَ بِٱلْأَجْوَازِ مِنْكَ خِيَامُهَا
فَمَا شِئْتَ مِنْ طَلٍّ غِذَاءً لِمُنْآدِ

وَمَا شِئْتَ مِنْ وَبْلٍ وَمَا شِئْتَ مِنْ نَدًى
سَحَابٌ عَلَى بَانَاتِهَا رَائِحٌ غَادِ

وَمَا شِئْتَ مِنْ ظِلٍّ ظَلِيلٍ وَمِنْ جَنًى [5]
شَهِيٍّ لَدَى ٱلْجَانِي يَمِيسُ بِمَيَّادِ

Your Wish

O garden of the riverbed
respond to the lady
of this hallowed ground,
she with the flashing

Smile   Cover her
in shade for a while
until the assembly
gathers by her side

And their tents nestle
along the banks
Then dew and rain
will moisten branches

As they sway
Mists will shroud
the moringa tree
at dawn and eve

Then the shade [5]
will start to deepen
from boughs laden
low with fruits

وَمِنْ نَاشِدٍ فِيهَا زَرُودَ وَرَمْلَهَا
وَمِنْ مُنْشِدٍ حَادٍ وَمِنْ مُنْشِدٍ هَادِ

For pilgrims seeking
the sands of Zarūd,
flanked by the chants
of drivers and guides

عُجْ بِٱلرَّكَائِبِ نَحْوَ بُرْقَةِ ثَهْمَدِ
حَيْثُ ٱلْقَضِيبُ ٱلرَّطْبُ وَٱلرَّوْضُ النَّدِي

حَيْثُ ٱلْبُرُوقُ بِهَا تُرِيكَ وَمِيضَهَا
حَيْثُ ٱلسَّحَابُ بِهَا يَرُوحُ وَيَغْتَدِي

وَٱرْفَعْ صُوَيْتَكَ بِٱلسُّحَيْرِ مُنَادِيًا
بِٱلْبِيضِ وَٱلْغِيدِ ٱلْحِسَانِ النُّهَّدِ

مِنْ كُلِّ فَاتِكَةٍ بِطَرْفٍ أَحْوَرٍ
مِنْ كُلِّ لَافِتَةٍ بِجِيدٍ أَغْيَدِ

تَهْوَى فَتُقْصِدُ كُلَّ قَلْبٍ هَائِمٍ [5]
يَهْوَى ٱلْحِسَانَ بِرَاشِقٍ وَمُهَنَّدِ

Blacksilver

Turn toward the hard
rock plain of Tháhmad
where willows and meadows
    are moist with dew

Where lightning flickers
before you and clouds
come early and
    by dusk are gone

Lift your voice
at the break of dawn
and call to each radiant
    lissome girl

Fatal the blacksilver
flash of her eyes,
gentle the bend
    of her neck as she turns

She hunts after [5]
the heart-dazed lover
laying him low
    with a glance of steel

تَعْطُو بِرَخْصٍ كَٱلدِّمَقْسِ مُنَعَّمٍ
بِٱلنَّدِّ وَٱلْمِسْكِ ٱلْفَتِيقِ مُقَرْمَدِ

تَرْنُو إِذَا لَحَظَتْ بِمُقْلَةِ شَادِنٍ
يُعْزَى لِمُقْلَتِهَا سَوَادُ ٱلْإِثْمِدِ

بِٱلْغُنْجِ وَٱلسِّحْرِ ٱلْقَتُولِ مُكَحَّلٍ
بِٱلتِّيهِ وَٱلْحُسْنِ ٱلْبَدِيعِ مُقَلَّدِ

هَيْفَاءُ مَا تَهْوَى ٱلَّذِي أَهْوَى وَلَا
تَفِ لِلَّذِي وَعَدَتْ بِصِدْقِ ٱلْمَوْعِدِ

[10] سَحَبَتْ غَدِيرَتَهَا شُجَاعًا أَسْوَدًا
لِتُخِيفَ مَنْ يَقْفُو بِذَاكَ ٱلْأَسْوَدِ

وَٱللَّهِ مَا خِفْتُ ٱلْمَنُونَ وَإِنَّمَا
خَوْفِي أَمُوتُ فَلَا أَرَاهَا فِي غَدِ

She extends you a hand
soft as undyed silk
anointed with
    ambergris and musk

She casts you the gaze
of a fawn gazelle
a glint of obsidian
    in her eyes

A collyrium of spells
across her brow,
neckline ablaze
    with beauty unheard

How slender she is,
not loving as I
do, nor true
    to her vow

She lets down her hair's [10]
black coils to
fix with dread
    one who'd track her

It isn't by God
my death I fear
but to die and
    never see her

23

سُحَيْرًا أَنَاخُوا بِوَادِي ٱلْعَقِيقِ
وَقَدْ قَطَعُوا كُلَّ فَجٍّ عَمِيقِ

فَمَا طَلَعَ ٱلْفَجْرُ إِلَّا وَقَدْ
رَأَوْا عَلَمًا لَائِحاً فَوْقَ نِيقِ

إِذَا رَامَهُ ٱلنَّسْرُ لَمْ يَسْتَطِعْ
فَمِنْ دُونِهِ كانَ بَيْضُ ٱلْأَنُوقِ

عَلَيْهِ زَخَارِفُ مَنْقُوشَةٌ
وَثِيقُ ٱلْقَوَاعِدِ مِثْلُ ٱلْعَقُوقِ

وَقَدْ كَتَبُوا أَسْطُرًا أَوْدَعُوهَا [5]
أَلَا مَنْ لِصَبٍّ غَرِيبٍ مَشُوقِ

Blaze

By dawn's edge they'd cut
  through every ravine
to kneel their camels
  in Wādilaqīq

At first pale light
  it appeared
high above them
  on a mountain peak

It towers beyond
  the eagle's glide,
cliff-buzzard's eggs
  nestled in its shadows

On great foundations
  it rises heavenward,
decked and blazoned
  like Castle 'Aqūq

On its walls they carved [5]
  a tale for the telling
and left it: Pity
  the love-lost stranger

لَهُ هِمَّةٌ فَوْقَ هٰذَا ٱلسِّمَاكِ
وَيُوطَأُ بِٱلْخُفِّ وَطْءَ ٱلْحَرِيقِ

وَمَسْكَنُهُ عِنْدَ هٰذَا ٱلْعُقَابِ
وَقَدْ مَاتَ فِي ٱلدَّمْعِ مَوْتَ ٱلْغَرِيقِ

قَدَ ٱسْلَمَهُ ٱلْحُبُّ لِلْحَادِثَاتِ
بِهٰذَا ٱلْمَكَانِ بِغَيْرِ شَقِيقِ

فَيَا وَارِدِينَ مِيَاهَ ٱلْقَلِيبِ
وَيَا سَاكِنِينَ بِوَادِي ٱلْعَقِيقِ

وَيَا طَالِبًا طَيْبَةً زَائِرًا [10]
وَيَا سَالِكِينَ بِهٰذَا ٱلطَّرِيقِ

أَفِيقُوا عَلَيْنَا فَإِنَّا رُزِينَا
بُعَيْدَ ٱلسُّحَيْرِ قُبَيْلَ ٱلشُّرُوقِ

بِبَيْضَاءَ غَيْدَاءَ بَهْنَانَةٍ
تَضَوَّعُ نَشْرًا كَمِسْكٍ فَتِيقِ

Who reached past Arcturus
    then was ground
underfoot like
    an ember

Who staked his home
    in Aquila's stars,
then sank drowning
    through his tears

Here in this place
    love turned him over
without a friend
    to the twisting fates

You who come down
    to Old Well,
you who find home
    in Wādilaqīq

You who search [10]
    for sweet Medina,
you treading this
    same hard ground

Revive me! Dawn
    then dusk and I

was robbed of a tender
    fragrant beauty

تَمَايَلَ سَكْرَى كَمِثْلِ ٱلْغُصُونِ
ثَنَتْهَا ٱلرِّيَاحُ كَمِثْلِ ٱلشَّقِيقِ

بِرِدْفٍ مَهُولٍ كَدِعْصِ ٱلنَّقَا
تَرَجْرَجُ مِثْلَ سَنَامِ ٱلْفَنِيقِ

[15]
فَمَا لَامَنِي فِي هَوَاهَا عَذُولٌ
وَلَا لَامَنِي فِي هَوَاهَا صَدِيقِ

وَلَوْ لَامَنِي فِي هَوَاهَا عَذُولٌ
لَكَانَ جَوَابِي إِلَيْهِ شَهِيقِ

فَشَوْقِي رِكَابِي وَحُزْنِي لِبَاسِي
وَوَجْدِي صَبُوحِي وَدَمْعِي غَبُوقِ

She sways tipsy
    as a willow touched
by the wind, as anemone
    petals part silken

With a sway of the hips
    like the sway of a dune
or the hump of a camel mare
    ambling in the haze

If you shame me, scold, [15]
    for loving her,

if you shame me, friend,
    I'll answer with a gasp

Longing's my mount
    solitude's my mantle,
my dawn wine's delirium,
    tears are for dusk

24

وَقَالَ وَٱنْشَدَنِي بَعْضُ ٱلْفُقَرَاءِ بَيْتًا لَا أَعْرِفُ لَهُ أَخاً وَهُوَ هٰذَا

كُلُّ ٱلَّذِي يَرْجُو نَوَالَكِ أُمْطِرُوا
مَا كَانَ بَرْقُكِ خُلَّبًا إِلَّا مَعِي

فَأَعْجَبَنِي وَقَفَوْتُ مَعْنَاهُ فَعَمِلْتُ أَبْيَاتًا فِي هٰذَا ٱلرَّوِيِّ وَضَمَّنْتُهَا هٰذَا ٱلْبَيْتَ بِكَمَالِهِ إِجَابَةً لِذٰلِكَ ٱلْفَقِيرِ رَحِمَهُ ٱللَّهُ فَقُلْتُ:

قِفْ بِٱلطُّلُولِ ٱلدَّارِسَاتِ بِلَعْلَعِ
وَٱنْدُبْ أَحِبَّتَنَا بِذَاكَ ٱلْبَلْقَعِ

قِفْ بِٱلدِّيَارِ وَنَادِهَا مُتَعَجِّبًا
مِنْهَا بِحُسْنِ تَلَطُّفٍ بِتَفَجُّعِ

عَهْدِي بِمِثْلِي عِنْدَ بَانِكِ قَاطِفًا
ثَمَرَ ٱلْقُدُودِ وَوَرْدَ رَوْضٍ أَيْنَعِ

Stay Now

A dervish recited a verse to me, the likes of which I'd never heard.

All who sought you
you showered with graces
Only for me did your
lightning flash faithless

It struck me and I followed its trail. I've composed verses using his rhyme, quoting his verse in full, as a response to that dervish, God rest his soul.

Stay at the ruins
in Lá'la'i fading,
and in that wilderness
grieve for those we loved

And at that campsite
call out her name,
your heart softly
torn away

O for the times
passed near her moringa,
picking her fruit,
her garden's red rose

كُلُّ ٱلَّذِي يَرْجُو نَوَالَكِ أُمْطِرُوا
مَا كَانَ بَرْقُكِ خُلَّبًا إِلَّا مَعِي

[5] قَالَتْ نَعَمْ قَدْ كَانَ ذَاكَ ٱلْمُلْتَقَى
فِي ظِلِّ أَفْنَانِي بِأَخْصَبِ مَوْضِعِ

إِذْ كَانَ بَرْقِي مِنْ بُرُوقِ مَبَاسِمٍ
وَٱلْيَوْمَ بَرْقِي لَمْعُ هٰذَا ٱلْيَرْمَعِ

فَٱعْتُبْ زَمَانًا مَا لَنَا مِنْ حِيلَةٍ
فِي دَفْعِهِ مَا ذَنْبُ مَنْزِلِ لَعْلَعِ

فَعَذَرْتُهَا لَمَّا سَمِعْتُ كَلَامَهَا
تَشْكُو كَمَا أَشْكُو بِقَلْبٍ مُوجَعِ

وَسَأَلْتُهَا لَمَّا رَأَيْتُ رُبُوعَهَا
مَسْرَى ٱلرِّيَاحِ ٱلذَّارِيَاتِ ٱلْأَرْبَعِ

All who sought you
you showered with graces
Only for me did your
lightning flash faithless

We used, she said, [5]
to come there together
in my branches' shadows
in that lush land

My lightning, once
a smile's flash,
is now a blaze
of barren stone

Blame time
relentless time!
What fault was it
of Lá'la'i?

I forgave her
as I heard her speak
grieving as I grieved
with wounded heart

I asked her when
I saw her meadows
pastures of the
scouring winds—

[10]

هَلْ أَخْبَرَتْكِ رِيَاحُهُمْ بِمَقِيلِهِمْ
قَالَتْ نَعَمْ قَالُوا بِذَاتِ ٱلْأَجْرَعِ

حَيْثُ ٱلْخِيَامُ ٱلْبِيضُ تُشْرِقُ بِٱلَّذِي
تَحْوِيهِ مِنْ تِلْكَ ٱلشُّمُوسِ ٱلطُّلَّعِ

Did they tell you where [10]
they'd rest at noon
Yes, she said,
at Sand Hill

Where white tents glow
from the light of
all those suns
ablaze within

25

وَا حَرَبَا مِنْ كَبِدِي وَا حَرَبَا
وَا طَرَبَا مِنْ خَلَدِي وَا طَرَبَا

فِي كَبِدِي نَارُ جَوًى مُحْرِقَةٌ
فِي خَلَدِي بَدْرُ دُجًى قَدْ غَرَبَا

يَا مِسْكُ يَا بَدْرُ وِيَا غُصْنَ نَقًا
مَا أَوْرَقَا مَا أَنْوَرَا مَا أَطْيَبَا

يَا مَبْسِمًا أَحبَبْتُ مِنْهُ ٱلْحَبَبَا
وِيَا رُضَابًا ذُقْتُ مِنْهُ ٱلضَّرَبَا

يَا قَمَرًا فِي شَفَقٍ مِنْ خَجَلٍ [5]
فِي خَدِّهِ لَاحَ لَنَا مُنْتَقِبَا

لَوْ أَنَّهُ يُسْفِرُ عَنْ بُرْقُعِهِ
كَانَ عَذَابًا فَلِهٰذَا ٱحْتَجَبَا

شَمْسُ ضُحًى فِي فَلَكٍ طَالِعَةٌ
غُصْنُ نَقًى فِي رَوْضَةٍ قَدْ نُصِبَا

ظِلْتُ لَهَا مِنْ حَذَرٍ مُرْتَقِبًا
وَٱلْغُصْنُ أَسْقِيهِ سَمَاءً صَيِّبَا

إِنْ طَلَعَتْ كَانَتْ لِعَيْنِي عَجَبًا
أَوْ غَرَبَتْ كَانَتْ لِحَيْنِي سَبَبَا

Vanished

Deep are the wounds and the rapture sharp
Love has ravaged me to the marrow

Yet by night a full moon shines
within my soul—musk and moon

And a branch on a dune,
so green and clear, so fragrant!

O how I loved the luster of his smile,
the nectar tasted in his kiss

A pale moon in sunset glow [5]
on his cheek from behind a veil

Had he lowered the veil, he'd
have sharpened the pain He let it be

She rose before me like a midday sun,
a branch on a dune become a garden

In fear I kept vigil, watering
that garden with a bursting sky

In wonder I behold her rise,
then, as she sets, I expire

مُذْ عَقَدَ ٱلْحُسْنُ عَلَى مَفْرِقِهَا [10]
تَاجاً مِنَ ٱلتِّبْرِ عَشِقْتُ ٱلذَّهَبَا

لَوْ أَنَّ إِبْلِيسَ رَأَى مِنْ آدَمٍ
نُورَ مُحَيَّاهَا عَلَيْهِ مَا أَبَى

لَوْ أَنَّ إِدْرِيسَ رَأَى مَا رَقَمَ ٱل
حُسْنُ بِخَدَّيْهَا إِذًا مَا كَتَبَا

لَوْ أَنَّ بِلْقِيسَ رَأَتْ رَفْرَفَهَا
مَا خَطَرَ ٱلْعَرْشُ وَلَا ٱلصَّرْحُ بِبَا

يَا سَرْحَةَ ٱلْوَادِي وَيَا بَانَ ٱلْغَضَا
أَهْدُوا لَنَا مِنْ نَشْرِكُمْ مَعَ ٱلصَّبَا

مُمَسَّكًا يَفُوحُ رَيَّاهُ لَنَا [15]
مِنْ زَهْرِ أَهْضَامِكَ أَوْ زَهْرِ ٱلرُّبَى

يَا بَانَةَ ٱلْوَادِي أَرِينَا فَنَنًا
فِي لِينِ أَعْطَافٍ لَهَا أَوْ قُضُبَا

رِيحُ صَبًا تُخْبِرُ عَنْ عَصْرِ صِبًا
بِحَاجِرٍ أَوْ بِمِنًى أَوْ بِقُبَا

أَوْ بِٱلنَّقَى فَٱلْمُنْحَنَى عِنْدَ ٱلْحِمَى
أَوْ لَعْلَعٍ حَيْثُ مَرَاتِعُ ٱلظِّبَا

لَا عَجَبٌ لَا عَجَبٌ لَا عَجَبًا
مِنْ عَرَبِيٍّ يَتَهَاوَى ٱلْعُرُبَا

يَفْنَى إِذَا مَا صَدَحَتْ قُمْرِيَّةٌ [20]
بِذِكْرِ مَنْ يَهْوَاهُ فِيهِ طَرَبَا

Beauty laced the strands of her hair [10]
in a gold tiara, gilding my fever

Had Iblīs seen her glow on Adam
he'd 've fallen down in prayer

Had Idrīs seen the mark of beauty
on her cheek, he'd 've written no more

Had Bilqīs seen her carpet
Sulaymân's hall would've slipped her mind

O sarh tree of the valley, moringa, tamarisk
send your fragrance on the Eastwind

A scent of musk, and a breath [15]
of the lowland and highland blossoms

Moringa of the riverbed, show me
a bough or wreath soft as her shoulder

The Eastwind tells of a time made young
at Hājir, Mína, or at Qúba

By the trail-bend dune not far from Híma,
at Lá'la' where gazelles graze

O do not do not do not wonder
at an Arab flirting with a beauty of the sands

When the turtledove cries lost love— [20]
he's gone

26

بِٱلْجِزْعِ بَيْنَ ٱلْأَبْرَقَيْنِ ٱلْمَوْعِدُ
فَأَنِخْ رَكَائِبَنَا فَذَاكَ ٱلْمَوْرِدُ

لَا تَطْلُبَنَّ وَلَا تُنَادِي بَعْدَهُ
يَا حَاجِرٌ يَا بَارِقٌ يَا ثَهْمَدُ

وَٱلْعَبْ كَمَا لَعِبَتْ أَوَانِسُ نُهَّدٌ
وَٱرْتَعْ كَمَا رَتَعَتْ ظِبَاءٌ شُرَّدُ

فِي رَوْضَةٍ غَنَّاءَ صَاحَ ذُبَابُهَا
فَأَجَابَهُ طَرَبًا هُنَاكَ مُغَرِّدُ

رَقَّتْ حَوَاشِيهَا وَرَقَّ نَسِيمُهَا [5]
فَٱلْغَيْمُ يَبْرُقُ وَٱلْغَمَامَةُ تَرْعُدُ

Vintage of Adam

Near the rock plain
    at Trail's Bend
our camels will kneel
    by home waters

There's no need to seek
    anywhere after
or call for Bāriq
    Tháhmad or Hājir

Revel like pert-
    breasted girls
or gazelles that pause
    to graze then wander

While a fly murmurs
    in the meadow
and a songbird trills
    in answer

The garden fringe, [5]
    breeze tender,
dark cloud glowing,
    thunder rumbling

وَٱلْوَدْقُ يَنْزِلُ مِنْ خِلَالِ سَحَابِهِ
كَدُمُوعِ صَبٍّ لِلْفِرَاقِ تَبَدَّدُ

وَٱشْرَبْ سُلَافَةَ خَمْرِهَا بِخُمَارِهَا
وَٱطْرَبْ عَلَى غَرِدٍ هُنَالِكَ يُنْشِدُ

وَسُلَافَةٍ فِي عَهْدِ آدَمَ أَخْبَرَتْ
عَنْ جَنَّةِ ٱلْمَأْوَى حَدِيثًا يُسْنَدُ

إِنَّ ٱلْحِسَانَ تَفَلْنَهَا مِنْ رِيقَةٍ
كَٱلْمِسْكِ جَادَ بِهَا عَلَيْنَا ٱلْخُرَّدُ

Rains cascading
    like the tears of a lover
torn apart from
    the one he loves

Drink this ancient
    wine, drink deeply
Let the song's
    spell take you . . .

Adam's vintage
    bearing word
down the gener-
    ations from Eden

This wine, scented
    with musk,
savored on the lips
    of women and girls

27

يَا أَيُّهَا ٱلْبَيْتُ ٱلْعَتِيقُ تعَالَى
نُورٌ لَكُم بِقُلُوبِنَا يَتَلَالَا

أَشْكُو إِلَيْكَ مَفَاوِزاً قَدْ جُبْتُهَا
أَرْسَلْتُ فِيهَا أَدْمُعِي إِرْسَالَا

أُمْسِي وَأُصْبِحُ لَا أَلَذُّ بِرَاحَةٍ
أَصِلُ ٱلْبُكُورَ وَأَقْطَعُ ٱلْآصَالَا

إِنَّ ٱلنِّيَاقَ وَإِنْ أَضَرَّ بِهَا ٱلْوَجَى
تَسْرِي وَتَرْقُلُ فِي ٱلسُّرَى إِرْقَالَا

هٰذِى ٱلرِّكَابُ إِلَيْكُمْ سَارَتْ بِنَا [5]
شَوْقًا وَمَا تَرْجُو بِذَاكَ وِصَالَا

Old Shrine

To you, old shrine,
    high above,
a light beckons
    from my heart

O the long,
    empty reaches
I've crossed, tears
    my messengers

Morning and evening
    I ride without rest
roping dawn to
    dusk to dawn

The camels stride
    through the night,
hoof-bruised and lame,
    hard-striding

They bear me to you [5]
    in longing, without
desire of ever
    arriving there

قَطَعَتْ إِلَيْكَ سَبَاسِبًا ورَمَايِلاً
وَجْدًا وَمَا تَشْكُو لِذَاكَ كَلَالَا

مَا تَشْتَكِي أَلَمَ ٱلْجَوَى وَأَنَا ٱلَّذِي
أَشْكُو ٱلْكَلَالَ لَقَدْ أَتَيْتُ مُحَالَا

Through the endless
    reach of sands
they race in a trance
    without complaint

No, I'm the one
    who groans
he's weary—
    absurd

28

بَــيْنَ ٱلـنَّـقَـا وَلَـعْـلَـعِ
ظِبَاءُ ذَاتِ ٱلْأَجْـرَعِ

تَـرْعَـى بِهَـا فِي خَمَـرٍ
خَمَـائِـلًا وَتَـرْتَـعِـي

مَـا طَـلَـعَـتْ أَهِـلَّـةٌ
بِأُفْقِ ذَاكَ ٱلْمَطْلَعِ

إِلَّا وَدَدْتُ أَنَّـهَـا
مِـنْ حَـذَرٍ لَمْ تَطْلُعِ

[5] وَلَا بَــدَتْ لَامِـعَـةٌ
مِنْ بَرْقِ ذَاكَ ٱلْيَرْمَعِ

إِلَّا ٱشْتَـهَيْتُ أَنَّـهَا
لِـمَـا بِـنَـا لَمْ تَـلْـمَـعِ

يَا دَمْعَتِي وَٱنْسَكِبِي
يَا مُقْلَتِي لَا تُقْلِعِي

يَا زَفْـرَتِي خُذْ صُعُدَا
يَا كَـبِـدِي تَـصَـدَّعِي

وَأَنْتَ يَا حَادِي ٱتَّئِدْ
فَٱلنَّـارُ بَـيْنَ أَضْلُعِي

No New Moon Risen

Between Náqa and Lá'la'
Ájran gazelles

Graze the hillsides,
in a covert, hidden

No new moon rises
on that horizon

Without me wishing
it wouldn't dare

Nor does the bare [5]
stone desert flash

Without me fearing
our exposure

May these eyes
pour tears forever

Sighs rise heavenward,
heart shatter!

Slowly now, driver,
my ribs burn

قَـدْ فَـنِـيَـتْ مِمَّـا جَـرَى
خَوْفَ ٱلْفِرَاقِ أَدْمُعِي

[10]

حَـتَّى إِذَا حَـلَّ ٱلـنَّـوَى
لَمْ تَـلْقَ عَـيْنَا تَـدْمَعُ

فَٱرْحَلْ إِلَى وَادِي ٱللِّوَى
مَـرْبَـعِـهِـمْ وَمَـصْـرَعِـي

إِنَّ بِــهِ أَحِــبَّــتِي
عِـنْـدَ مِـيَـاهِ ٱلْأَجْــرَعِ

وَنَــادِهِــمْ مَــنْ لِـفَـتًى
ذِي لَـوْعَـةٍ مُــوَدَّعِ

رَمَــتْ بِـهِ أَشْـجَـانُـهُ
بَـهْـمَـاءَ رَسْـمٍ بَلْـقَعِ

[15]

يَـا قَـمَـراً تَحْـتَ دُجًـى
خُـذْ مِـنْـهُ شَيْـئًا وَدَعِ

وَزَوِّدِيــــــهِ نَــظْــرَةً
مِنْ خَلْفِ ذَاكَ ٱلْبُرْقُعِ

لِأَنَّــهُ يَـضْـعُـفُ عَـنْ
دَرْكِ ٱلْجَـمَـالِ ٱلْأَرْوَعِ

I wept and wept [10]
at the thought of their leaving

And now they're gone
I can give no more

Journey to the swale
of the twisting dune

Where they graze
where I lie fallen

There by Ájran waters
are those I love

So tell of a man
left torn apart

Cast down in sorrow [15]
before the ruin

O hidden moon
take something from him

But leave him a glimpse
from behind the veil

(For he couldn't bear
to behold such beauty)

أَوْ عَلِّلِيهِ بِٱلْمُنَى
عَسَاهُ يَحْيَا وَيَعِي

[20]

مَا هُوَ إِلَّا مَيِّتٌ
بَيْنَ ٱلنَّقَا وَلَعْلَعِ

فَمُتُّ يَأْسًا وَأَسًى
كَمَا أَنَا فِي مَوْضِعِي

مَا صَدَقَتْ رِيحُ ٱلصَّبَا
حِينَ أَتَتْ بِٱلْخُدَعِ

قَدْ تَكْذِبُ ٱلرِّيحُ إِذَا
تُسْمِعُ مَا لَمْ يُسْمَعِ

And a potion of hope
to restore him to life

And to his senses
He is just a creature

Dead on the trail [20]
between Náqa and Lá'la'

Dead from despair,
dead from grief

Dead like me
in the place I stand

What the Eastwind promised
was illusion

When she led you to hear
what wasn't spoken

29

بِأَبِي ٱلْغُصُونُ ٱلْمَائِسَاتُ عَوَاطِفَا
أَلْعَاطِفَاتُ عَلَى ٱلْخُدُودِ سَوَالِفَا

أَلْمُرْسِلَاتُ مِنَ ٱلشُّعُورِ غَدَائِرًا
أَللَّيِّنَاتُ مَعَاقِدًا وَمَعَاطِفَا

أَلسَّاحِبَاتُ مِنَ ٱلدَّلَالِ ذَلَاذِلاً
أَللَّابِسَاتُ مِنَ ٱلْجَمَالِ مَطَارِفَا

أَلْبَاخِلَاتُ بِحُسْنِهِنَّ صِيَانَةً
أَلْوَاهِبَاتُ مَتَالِدًا وَمَطَارِفَا

أَلْمُؤْنِقَاتُ مَضَاحِكًا وَمَبَاسِمًا [5]
أَلطَّيِّبَاتُ مُقَبَّلاً وَمَرَاشِفَا

Circling

I swear by my father's
    life they sway
like boughs, strands
    along the cheeks

As their tresses
    gently fall
Soft and supple
    through shoulder and wrist

They walk forth trailing
    flirtatious pride
in gowns of luxuriant
    silken splendor

Cautious, they hold back
    their beauty but give
of their treasures freely,
    old and new

A laugh's glamour, [5]
    a welcoming smile,
the ambrosial elixir
    of a kiss

أَلنَّاعِمَاتُ مُجَرَّدًا وَٱلْكَاعِبَا
تُ مُنَهَّدًا وَٱلْمُهْدِيَاتُ طَرَائِفَا

أَلْخَالِبَاتُ بِكُلِّ سِحْرٍ مُعْجِبٍ
عِنْدَ ٱلْحَدِيثِ مَسَامِعًا وَلَطَائِفَا

أَلسَّاتِرَاتُ مِنَ ٱلْحَيَاءِ مَحَاسِنًا
تَسْبِي بِهَا ٱلْقَلْبَ ٱلتَّقِيَّ ٱلْخَائِفَا

أَلْمُبْدِيَاتُ مِنَ ٱلثُّغُورِ لَآلِيًا
تَشْفِي بِرِيقَتِهَا ضَعِيفًا تَالِفَا

[10] أَلرَّامِيَاتُ مِنَ ٱلْعُيُونِ رَوَاشِقًا
قَلْبًا خَبِيرًا بِٱلْحُرُوبِ مُثَاقِفَا

أَلْمُطْلِعَاتُ مِنَ ٱلْجُيُوبِ أَهِلَّةً
لَا يُلْفَيَنَّ مَعَ ٱلتَّمَامِ كَوَاسِفَا

A word, a phrase
    or plaintive call
to enchant the ear
    and bind the soul

A woman's embrace,
    a girl's charms,
graces giving
    wonder on wonder

With modest veils
    over such beauty
as would ruin
    a God-fearing man

O how their teeth
    glow with a liquor
that would bring
    back the dead!

Their eyes' arrows [10]
    piercing the heart
of a man long-
    practiced in war

New moons rising
    from their bodices—
Once full they'll
    never fade

أَلْمُنْشِئَاتُ مِنَ ٱلدُّمُوعِ سَحَائِبًا
أَلْمُسْمِعَاتُ مِنَ ٱلزَّفِيرِ قَوَاصِفَا

يَا صَاحِبَيَّ بِمُهْجَتِي خُمْصَانَةٌ
أَسْدَتْ إِلَيَّ أَيَادِيًا وَعَوَارِفَا

نُظِمَتْ نِظَامَ ٱلشَّمْلِ فَهِيَ نِظَامُنَا
عَرَبِيَّةٌ عَجْمَاءُ تُلْهِي ٱلْعَارِفَا

مَهْمَا رَنَتْ سَلَّتْ عَلَيْكَ صَوَارِمًا [15]
وَيُرِيكَ مَبْسِمُهَا بَرِيقًا خَاطِفَا

يَا صَاحِبَيَّ قِفَا بِأَكْنَافِ ٱلْحِمَى
مِنْ حَاجِرٍ يَا صَاحِبَيَّ قِفَا قِفَا

حَتَّى أُسَايِلَ أَيْنَ سَارَتْ عِيسُهُمْ
فَقَدِ ٱقْتَحَمْتُ مَعَاطِبًا وَمَتَالِفَا

And tears bursting
    in cascades,
and sighs deep
    as rolling thunder

O my companions,
    my bones' marrow!
for a slender girl
    who gave me her favor

She joins all
    to all in harmony
Arabic or Persian
    she'd charm the sage

Wherever she gazes [15]
    she bares a sword
Lightning shimmers
    in her smile

Halt, dear friends,
    at the borders
of Híma, near Hājir,
    halt there, please

That I may ask where
    their red-roans turn
I've ridden through peril
    and the shadow of death

وَمَعَالِمًا وَمَجَاهِلاً بِشِمِلَّةٍ
تَشْكُو ٱلْوَجَا وَسَبَاسِبًا وَتَنَائِفَا

مَطْوِيَّةُ ٱلْأَقْرَابِ أَذْهَبَ سَيْرُهَا
بِحَثِيثَةٍ مِنْهَا قُوىً وَسَدَائِفَا

[20] حَتَّى وَقَفْتُ بِهَا بِرَمْلَةِ حَاجِرٍ
فَرَأَيْتُ نُوقًا بِٱلْأُثَيْلِ خَوَالِفَا

يَقْتَادُهَا قَمَرٌ عَلَيْهِ مَهَابَةٌ
فَطَوَيْتُ مِنْ حَذَرٍ عَلَيْهِ شَرَاسِفَا

قَمَرٌ تَعَرَّضَ فِي ٱلطَّوَافِ فَلَمْ أَكُنْ
بِسِوَاهُ عِنْدَ طَوَافِهِ بِي طَائِفَا

يَمْحُو بِفَاضِلِ بُرْدِهِ آثَارَهُ
فَتُحَارُ لَو كُنْتَ ٱلدَّلِيلَ ٱلْقَائِفَا

Past the last way-stone
    into trackless spaces
on a hard-strider groaning
    through the desert void,

Flanks gaunt
    hump hollowed
forces spent
    from her journey's pace

I brought her to halt [20]
    at Hājir's sands
near Tamarisk, seeing
    nurslings and mares

Led by a moon
    of ghastly mien
I folded toward him
    in desire and fear

He appeared
    in the circling as
around him I turned,
    he around me

His footprints effaced
    by the edge of his robe,
so baffling should you
    seek to follow

30

بِأُثَيْلَاتِ ٱلنَّقَا سِرْبُ قَطَا
ضَرَبَ ٱلْحُسْنُ عَلَيْهِ طُنُبَا

وَبِأَجْوَازِ ٱلْفَلَا مِنْ إِضَمٍ
نَعَمٌ تَرْعَى لَدَيْهَا وَظِبَى

يَا خَلِيلَيَّ قِفَا وَٱسْتَنْطِقَا
رَسْمَ دَارٍ بَعْدَهُمْ قَدْ خَرِبَا

وَٱنْدُبَا قَلْبَ فَتًى فَارَقَهُ
يَوْمَ بَانُوا وَٱبْكِيَا وَٱنْتَحِبَا

عَلَّهُ يُخْبِرُ حَيْثُ يَمَّمُوا
أَلِجَرْعَاءِ ٱلْحِمَى أَمْ لِقُبَا [5]

Like Sába's Lost Tribes

In the tamarisk stand
    near White Dune
sand grouse shelter
    and beauty camps

Within a desert
    slashed by ravines
camels graze
    among gazelles

O my two
    friends, halt
here and question
    these ruins

As you grieve
    for a young man
who lost his heart
    when she went away

Have they set out [5]
    for Híma's sands
or might they be headed
    to Qúba instead?

رَحَّلُوا ٱلْعِيسَ وَلَمْ أَشْعُرْ بِهِمْ
أَلِسَهْوٍ كَانَ أَمْ طَرْفٍ نَبَا

لَمْ يَكُنْ ذَاكَ وَلَا هٰذَا وَمَا
كَانَ إِلَّا وَلَهٌ قَدْ غَلَبَا

يَا هُمُومًا شَرَدَتْ وَٱفْتَرَقَتْ
خَلْفَهُمْ تَطْلُبُهُمْ أَيْدِي سَبَا

أَيُّ رِيحٍ نَسَمَتْ نَادَيْتُهَا
يَا شَمَالاً يَا جَنُوبًا يَا صَبَا

[10] هَلْ لَدَيْكُمْ خَبَرٌ مِمَّا بِنَا
قَدْ لَقِينَا مِنْ نَوَاهُمْ نَصَبَا

أَسْنَدَتْ رِيحُ ٱلصَّبَا أَخْبَارَهَا
عَنْ نَبَاتِ ٱلشِّيحِ عَنْ زَهْرِ ٱلرُّبَا

I didn’t notice them
    saddling to leave—
Did my senses fail me
    or my attention?

It wasn’t this
    and wasn’t that
but a conflagra-
    tion of desire

And O my cares—
    how you dispersed,
scattering after them
    like Sába’s lost tribes!

I call the fragrant
    winds as they pass:
Northwind, South,
    Sweet-scented East!

Has news of us, [10]
    so weary and spent
in their absence,
    reached you?

The Eastwind brought
    the absinthe’s word
taken it in turn
    from the mountain flower

أَنَّ مَنْ أَمْرَضَهُ دَاءُ ٱلْهَوَى
فَلْيُعَلَّلْ بِأَحَادِيثِ ٱلصِّبَا

ثُمَّ قَالَتْ يَا شَمَالُ خَبِّرِي
مِثْلَمَا خَبَّرْتُهُ أَوْ أَعْجَبَا

ثُمَّ أَنْتِ يَا جَنُوبُ حَدِّثِي
مِثْلَ مَا حَدَّثْتُهُ أَوْ أَعْذَبَا

[15]

قَالَتِ ٱلشَّمْأَلُ عِنْدِي فَرَجٌ
شَارَكَتْ فِيهِ ٱلشَّمَالُ ٱلْأَزْيَبَا

كُلُّ سُوءٍ فِي هَوَاهُمْ حَسُنَا
وَعَذَابٍ بِرِضَاهُم عَذُبَا

فَإِلَى مَا وَعَلَى مَا وَلِمَا
تَشْتَكِي ٱلْبَثَّ وَتَشْكُو ٱلْوَصَبَا

Whoever suffers
love's ills
hadiths of young
passion may heal

Give us a word
like the one given,
she said to the Northwind,
or more wondrous still

And you, then, wind
from the South,
bring news as sweet
as mine or sweeter

I bring you, South [15]
said, glad tidings
shared by the North
and Southwest

All wrongs endured
become graces,
all pain, if it pleases them,
turns to pleasure

Till when and why
do you lament
their leaving and
count your wounds?

وَإِذَا مَـا وَعَـدُوكُـمْ مَـا تَـرَى
بَــرْقَــهُ إِلَّا بَـرِيـقًـا خُـلَّـبَـا

رَقَـمَ ٱلْغَيْمُ عَلَى رُدْنِ ٱلْغَمَا
مِـنْ سَنَا ٱلْـبَـرْقِ طِـرَازاً مُذْهَبَا

[20] فَـجَـرَتْ أَدْمُـعُـهَـا مِـنْـهَـا عَـلَى
صَـحْـنِ خَـدَّيْـهَـا فَـأَذْكَـتْ لَهَبَا

وَرْدَةٌ نَـابِـتَـةٌ مِــنْ أَدْمُــعِ
نَـرْجِـسٌ يُمْـطِـرُ غَـيْثًـا عَـجَـبَـا

وَمَـتَى رُمْـتَ جَـنَـاهَـا أَرْسَـلَـتْ
عَطْفَ صُدْغَيْهَا عَلَيْهَا عَقْرَبَا

تُشْرِقُ ٱلشَّمْسُ إِذَا مَا ٱبْتَسَمَتْ
رَبِّ مَـا أَنْــوَرَ ذَاكَ ٱلْحَـبَـبَـا

Whatever they promise
    you see in the lightning
only the flash
    of a rainless cloud

There on the fringe
    of dark, the cloud
wove a filigree
    of pure gold

Then sent tears [20]
    running along
its cheeks, then
    kindled a flame

Eyes as black
    as narcissi shone
and a rose appeared
    upon her cheek

If you seek it
    she will lower
her scorpion curls
    over her temples

The sun rises
    in her smile
How clearly, lord,
    her moist teeth shine!

يَطْلُعُ ٱللَّيْلُ إِذَا مَا سَدَلَتْ
فَاحِمًا جَثْلاً أَثِيثًا غَيْهَبَا

[25] يَتَجَارَى ٱلنَّحْلُ مَهْمَا تَفَلَتْ
رَبِّ مَا أَعْذَبَ ذَاكَ ٱلشَّنَبَا

وَإِذَا مَالَتْ أَرَتْنَا فَنَنًا
أَوْ رَنَتْ سَلَّتْ مِنَ ٱللَّحْظِ ظُبَا

كَم تُنَاغِي بِٱلنَّقَا مِنْ حَاجِرٍ
يَا سَلِيلَ ٱلْعَرَبِيِّ ٱلْعُرُبَا

أَنَا إِلَّا عَرَبِيٌّ وَلِذَا
أَعْشَقُ ٱلْبِيضَ وَأَهْوَى ٱلْعَرَبَا

لَا أُبَالِي شَرَّقَ ٱلْوَجْدُ بِنَا
حَيْثُ مَا كَانَتْ بِهِ أَوْ غَرَّبَا

Night falls
    as she loosens
the plush jet
    black of her hair

She spits and brings [25]
    bliss to the bees
Much sweeter, lord,
    the nectar of her kiss

Like a willow
    in the wind she moves
Her glance bares
    a glimmering sword

How far will you go,
    Arab son,
courting the women
    by Hājir's white sands!

I'm but an Arab
    born to love
bright beauties
    of my kind

Whether passion
    rises within me
or sets, no matter—
    so long as they're there

كُلَّمَا قُلْتُ أَلَا قَالُوا أَمَا [30]

وَإِذَا مَا قُلْتُ هَلْ قَالُوا أَبَا

وَمَتَى مَا أَنْجَدُوا أَوْ أَتْهَمُوا

أَقْطَعُ ٱلْبِيدَ أَحُثُّ ٱلطَّلَبَا

سَامِرِيُّ ٱلْوَقْتِ قَلْبِي كُلَّمَا

أَبْصَرَ ٱلْآثَارَ يَبْغِي ٱلْمَذْهَبَا

وَإِذَا هُم غَرَّبُوا أَوْ شَرَّقُوا

كَانَ ذَا ٱلْقَرْنَيْنِ يَقْفُو ٱلسَّبَبَا

كَمْ دَعَوْنَا لِوِصَالٍ رَغَبًا

كَمْ دَعَوْنَا مِنْ فِرَاقٍ رَهَبَا

يَا بَنِي ٱلزَّوْرَاءِ هٰذا قَمَرٌ [35]

عِنْدَكُمْ لَاحَ وَعِنْدِي غَرَبَا

Isn't it? I said [30]

They said *it isn't*

And when I asked *maybe . . .*

they added *not*

Whenever they rode

toward highland or plain

I tore through the desert

in fierce pursuit

My heart's the Sāmiri

of the moment

Discerning the trace

it casts for gold

East or west

I'm on their trail

like Iskándar gliding

on heaven's cords

When we were with her

we cried out in pleasure

then in her absence

cried out in fear

O sons of Zawrā— [35]

behold the full moon

rising above you

as it slips my horizon

حَــرَبِي وَٱللهِ مِـنْـهُ حَـرَبِي
كَمْ أُنَادِي خَلْفَهُ وَا حَرَبَا

لَهْفَ نَفْسِي لَهْفَ نَفْسِي لِفَتىً
كُلَّمَا غَـنَّى حَمَـامٌ غُيِّبَا

Woe is me,

I call in their wake,

woe is me . . .

ruination!

Woe O woe,

woe for a lad

At the cry of a dove

he's gone

31

أَضَاءَ بِذَاتِ ٱلْأَضَا بَارِقٌ
مِنَ ٱلنُّورِ فِي جَوِّهَا خَافِقُ

وَصَلْصَلَ رَعْدُ مُنَاجَاتِهِ
فَأَرْسَلَ مِدْرَارَهُ ٱلْوَادِقُ

تَنَادَوْا أَنِيخُوا فَلَمْ يَسْمَعُوا
فَصِحْتُ مِنَ ٱلْوَجْدِ يَا سَائِقُ

أَلَا فَٱنْزِلُوا هٰهُنَا وَأَرْبَعُوا
فَإِنِّي بِمَنْ عِنْدَكُمْ وَامِقُ

[5] بَهَيْفَاءَ غَيْدَاءَ رُعْبُوبَةٍ
فُؤَادُ ٱلشَّجِيِّ لَهَا تَائِقُ

يَفُوحُ ٱلنَّدِيُّ لَدَى ذِكْرِهَا
فَكُلُّ لِسَانٍ بِهَا نَاطِقُ

Áda Trail

Lightning lit up Dhāt-
al-Áda, flashes shuddering
steep valley sides

A chain of rumbling
across the sky, then
thunder unleashed rains!

Kneel the camels! they shout
to all—but no one hears
Driver, I scream

Graze the camels!
For the love of a girl
in your care, a slender thing—

Soft her gestures, delicate [5]
her walk—the heart of a
sad soul breaks

Mention her and we sigh
Every tongue
whispers her name

فَـلَـوْ أَنَّ مَجْلِسَـهَـا هَـضْـمَـةٌ
وَمَـقْـعَـدُهَـا جَـبَـلٌ حَـالِـقٌ

لَـكَـانَ ٱلْـقَـرَارُ بِهَـا حَالِقًا
وَلَنْ يُدْرِكَ ٱلْحَالِقَ ٱلرَّامِقُ

فَـكُـلُّ خَــرَابٍ بِهَـا عَـامِـرٌ
وَكُـلُّ سَـرَابٍ بِهَـا غَـادِقُ

وَكُــلُّ رِيَــاضٍ بِهَــا زَاهِــرٌ [10]
وَكُــلُّ شَــرَابٍ بِهَـا رَائِــقُ

فَلَيْلِيَ مِنْ وَجْهِهَا مُشْرِقٌ
وَيَوْمِيَ مِنْ شَعْرِهَا غَاسِقُ

لَقَد فَلَقَتْ حَبَّةَ ٱلْقَلْبِ إِذْ
رَمَـاهَـا بِـأَسْـهُـمِـهِ ٱلْـفَـالِـقُ

عُيُونٌ تـعَـوَّدْنَ رَشْقَ ٱلْحَشَا
فَـلَـيْـسَ يَـطِـيشُ لَهَـا رَاشِـقُ

She makes her home on
a bald-cap mountain
Were she camped below

Lowlands would rise
and the heights would soar
beyond the gaze

Every ruin, she brings
to life, she turns mirage
into quenching rains

With her, every garden [10]
bursts into flower
All wine is pure

Her countenance illu-
mines my night, dark
in the fall of her hair's my day

The Sunderer split my
heart down center
when she let her arrows fly

With eyes adept at
finding their target
she buried the arrows inside

فَمَا هَامَةٌ فِي خَرَابِ ٱلْبِقَاعِ
وَلَا سَاقُ حُرٍّ وَلاَ نَاعِقُ

بِـأَشْـأَمَ مِـنْ بَـازِلٍ رَحَّـلُـوا [15]
لِيَحْمِلَ مَنْ حُسْنُهُ فَائِقُ

وَيُتْرَكُ صَبٌّ بِذَاتِ ٱلْأَضَا
قَتِيلاً وَفِي حُبِّهِمْ صَادِقُ

No owl in a ruin

No turtledove either

No, not even a crow

Is more baleful [15]

than an old camel

saddled to carry

That fatal beauty away

and leave a man

still loving

Dead on Áda trail

يُذَكِّرُنِي حَالَ ٱلشَّبِيبَةِ وَٱلشَّرْخِ
حَدِيثٌ لَنَا بَيْنَ ٱلْحَدِيثَةِ وَٱلْكَرْخِ

فَقُلْتُ لِنَفْسِي بَعْدَ خَمْسِينَ حِجَّةً
وَقَدْ صِرْتُ مِنْ طُولِ ٱلتَّفَكُّرِ كَٱلْفَرْخِ

تُذَكِّرُنِي أَكْنَافَ سَلْعٍ وَحَاجِرٍ
وَتَذْكُرُ لِي حَالَ ٱلشَّبِيبَةِ وَٱلشَّرْخِ

وَسَوْقِي ٱلْمَطَايَا مُنْجِدًا ثُمَّ مُتْهِمًا
وَقَدْحِي لَهَا نَارَ ٱلْعَفَارِ مَعَ ٱلْمَرْخِ

Fifty Years

Brought back to the prime
    of my life and youth
by words spoken
    between Hadītha and Karkh

After fifty years
    of hard thinking
I've become like
    a fledgling bird

Brought back to the folds
    of Splitrock and Hājir
back to the prime
    of my life and youth

When I led camels
    to Najd and Tihām
and lit for her a fire
    of flametree and markh

33

أُطَــارِحُ كُــلَّ هَــاتِفَــةٍ بِأَيْكٍ
عَلَى فَنَنٍ بِأَفْنَانِ ٱلشُّجُونِ

فَتَبْكِي إِلْفَهَا مِنْ غَيْرِ دَمْعٍ
وَدَمْعُ ٱلْحُزْنِ يَهْمُلُ مِنْ جُفُونِي

أَقُولُ لَهَا وَقَدْ سَمَحَتْ جُفُونِي
بِأَدْمُعِهَا تُخَبِّرُ عَنْ شُؤُونِ

أَعِنْدَكِ بِٱلَّذِي أَهْـوَاهُ عِلْمٌ
وَهَلْ قَالُوا بَأَفْيَاءِ ٱلْغُصُونِ

Drowning Eyes

I trade cries
    with a dove
in a tangle thick
    with woe

Tearlessly she
    mourns
her only one
    as my eyes stream

I ask as my drown-
    ing lashes reveal
the wreckage of
    my mind   What news

Do you have
    of those I love?
are they safe
    in branches' shade?

34

عِنْدَ ٱلْكُثَيِّبِ مِنْ جِبَالِ زَرُودِ
صِيدٌ وَأُسْدٌ مِنْ لِحَاظِ ٱلْغِيدِ

صَرْعَى وَهُمْ أَبْنَاءُ مَلْحَمَةِ ٱلْوَغَى
أَيْنَ ٱلْأُسُودُ مِنَ ٱلْعُيُونِ ٱلسُّودِ

فَتَكَتْ بِهِمْ لَحَظَاتُهُنَّ وَحَبَّذَا
تِلْكَ ٱلْمَلَاحِظُ مِنْ بَنَاتِ ٱلصِّيدِ

Sweet the Gaze

Lions and other
    beasts of prey
touched by the glances
    of beautiful women

Smitten near Zarūd—
    these sons of carnage!
What are lions
    before dark eyes?

A glance took them
    by mortal surprise
Sweet the gaze
    of the hunter's child

35

ثَــلَاثُ بُــدُورٍ مَـا يُـــزَنُّ بِزِينَـةٍ
خَرَجْنَ إِلَى ٱلتَّنْعِيمِ مُعْتَجِرَاتِ

حَسَرْنَ عَنَ ٱمْثَالِ ٱلشُّمُوسِ إِضَاءَةً
وَلَـبَّيْنَ بِـٱلْإِهْـلَالِ مُعْتَـمِرَاتِ

وَأَقْبَلْـنَ يَمْشِينَ ٱلرُّوَيْدَا كَمِثْلِ مَا
تَمَشَّى ٱلْقَطَا فِي أَلْحُفِ ٱلْحَبَرَاتِ

You Now

Three moons needing
no adornment
rose over Tanʿīm,
faces veiled

Lowering the veils they
glowed like the sun
I'm here for you now
by the stations they chanted

They passed with a gait
like that of sandgrouse,
skipping along
in dappled gowns

أَلَا يَا ثَـرَى نَجْـدٍ تَـبَـارَكْـتَ مِـنْ نَجْدِ
سَقَتْكَ سَحَابُ ٱلْمُزْنِ جَوْدًا عَلَى جَوْدِ

وَحَـيَّـاكَ مَـنْ أَحْـيَـاكَ خَمْـسِـينَ حِـجَّـةً
بِـعَـوْدٍ عَـلَـى بَـدْءٍ وَبَـــدْءٍ عَـلَـى عَـوْدِ

قَـطَـعْـتُ إِلَـيْـهَـا كُـلَّ قَـفْـرٍ وَمَـهْـمَـةٍ
عَلَى ٱلنَّاقَةِ ٱلْكَوْمَاءِ وَٱلْجَـمَـلِ ٱلْعَوْدِ

إِلَى أَنْ تَرَاءَى ٱلْبَرْقُ مِنْ جَانِبِ ٱلْحِمَى
وَقَـدْ زَادَنِي مَـسْـرَاهُ وَجْـدًا عَـلَـى وَجْـدِ

Lightning over Gháda

Earth of the highlands
how blessed you are,
quenched by the gentle
comfort of rains

He greets you again
—long-life greetings—
who has greeted you
for fifty years

And always returns
to the beginning
and always begins
again to return

I've ridden through wastelands
and empty quarters
on high-humped mares
or long-toothed camels

Till evening's flash
over Híma
split me apart
with longing

37

يَا خَلِيلَيَّ أَلِمَّا بِٱلْحِمَى
وَٱطْلُبَا نَجْدًا وَذَاكَ ٱلْعَلَمَا

وَرِدَا مَاءً بِخَيْمَاتِ ٱللِّوَى
وَٱسْتَظِلَّا ضَالَهَا وَٱلسَّلَمَا

فَإِذَا مَا جِئْتُمَا وَادِي مِنًى
فَٱلَّذِي قَلْبِي بِهِ قَدْ جِئْتُمَا

أَبْلِغَا عَنِّي تَحِيَّاتِ ٱلْهَوَى
كُلَّ مَنْ حَلَّ بِهِ أَوْ سَلَّمَا

وَٱسْمَعَا مَاذَا يُجِيبُونَ بِهِ [5]
وَأَخْبِرَا عَنْ دَنِفِ ٱلْقَلْبِ بِمَا

Come Down to the Waters

Pass by al-Híma,
  friends, in search
of Najd and its
  lonesome waymark

Come down to the waters
  at Twisting Sands
down to the lote shade
  and absinthe

When you reach
  Mína's valley
you'll be in the place
  that holds my heart

To all who arrive
  bring greetings
and blessings of peace
  on my behalf

Hearken to each [5]
  report that reaches you
and tell in turn
  of a haggard man

يَشْتَكِيهِ مِنْ صَبَابَاتِ ٱلْهَوَى
مُعْلِنًا مُسْتَخْبِرًا مُسْتَفْهِمَا

Who opens his heart

    and pleads for a word,

asking only

    why . . . why

38

أَحَـبُّ بِـلَادِ ٱللهِ لِي بَـعْـدَ طَيْبَةٍ
وَمَـكَّـةَ وَٱلْأَقْـصَـى مَـدِيـنَـةُ بَـغْـدَانِ

وَمَـالِيَ لَا أَهْوَى ٱلسَّلَامَ وَلِي بِهَا
إِمَـامُ هُـدىً دِيـنِي وَعَـقْـدِي وَإِيمَـانِي

وَقَدْ سَكَنَتْهَا مِنْ بُنَيَّاتِ فَارِسٍ
لَـطِـيـفَـةُ إِيمَـــاءٍ مَـرِيـضَـةُ أَجْـفَـانِ

تُحَيِّ فَتُحْيِي مَنْ أَمَاتَتْ بِلَحْظِهَا
فَجَاءَتْ بِحُسْنَى بَعْدَ حُسْنٍ وَإِحْسَانِ

A Persian Girl

After Medina,
    Mecca and Jerusalem,
Baghdad's God's city
    I love the most

Why wouldn't I
    love that city
of peace   My imām's
    there to guide me

There lives a girl
    a Persian pearl
of delicate gesture
    and languid eye

Who kills with a glance
    then revives with a word
tempering fierce beauty
    with compassion

39

نَفْسِي ٱلْفِدَاءُ لَبِيضٍ خُرَّدٍ عُرُبٍ
لَعِبْنَ بِي عِنْدَ لَثْمِ ٱلرُّكْنِ وَٱلْحَجَرِ

مَا تَسْتَدِلُّ إِذَا مَا تِهْتَ خَلْفَهُمُ
إِلَّا بِرِيحِهِمْ مِنْ طَيِّبِ ٱلْأَثَرِ

وَلَا دَجَا بِيَ لَيْلٌ مَا بِهِ قَمَرٌ
إِلَّا ذَكَرْتُهُمُ فَسِرْتُ فِي ٱلْقَمَرِ

وَإِنَّمَا حِينَ أَمْشِي فِي رِكَابِهِمُ
فَٱللَّيْلُ عِنْدِيَ مِثْلُ ٱلشَّمْسِ فِي ٱلْبُكَرِ

[5] غَازَلْتُ مِنْ غَزَلِي مِنْهُنَّ وَاحِدَةً
حَسْنَاءَ لَيْسَ لَهَا أُخْتٌ مِنَ ٱلْبَشَرِ

Day Falls Night

I'd give all I am
    for those ravishing girls
who teased me where
    we kissed the stone

When you lose yourself
    in their wake
a fragrant trace
    on the wind will guide you

When moonless night
    drags dark upon me
I recall them and walk
    bathed in light

When I ride with them
    in the falling dark
my night shines
    like the rising sun

I whispered love [5]
    to one of them,
a beauty far
    beyond compare

إِنْ أَسْفَرَتْ عَنْ مُحَيَّاهَا أَرَتْكَ سَنًا
مِثْلَ ٱلْغَزَالَةِ إِشْرَاقًا بِلَا غِيَرِ

لِلشَّمْسِ غُرَّتُهَا لِلَّيْلِ طُرَّتُهَا
شَمْسٌ وَلَيْلٌ مَعًا مِنْ أَعْجَبِ ٱلصُّوَرِ

فَنَحْنُ بِٱللَّيْلِ فِي ضَوْءِ ٱلنَّهَارِ بِهِ
وَنَحْنُ فِي ٱلظُّهْرِ فِي لَيْلٍ مِنَ ٱلشَّعَرِ

When she opens her veil

    her face shines—

Sunblaze—lighting

    unfading sky

Strands of hair

    along her forehead—

sun by night, in-

    explicable

By night the light

    of day in her shines

By day night falls

    with the dark of her hair

40

طَلَعَتْ بَيْنَ أَذْرِعَاتٍ وَبُصْرَى
بِنْتُ عَشْرٍ وَأَرْبَعٍ لِيَ بَدْرَا

قَدْ تَعَالَتْ عَلَى ٱلزَّمَانِ جَلَالًا
وَتَسَامَتْ عَلَيْهِ فَخْرًا وَكِبْرَا

كُلُّ بَدْرٍ إِذَا تَنَاهَى كَمَالًا
جَاءَهُ نَقْصُهُ لِيَكْمُلَ شَهْرَا

غَيْرُ هٰذِي فَمَا لَهَا حَرَكَاتٌ
فِي بُرُوجٍ فَمَا تُشَفِّعُ وِتْرَا

[5] حُقَّةٌ أُودِعَتْ عَبِيرًا وَنَشْرًا
رَوْضَةٌ أَنْبَتَتْ رَبِيعًا وَزَهْرَا

Odd to Even

Between Adhri'āt
    and Búsra she appeared,
a girl of fourteen,
    full moon rising

In pride and glory
    she surpasses
the ebb and flow
    of time itself

Every moon
    when it waxes full
must wane again
    to complete its turn

But this moon runs
    through no constellations
and knows no doubling
    from odd to even

It's you who bring [5]
    each sweet fragrance
you, who give the
    spring its blossom

إِنْتَهَى ٱلْحُسْنُ فِيكِ أَقْصَى مَدَاهُ
مَا بِوُسْعِ ٱلْإِمْكَانِ مِثْلُكِ أُخْرَى

Beauty in you

    has become complete

There's none like you

    in creation

41

رَعَـى ٱللهُ طَـيْـرًا عَـلَـى بَـانَـةٍ
قَدَ ٱفْصَحَ لِي عَنْ صَحِيحِ ٱلْخَبَرْ

بِــأَنَّ ٱلْأَحِــبَّــةَ شَــدُّوا عَـلَـى
رَوَاحِـلِـهِـمْ ثُمَّ رَاحُــوا سَـحَـرْ

فَسِرْتُ وَفِي ٱلْقَلْبِ مِنْ أَجْلِهِمْ
جَـحِـيـمٌ لِـبَـيْـنِـهِـمُ تَـسْـتَـعِـرْ

أُتَـابِـعُـهُـمْ فِي ظَـلَامِ ٱلـدُّجَـى
أُنَــادِي بِهِـمْ ثُمَّ أَقْـفُـو ٱلْأَثَــرْ

وَمَــا لِي دَلِـيـلٌ عَـلَـى إِثْـرِهِـمْ [5]
سِـوَى نَـفَـسٍ مِـنْ هَـوَاهُـمْ عَـطِرْ

My Only Guide

God save that bird
high in a moringa

who called out the news
sharp and clear

that those I loved
had cinched their saddles

and set off by camel
at the break of dawn

leaving me, heart
afire, in their wake

In the moonless dark
I raced in pursuit

calling after,
close on their traces

tracking and tracking— [5]
my only guide

a fragrant breath
on the wind of desire

رَفَعْنَ ٱلسِّجَافَ أَضَاءَ ٱلدُّجَى
فَسَارَ ٱلرِّكَابُ لِضَوْءِ ٱلْقَمَرْ

فَأَرْسَلْتُ دَمْعِي أَمَامَ ٱلرِّكَابِ
فَقَالُوا مَتَى سَالَ هٰذَا ٱلنَّهَرْ

وَلَمْ يَسْتَطِيعُوا عُبُورًا فَقُلْتُ
دُمُوعِي جَرَيْنَ بِهٰذَا دِرَرْ

كَأَنَّ ٱلرُّعُودَ لِلَمْعِ ٱلْبُرُوقِ
وَسَيْرَ ٱلْغَمَامِ لِصَوْبِ ٱلْمَطَرْ

[10] وَجِيبُ ٱلْقُلُوبِ لِبَرْقِ ٱلثُّغُورِ
وَسَكْبُ ٱلدُّمُوعِ لِرَكْبٍ نَفَرْ

When they lowered their veils
they lit the dark—

flooding the riders
in a sudden full moon

My tears rained down,
blocking the way

Since when, they asked,
does a river run here?

The tears, I say—
as they seek

and fail to cross it—
are endless As

if the thunder
and lightning flares

and clouds roiling
in the pouring rain

were hearts beating, [10]
the flash of a smile

and a burst of tears
for those gone away

فَيَا مَنْ يُشَبِّهُ لِينَ ٱلْقُدُودِ
بِلِينِ ٱلْقَضِيبِ ٱلرَّطِيبِ ٱلنَّضِرْ

وَلَوْ عَكَسَ ٱلْأَمْرَ مِثْلَ ٱلَّذِي
فَعَلْتُ لَكَانَ سَلِيمَ ٱلنَّظَرْ

فَلِينُ ٱلْغُصُونِ لِلِينِ ٱلْقُدُودِ
وَوَرْدُ ٱلرِّيَاضِ لِوَرْدِ ٱلْخَفَرْ

You who liken
the lover's cheek

to the dewy softness
of a new spring bough

turn it around
as I've done and you'll see

a bough's pliant
as a lover's limbs

Blush red's
the garden rose

42

يَا أُولِي ٱلْأَلْبَابِ يَا أَهْلَ ٱلنُّهَى
هِمْتُ مَا بِيْنَ ٱلْمَهَاةِ وَٱلْمَهَا

مَنْ سَهَا عَنِ ٱلْسُّهَا فَمَا سَهَا
مَنْ سَهَا عَنِ ٱلْمَهَاةِ قَدْ سَهَا

سِرْ بِهِ بِسِرْبِهِ لِسِرْبِهِ
فَٱللُّهَى تَفْتَحُ بِٱلْحَمْدِ ٱللَّهَى

إِنَّهَا مِنْ فَتَيَاتٍ عُرُبٍ
مِنْ بَنَاتِ ٱلْفُرْسِ أَصْلاً إِنَّهَا

نَظَمَ ٱلْحُسْنُ مِنَ ٱلدُّرِّ لَهَا   [5]
أَشْنَبًا أَبْيَضَ صَافٍ كَٱلْمَهَا

Sign Masters

Wise ones! Sign-
    masters! I wander,
dazed, between
    Onyx and Oryx

Distracted, he
    who can't see the sun,
not Súha, that faint
    horizon spark

Take him to offer
    his heart for his herd
Oblations open
    the throat in praise

She's an Arab
    beauty and yet
pure Persian
    she is as well

Beauty composed her [5]
    a harmony in pearl,
her teeth gleaming
    clear as crystal

رَابَـنِي مِـنْـهَـا سُـفُـورٌ رَاعَـنِي
عِـنْـدَهُ مِـنْـهَـا جَمَــالٌ وَبَهَــا

فَأَنَا ذُو ٱلْمَـوْتَـتَـيْنِ مِنْهُـمَا
هٰـكَـذَا ٱلْـقُـرْآنُ قَـدْ جَـاءَ بِهَا

قُلْتُ مَا بَالُ سُفُورٍ رَابَنِي
مَوْعِدُ ٱلْأَقْـوَامِ إِشْـرَاقُ ٱلْمَهَا

قُلْتُ إِنِّي فِي حِمىً مِنْ فَاحِمٍ
سَـاتِـرٍ فَـلْـتُـرْسِـلِـيـهِ عِـنْـدَهَـا

شِـعْـرُنَـا هٰــذَا بِـلَا قَـافِـيَـةٍ [10]
إِنَّمَــا قَـصْـدِيَ مِـنْـهُ حَـرْفُ هَـا

غَرَضِي لَفْظَةُ هَا مِنْ أَجْلِهَا
لَسْتُ أَهْوَى ٱلْبَيْعَ إِلاَّ هَا وَهَا

She lowered her veil
    and a fearsome beauty
drew me toward her
    yet held me back

I'm the one
    with two deaths to die,
both told here
    in this Qur'an

Frightened by
    a lowered veil?
A battlefield's
    a rising sun

My sanctuary,
    I said, is night's
black curtain
    So let it fall

These verses have [10]
    no rhyme, the sound
of *her*'s their only
    aspiration

She is the sign,
    the signification
Her for *her*'s
    my only offer

43

وَلَا أَنْسَ يَوْمًا عِنْدَ وَانَةَ مَنْزِلِي
وَقَوْلِي لِرَكْبٍ رَائِحِينَ وَنُزَّلِ

أَقِيمُوا عَلَيْنَا سَاعَةً نَشْتَفِي بِهَا
فَإِنِّي وَمَنْ أَهْوَاهُمُ فِي تَعَلُّلِ

فَإِنْ رَحَلُوا سَارُوا بِأَيْمَنِ طَائِرٍ
وَإِنْ نَزَلُوا حَلُّوا بِأَخْصَبِ مَنْزِلِ

وَبِٱلشِّعْبِ مِنْ وَادِي قَنَاةٍ لَقِيتُهُمْ
وَعَهْدِي بِهِمْ بَيْنَ ٱلنَقَا وَٱلْمُشَلَّلِ

يُرَاعُونَ مَرْعَى ٱلْعِيسِ حَيْثُ وَجَدْنَهُ [5]
وَلَيْسَ يُرَاعُوا قَلْبَ صَبٍّ مُضَلَّلِ

Parting's Hour

I'll never forget
Camp Wân and my word
to the riders leading
my love away

Stay a while
for by my love!
I need some respite
and time to heal

If they ride, let it be
with fortune
If they halt, let it be
on fertile land

I met them in Qánat
valley and stayed
with them from
Náqa to Arroyo

They tend to roans [5]
grazing the pasture
but not to a lover
dazed and lost

فَيَا حَادِيَ ٱلْأَجْمَالِ رِفْقًا عَلَى فَتًى
تَـرَاهُ لَـدَى ٱلتَّوْدِيعِ كَـاسِرَ حَنْظَلِ

يُخَالِفُ بَيْنَ ٱلرَّاحَتَيْنِ عَلَى ٱلْحَشَا
يُسَكِّنُ قَلْبًا طَـارَ مِنْ صِرِّ مَحْمَلِ

يَقُولُونَ صَبْرًا وَٱلْأَسَى غَيْرُ صَابِرٍ
فَـمَا حِيلَتِي وَٱلـصَّـبْـرُ عَـنِّي بِمَعْزِلِ

وَلَـوْ كَـانَ لِي صَبْرٌ وَكُنْتُ بِحُكْمِهِ
لَمَا صَبرَتْ نَفْسِي فَكَيْفَ وَلَيْسَ لِي

Have mercy, driver,
on a young man
splitting bittergourd
at parting's hour

One hand he clutches
to his chest
The other calms
a heart tearing free

As the saddle groans
Patience! they say,
but grief knows not
what this means

And if I'd ever
been under its sway
I'd have lost it
So what of me now?

44

طَلَعَ ٱلْبَدْرُ فِي دُجَى ٱلشَّعَرِ
وَسَقَى ٱلْوَرْدَ نَرْجِسُ ٱلْحَوَرِ

غَادَةٌ تَاهَتِ ٱلْحِسَانُ بِهَا
وَزَهَا نُورُهَا عَلَى ٱلْقَمَرِ

هِيَ أَسْنَى مِنَ ٱلْمَهَاةِ سَنًا
صُورَةٌ لَا تُقَاسُ بِٱلصُّوَرِ

فَلَكُ ٱلنُّورِ دُونَ أَخْمَصِهَا
تَاجُهَا خَارِجٌ عَنِ ٱلْأُكَرِ

إِنْ سَرَتْ فِي ٱلضَّمِيرِ يَجْرَحُهَا
ذٰلِكَ ٱلْوَهْمُ كَيْفَ بِٱلْبَصَرِ [5]

Chimera

A full moon rises
    in the dark of her hair
Her eyes, black narcissi,
    moisten the rose

Other beauties
    in her flowering vanish
Her light darkens
    the light of the moon

More beautiful than
    all gazelles is she,
a form beyond
    all measure and form

The sphere of light
    turns at her feet
Her diadem gleams
    beyond the stars

If thought's whisper [5]
    might wound her
harsher still
    would be the gaze

لُعْبَةٌ ذِكْرُنَا يُذَوِّبُهَا
لَطُفَتْ عَنْ مَسَارِحِ ٱلنَّظَرِ

طَلَبَ ٱلنَّعْتُ أَنْ يُبَيِّنَهَا
فَتَعَالَتْ فَعَادَ ذَا حَصَرِ

وَإِذَا رَامَ أَنْ يُكَيِّفَهَا
لَمْ يَزَلْ نَاكِصاً عَلَى ٱلْأَثَرِ

إِنْ أَرَاحَ ٱلْمَطِيَّ طَالِبُهَا
لَمْ يُرِيحُوا مَطِيَّةَ ٱلْفِكَرِ

[10] رَوْحَنَتْ كُلَّ مَنْ أُشِبَّ بِهَا
نَقْلَةً عَنْ مَرَاتِبِ ٱلْبَشَرِ

غَيْرَةً أَنْ يُشَابَ رَائِقُهَا
بِٱلَّذِي فِي ٱلْحِيَاضِ مِنْ كَدَرِ

Chimera—recall her
    and she's gone—
too quick for thought
    or observation

Words would describe her
    but she rises
always just beyond
    and leaves them a'stammer

They'd place her
    but she steals away
leaving them baffled
    by her traces

Riders pursuing
    might ease their pace
but no one can ease
    a racing mind

All who love her [10]
    she revives,
then takes beyond
    the bounds of mortal being

Unwilling to lavish
    her nectared kiss
on a would-be lover
    in the mire

45

أَحْبَابَنَا أَيْنَ هُمُ
بِاللهِ قُولُوا أَيْنَ هُمْ

كَمَا رَأَيْتُ طَيْفَهُمْ
فَهَلْ تُرِينِي عَيْنَهُمْ

فَكَمْ وَكَمْ أَطْلُبُهُمْ
وَكَمْ سَأَلْتُ بَيْنَهُمْ

حَتَّى أَمِنْتُ بِينَهُمْ
وَمَا أَمِنْتُ بَيْنَهُمْ

لَعَلَّ سَعْدِي حَايِلٌ [5]
بَيْنَ ٱلنَّوَى وَبَيْنَهُمْ

لِتَنْعَمَ ٱلْعَيْنُ بِهِمْ
فَلَا أَقُولُ أَيْنَ هُمْ

Where Gone

Where are my true loves now? By God
tell me where they've gone

I have seen their apparition
Show me their true form!

How long have I sought among them
asking where they are

To be assured in their presence
but in the end—never sure

Perhaps my star will intervene [5]
twixt the here and far

My eyes rejoice, and my tongue
ask where O where no more

بَيْنَ ٱلْحَشَا وَٱلْعُيُونِ ٱلنُّجْلِ حَرْبُ هَوًى
وَٱلْقَلْبُ مِنْ أَجْلِ ذَاكَ ٱلْحَرْبِ فِي حَرَبِ

لَمْيَاءُ لَعْسَاءُ مَعْسُولٌ مُقَبَّلُهَا
شَهَادَةُ ٱلنَّحْلِ مَا تُلْقِي مِنَ ٱلضَّرَبِ

رَيَّا ٱلْمُخَلْخَلِ دَيْجُورٌ عَلَى قَمَرٍ
فِي خَدِّهَا شَفَقٌ غُصْنٌ عَلَى كُثُبِ

حَسْنَاءُ حَالِيَةٌ لَيْسَتْ بِغَانِيَةٍ
تَفْتَرُّ عَنْ بَرَدٍ ظُلْمٍ وَعَنْ شَنَبِ

تَصُدُّ جِدًّا وَتَلْهُو بِٱلْهَوَى لَعِبًا [5]
وَٱلْمَوْتُ مَا بَيْنَ ذَاكَ ٱلْجِدِّ وَٱللَّعِبِ

مَا عَسْعَسَ ٱللَّيْلُ إِلَّا جَاءَ يَعْقُبُهُ
تَنَفُّسُ ٱلصُّبْحِ مَعْلُومٌ مِنَ ٱلْحُقَبِ

وَلَا تَمُرُّ عَلَى رَوْضٍ رِيَاحُ صَبًا
يَحْوِي عَلَى كَاعِبَاتٍ خُرَّدٍ عُرُبِ

Cool Lightning

There's a wrench in my gut
  and a tear in my eye—
    my heart rages between

Deep red are her lips,
  her kisses sweet as
    clear honey from bees

Her anklets entice like a cloud
  on a moon—sunset
    on her cheek, branch on a dune

Single and yet her
  bangles sparkle, cool
    lightning is her smile

She guards herself in earnest [5]
  and in love she plays
    Death waits between

No night draws dark without
  the breath of dawn rising
    This we know of old

No wind from the East falls
  on a garden guarding maidens
    with budding breasts

إِلَّا أَمَالَتْ وَنَمَّتْ فِي تَنَسُّمِهَا
بِمَا حَمَلْنَ مِنَ ٱلْأَزْهَارِ وَٱلْقُضُبِ

سَأَلْتُ رِيحَ ٱلصَّبَا عَنْهُمْ لِتُخْبِرَنِي
قَالَتْ وَمَا لَكَ فِي ٱلْإِخْبَارِ مِنْ أَرَبِ

[10] فِي ٱلْأَبْرَقَيْنِ وَفِي بَرْكِ ٱلْغِمَادِ وَفِي
بَرْكِ ٱلْغَمِيمِ تَرَكْتُ ٱلْحَيَّ عَنْ كَثَبِ

لَا تَسْتَقِلُّ بِهِمْ أَرْضٌ فَقُلْتُ لَهَا
أَيْنَ ٱلْمَفَرُّ وَخَيْلُ ٱلشَّوْقِ فِي ٱلطَّلَبِ

هَيْهَاتَ لَيْسَ لَهُمْ مَغْنًى سِوَى خَلَدِي
فَحَيْثُ كُنْتُ يَكُونُ ٱلْبَدْرُ فَارْتَقِبِ

أَلَيْسَ مَطْلَعُهَا وَهْيَ وَمَغْرِبُهَا
قَلْبِي فَقَدْ زَالَ شُؤْمُ ٱلْبَانِ وَٱلْغَرَبِ

مَا لِلْغُرَابِ نَعِيقٌ فِي مَنَازِلِنَا
وَمَالَهُ فِي نِظَامِ ٱلشَّمْلِ مِنْ نَدَبِ

Without stirring the leaves
 and wafting the perfume
  it gathers and passes on

I asked the Eastwind about them
 And who are you to want
  to know? she answered

I left them at Twin Flash— [10]
 and at the relays of Ghimād
  and Ghamīm, close by

It's said no land can hold them
 But they will never elude
  the cavalries of my longing

They hide in my soul
 and here where I am, look!
  the full moon rises

In my mind, then sets
 in my heart Gone's
  the curse of willow and moringa

And here where we dwell
 no crow can caw, ruing
  our embrace as one

47

حَمَامَةَ ٱلْبَانِ بِذَاتِ ٱلْغَضَا
ضَاقَ لِمَا حَمَّلْتِنِيهِ ٱلْفَضَا

مَنْ ذَا ٱلَّذِي يَحْمِلُ شَجْوَ ٱلْهَوَى
مَنْ ذَا ٱلَّذِي يَجْرَعُ مُرَّ ٱلْقَضَا

أَقُولُ مِنْ وَجْدٍ وَمِنْ لَوْعَةٍ
يَا لَيْتَ مَنْ أَمْرَضَنِي مَرَّضَا

مَرَّ بِبَابِ ٱلدَّارِ مُسْتَهْزِئاً
مُسْتَخْفِيًا مُعْتَجِرًا مُعْرِضَا

[5] مَا ضَرَّنِي تَعْجِيرُهُ إِنَّمَا
أَضَرَّ بِي مِنْ كَوْنِهِ أَعْرَضَا

The Turning

Moringa dove cooing
in Dhāt al-Ghāda—
no world can hold
your song

Who can bear
love's sorrows
or down fate's
bitter potion?

Heartsplit I cry,
O you who put me
through all this
will you care for me now?

He passed by
my door laughing,
hid his face
then turned away

It wasn't his hiding [5]
that hurt, no
It was the turning,
the turning away

48

يَا حَادِيَ ٱلْعِيسِ بِسَلْعٍ عَرِّجِ
وَقِفْ عَلَى ٱلْبَانَةِ بِٱلْمُدَرَّجِ

وَنَادِهِمْ مُسْتَعْطِفًا مُسْتَلْطِفًا
يَا سَادَاتِي هَلْ عِنْدَكُمْ مِنْ فَرَجِ

بِرَامَةٍ بَيْنَ ٱلنَّقَا وَحَاجِرٍ
جَارِيَةٌ مَقْصُورَةٌ فِي هَوْدَجِ

يَا حُسْنَهَا مِنْ طَفْلَةٍ غُرَّتُهَا
تُضِيءُ لِلطَّارِقِ مِثْلِ ٱلسُّرُجِ

[5] لُؤْلُؤَةٌ مَكْنُونَةٌ فِي صَدَفٍ
مِنْ شَعَرٍ مِثْلَ سَوَادِ ٱلسَّبَجِ

لُؤْلُؤَةٌ غَوَّاصُهَا ٱلْفِكْرُ فَمَا
يَنْفَكُّ فِي أَعْمَاقِ تِلْكَ ٱللُّجَجِ

يَحْسَبُهَا نَاظِرُهَا ظَبْيَ نَقًا
مِنْ جِيدِهَا وَحُسْنِ ذَاكَ ٱلْغَنَجِ

كَأَنَّهَا شَمْسُ ضُحىً فِي حَمَلٍ
قَاطِعَةً أَقْصَى مَعَالِي ٱلدَّرَجِ

إِنْ حَسَرَتْ بُرْقُعَهَا أَوْ سَفَرَتْ
أَزْرَتْ بِأَنْوَارِ ٱلصَّبَاحِ ٱلْأَبْلَجِ

Brave

Turn at Splitrock, driver, then halt
by the moringa in Mudárraj

Call out: Ladies, would you
grant us sweet release?

Near Râma, Hājir, and White Dune
a shy-eyed girl rides in a palanquin

She lights the way like a lamp
for a man walking the night

Pearl in a shell of jet black hair— [5]
The mind dives after, sinking deep

Neck supple, gestures coquette,
like a gazelle of the shifting sands

Like the forenoon sun arcing
over Aries

When she lowers her veil, she covers
dawn in her morning light

[10]

نَادَيْتُهَا بَيْنَ ٱلْحِمَى وَرَامَةٍ
مَنْ لِفَتًى حَلَّ بِسَلْعٍ يَرْتَجِي

مَنْ لِفَتًى مُتَيَّمٍ فِي مَهْمَهٍ
مُوَلَّهٍ مُدَلَّهِ ٱلْعَقْلِ شَجِي

مَنْ لِفَتًى عَبْرَتُهُ مُغْرِقَةٌ
أَسْكَرَهُ خَمْرٌ بِذَاكَ ٱلْفَلَجِ

مَنْ لِفَتًى زَفْرَتُهُ مُحْرِقَةٌ
تَيَّمَهُ جَمَالُ ذَاكَ ٱلْبَلَجِ

قَدْ لَعِبَتْ أَيْدِي ٱلْهَوَى بِقَلْبِهِ
فَمَا عَلَيْهِ فِي ٱلَّذِي مِنْ حَرَجِ

I cried out between Híma and Râma, [10]

Who's here for a lad who halts and hopes

At Sal‘ For one in a desert maze,

haggard, haunted, forlorn?

For one drowned in his tears,

drunk on the wine of her open mouth?

For one burned in sighs,

lost in the glow between her eyes?

Desire's hand played on his heart

Where is his crime?

مَنْ لِي بِمَخْضُوبَةِ ٱلْبَنَانِ
مَنْ لِي بِمَعْسُولَةِ ٱللِّسَانِ

مِنْ كَاعِبَاتٍ ذَوَاتِ خِدْرٍ
نَوَاعِمٍ نُهَّدٍ حِسَانِ

بُدُورُ تَمٍّ عَلَى غُصُونٍ
هُنَّ مِنَ ٱلنَّقْصِ فِي أَمَانِ

فِي رَوْضَةٍ مِنْ دِيَارِ جِسْمِي
حَمَامَةٌ فَوْقَ غُصْنِ بَانِ

[5] تَذُوبُ عِشْقًا تَمُوتُ شَوْقًا
لَمَّا شَجَاهَا ٱلَّذِي شَجَانِي

تَنْدُبُ إِلْفًا تَذُمُّ دَهْرًا
رَمَاهَا قَصْدًا بِمَا رَمَانِي

فِرَاقُ جَارٍ وَنَأْيُ دَارٍ
فَوَا زَمَانِي عَلَى زَمَانِي

مَنْ لِي بِمَنْ تَرْتَضِي عَذَابِي
مَا لِي بِمَا تَرْتَضِي يَدَانِ

In the Ruins of My Body

Who'll show me her henna'd hand?
Who her honey'd tongue?

Such an enticing girl she is,
and in her beauty guarded well

Full moons on a flowering bough—
those like her will never fade

In the ruins of my body there's
a garden dove high in a moringa

She dies longing, dissolved in desire, [5]
stricken with what struck me

Her mate she mourns and blames time's
arrow buried in both our hearts

The near are gone, home's far away
Time has taken all that was

Who's with me as she commends my pain
Before her, all my power fades

50

وَغَـــادِرَةٍ قَـدْ غَـــادَرَتْ بِـغَـدَائِـرٍ
شَبِيهَ ٱلْأَفَـاعِـي مَـنْ أَرَادَ سَبِيلَا

سَلِيمًـا وَتَـلْـوِي لِينَـهَا فَتُـذِيبُـهُ
وَتَـتْـرُكُـهُ فَـوْقَ ٱلْـفِـرَاشِ عَلِيلَا

رَمَتْ بِسِهَامِ ٱللَّحْظِ عَنْ قَوْسِ حَاجِبٍ
فَمِنْ أَيِّ شِقٍّ جِئْتَ كُنْتَ قَتِيلَا

Done

Double-dealer with curls like snakes
she left a man who sought the way

Coiled him in her ringlets
and left him stricken on the bed

Prey to her glances from every side
Whichever way you've come, you're done

51

بِـذَاتِ ٱلْأَضَـا وَٱلْـمَـأْزِمَـيْنِ وَبَـارِقِ
وَذِي سَـلَـمٍ وَٱلْأَبْـرَقَـيْنِ لِـطَـارِقِ

بُـرُوقُ سُيُوفٍ مِنْ بُـرُوقِ مَبَاسِـمٍ
نَـوَافِجُ مِسْكٍ مَا أُبِيحَتْ لِنَاشِقِ

فَإِنْ حُورِبُوا سَلُّوا سُيُوفَ لِحَاظِهِمْ
وَإِنْ سُولِمُوا هَدُّوا عُقُودَ ٱلْمَضَائِقِ

فَـنَـالُـوا وَنِـلْـنَـا لَـذَّتَـيْنِ تَـسَـاوَتَـا
فَمُلْكٌ لِمَعْشُوقٍ وَمُلْكٌ لِعَاشِقِ

Nightwalker

For a nightwalker
at Ma'zimáyn or Áda,
at Flashrock, Ridge
or Abraqáyn

There are swords
flashing through smiles
and pouches of musk
forbidden the senses

Resist and they'll
unsheathe their glances
Give in and they
will shatter the chains

We took and they
took equal pleasure—
Kingdoms for the beloved
and for the lover

52

رَضِيتُ بِرَضْوَى رَوْضَةً وَمُنَاخَا
فَإِنَّ بِهِ مَرْعًى وَفِيهِ نُقَاخَا

عَسَى أَهْلُ وُدِّي يَسْمَعُونَ بِخِصْبِهِ
فَيَتَّخِذُوهُ مَرْبَعًا وَمُنَاخَا

فَإِنَّ لَنَا قَلْبًا بِهِنَّ مُعَلَّقًا
إِذَا مَا حَدَى ٱلْحَادِي بِهِنَّ أَصَاخَا

وَإِنْ هُمْ تَنَادَوْا لِلرَّحِيلِ وَقَوَّزُوا
سَمِعْتَ لَهُ خَلْفَ ٱلرِّكَابِ صُرَاخَا

فَإِنْ قَصَدُوا ٱلزَّوْرَاءَ كَانَ أَمَامَهُمْ [5]
وَإِنْ يَمَّمُوا ٱلْجَرْعَاءَ ثَمَّ أَنَاخَا

Rídwa

Happy the thought
    of Rídwa's pastures
where the traveler finds
    cool waters and rest

My love's party might
    have heard of the place,
kneeled camels there
    and encamped

Wherever they go
    my soul clings
as they chant
    their camels on

And when amid shouts
    they break toward desert
you can hear it
    howling on their trail

If they move toward Zawrā' [5]
    that's where it leads them
If it's Jawrā' they seek
    it awaits them there

فَمَا ٱلطَّيْرُ إِلَّا حَيْثُ كَانُوا وَخَيَّمُوا
فَــإِنَّ لَــهُ فِي حَـيِّـهِـنَّ فِـرَاخَـا

تَحَارَبَ خَوْفٌ لِي وَخَوْفٌ مِنْ أَجْلِهَا
وَمَـا وَاحِـدٌ عَـنْ قِـرْنِـهِ يَـتَـرَاخَـا

إِذَا خَـطَـفَـتْ أَبْـصَـارَنَـا سُبُـحَـاتُـهَـا
أَصَمَّ لَهَا صَوْتُ ٱلشَّهِيقِ صِمَاخَا

Wherever they are

  wherever they camp

the bird follows

  For its chicks are there

Two fears ceaselessly

  vie within me,

fear for myself

  and fear for her

Lest her splendor

  shatter my gaze

and she be deafened

  by my sighs

53

إِذَا مَا ٱلْتَقَيْنَا لِلْوَدَاعِ حَسِبْتَنَا
لَدَى ٱلضَّمِّ وَٱلتَّعْنِيقِ حَرْفًا مُشَدَّدَا

فَنَحْنُ وَإِنْ كَانَتْ مُثَنًّى شُخُوصُنَا
فَمَا تُبْصِرُ ٱلْأَبْصَارُ إِلَّا مُوَحَّدَا

وَمَا ذَاكَ إِلَّا مِنْ نُحُولِي وَنُورِهِ
فَلَوْلَا أَنِينِي مَا رَأَتْ لِيَ مَشْهَدَا

Like a Doubled Letter

Parting we cling to each
other and intertwine
like a doubled letter

Although our shapes
are two we appear
as one alone

He's light and I am shadow
If I didn't moan
you'd never see me

54

وَقَالُوا شُمُوسٌ بِدَارِ ٱلْفَلَكْ
وَهَلْ مَنْزِلُ ٱلشَّمْسِ إِلَّا ٱلْفَلَكْ

إِذَا قَامَ عَرْشٌ عَلَى سَاقِهِ
فَلَمْ يَبْقَ إِلَّا ٱسْتِوَاءُ ٱلْمَلِكْ

إِذَا خَلَصَ ٱلْقَلْبُ مِنْ جَهْلِهِ
فَمَا هُوَ إِلَّا نُزُولُ ٱلْمَلَكْ

تَمَلَّكَنِي وتَمَلَّكْتُهُ
فَكُلٌّ لِصَاحِبِهِ قَدْ مَلَكْ

[5] فَكَوْنِيَ مِلْكًا لَهُ بَيِّنٌ
وَمِلْكِي لَهُ قَوْلُهُ هَيْتَ لَكْ

فَيَا حَادِيَ ٱلْعِيسِ عَرِّجْ بِنَا
وَلَا تَعْدُ بِٱلرَّكْبِ دَارَ ٱلْفَلَكْ

أَعَلَّكَ دَارٌ عَلَى شَاطِئٍ
بِقُرْبِ ٱلْمُسَنَّى وَمَا عَلَّلَكْ

فَلَيْتَ ٱلَّذِي بِي وَحُمِّلْتُهُ
مِنَ ٱلْحُبِّ رَبُّ ٱلْهَوَى حَمَّلَكْ

فَلَيْسَ زَرُودٌ وَلَا حَاجِرٌ
وَلَا سَلَمٌ مَنْزِلٌ أَنْحَلَكْ

Dár al-Fálak

Those suns, they tell us, are in Dār al-Fálak
Beyond what heaven should a sun be set?

When the throne rests firm on its pillars,
the king has only to take his place

When the heart abandons its last delusion
it's only an angel descending

I am his and he is mine
We belong to each other

I'm his, clearly, but is he mine? [5]
Come to me now, he's saying

Red-roan driver, hold on!
Don't miss the turn at Dār al-Fálak

May a riverbank camp near Musánna cast
a spell on you and never let go

The love I've borne, the pain endured—
may the lord of desire put you through it

It wasn't Zarūd, Hājir, or Sálam
that left you, lover, drawn as a ghost

[10]

ظَلِلْتَ لِحَرِّ ٱلْهَوَى طَالِبًا
سَحَابَ ٱلْوِصَالِ فَمَا ظَلَّلَكْ

أَذَلَّكَ عِزٌّ لِسُلْطَانِهِ
فَلَيْتَ كَمَا ذَلَّلَكَ ذَلَّ لَكْ

وَيَا لَيْتَهُ إِذْ أَبَى عِزُّهُ
تَدَلُّلَهُ لَيْتَهُ دَلَّلَكْ

In the scorching heat, you searched in vain [10]
for a cloud of union to shade you

May the one who subjected you
grant you affection

But if pride restrains him
let him embolden you

أَغِيبُ فَيُفْنِي ٱلشَّوْقُ نَفْسِي فَأَلْتَقِي
فَلَا أَشْتَفِي فَٱلشَّوْقُ غَيْبًا وَمَحْضَرَا

وَيُحْدِثُ لِي لُقْيَاهُ مَا لَمْ أَظُنَّهُ
فَكَانَ ٱلشِّفَا دَاءً مِنَ ٱلْوَجْدِ آخَرَا

لِأَنِّيَ أَرَى شَخْصاً يَزِيدُ جَمَالُهُ
إِذَا مَا ٱلْتَقَيْنَا نَضْرَةً وَتَكَبُّرَا

فَلَا بُدَّ مِنْ وَجْدٍ يَكُونُ مُقَارِنًا
لِمَا زَادَ مِنْ حُسْنٍ نِظَامًا مُحَرَّرَا

No Cure

Without him I die
    and with him's no better
With or without him
    longing's the same

I found him, finding
    what I hadn't foreseen,
the cure and disease
    as equal fevers

His silhouette flares
    as we draw near
each other and
    burns more proud

The deeper the harmony
    the sharper the pain
Measure for measure
    as decreed

56

ٱلْقَصْرُ ذُو ٱلشُّرُفَاءِ مِنْ بَغْدَادِ
لَا ٱلْقَصْرُ ذُو ٱلشُّرَفَاتِ مِنْ سِنْدَادِ

وَٱلتَّاجُ مِنْ فَوْقِ ٱلرِّيَاضِ كَأَنَّهُ
عَذْرَاءُ قَدْ جُلِيَتْ بِأَعْطَرِ نَادِ

وَٱلرِّيحُ تَلْعَبُ بِٱلْغُصُونِ فَتَنْتَشِي
وَكَأَنَّهُ مِنْهَا عَلَى مِيعَادِ

وَكَأَنَّ دِجْلَةَ سِلْكُهَا فِي جِيدِهَا
وَٱلْبَعْلُ سَيِّدُنَا ٱلْإِمَامُ ٱلْهَادِي

أَلنَّاصِرُ ٱلْمَنْصُورُ خَيْرُ خَلِيفَةٍ [5]
لَا يَمْتَطِي فِي ٱلْحَرْبِ مَتْنَ جَوَادِ

Baghdad Song

I long for Baghdād's
    palace of the brave
(not for the battlements
    of old Sindād)

It crowns the gardens
    cascading below—
a virgin revealed
    in a perfumed chamber

The branches are stirred
    by the wind and bend,
lovers joined
    together at last

The river Tigris
    adorns her
Her lord's our master
    imâm and guide—

Násir, Mansúr, [5]
    best of the caliphs,
who never rode out
    for war

صَلَّى عَلَيْهِ ٱللهُ مَا صَدَحَتْ بِهِ
وَرْقَا مُطَوَّقَةٌ عَلَى مَيَّادِ

وَكَذَاكَ مَا بَرَقَتْ بُرُوقُ مَبَاسِمٍ
سَحَّتْ لَهَا مِنْ مُقْلَتَيَّ غَوَادِ

مِنْ خُرَّدٍ كَٱلشَمْسِ أَقْلَعَ غَيْثُهَا
فَبَدَتْ بِأَضْوَا مُسْتَنِيرٍ بَادِ

God bless him
    long as a dove
on a bough coos
    and sways

Long as smiles
    flash lightning
(my eyes responding
    like the morning rain)

From a bride like
    the sun when the mists
part, unveiling
    herself in splendor

57

أَلَا يَا نَسِيمَ ٱلرِّيحِ بَلِّغْ مَهَا نَجْدٍ
بِأَنِّي عَلَى مَا تَعلَمُونَ مِنَ ٱلْعَهْدِ

وَقُلْ لِفَتَاةِ ٱلْحَيِّ مَوْعِدُنَا ٱلْحِمَى
غُدَيَّةَ يَوْمِ ٱلسَّبْتِ عِنْدَ رُبَا نَجْدِ

عَلَى ٱلرَّبْوَةِ ٱلْحَمْرَاءِ مِنْ جَانِبِ ٱلصُّوَى
وعَنْ أَيْمَنِ ٱلْأَفْلَاجِ وَٱلْعَلَمِ ٱلْفَرْدِ

فَإِنْ كَانَ حَقًّا مَا تَقُولُ وَعِنْدَهَا
إِلَيَّ مِنَ ٱلشَّوْقِ ٱلْمُبَرِّحِ مَا عِنْدِي

[5] إِلَيْهَا فَفِي حَرِّ ٱلظَّهِيرَةِ نَلْتَقِي
بِخَيْمَتِهَا سِرًّا عَلَى أَصْدَقِ ٱلْوَعْدِ

فَتُلْقِي وَنُلْقِي مَا نُلَاقِي مِنَ ٱلْهَوَى
وَمِنْ شِدَّةِ ٱلْبَلْوَى وَمِنْ أَلَمِ ٱلْوَجْدِ

أَأَضْغَاثُ أَحْلَامٍ أَبُشْرَى مَنَامَةٍ
أَنُطْقُ زَمَانٍ كَانَ فِي نُطْقِهِ سَعْدِي

لَعَلَّ ٱلّذِي سَاقَ ٱلْأَمَانِي يَسُوقُهَا
عِيَانًا فَيُهْدِي رَوْضُهَا لِي جَنَى ٱلْوَرْدِ

Red Rise

Eastwind fragrance, bring the gazelles of Najd
this word, that I, as they know me, am faithful

Tell the girl of the tribe we'll meet early
Saturday morning, in the Najdian hills

Near the trail-stone at the red rise
to the right of the flood beds and lonely ruin

If, as you say, it's true that she suffers
the same desire as I do and burns

We'll shade together in her tent [5]
fulfilling the promise we made

We'll tell of our longings, our tribulations
our trances, aches, and fevers—dream

stuff? signs from sleep bright with promise?
voice of a time that foretold my fortune?

May wishes' shepherd lead them to day—
and her garden enclose me in rose

58

أَلَا هَلْ إِلَى ٱلزُّهْرِ ٱلْحِسَانِ سَبِيلُ
وَهَلْ لِي عَلَى آثَارِهِنَّ دَلِيلُ

وَهَلْ لِي بِخَيْمَاتِ ٱللِّوَى مِنْ مُعَرَّسٍ
وَهَلْ لِي فِي ظِلِّ ٱلْأُثَيْلِ مَقِيلُ

فَقَالَ لِسَانُ ٱلْحَالِ يُخْبِرُ أَنَّهَا
تَقُولُ تَمَنَّ مَا إِلَيْهِ سَبِيلُ

وِدَادِي صَحِيحٌ فِيكِ يَا غَايَةَ ٱلْمُنَى
وَقلبِي مِنْ ذَاكَ ٱلْوِدَادِ عَلِيلُ

تَعَالَيْتِ مِنْ بَدْرٍ عَلَى ٱلْقَلْبِ طَالِعٍ
وَلَيْسَ لَهُ بَعْدَ ٱلطُّلُوعِ أُفُولُ [5]

Is There a Way

Is there a way
    to those radiant graces,
a guide who'd track them
    to their place of rest

A haven from midday
    sun in the shade
of the persica by
    those tents near the dune?

A voice within
    told me her answer
Hope for what
    you may attain!

My love for you
    is strong and in it
I'm stricken   You
    are my desire

You are the full moon [5]
    risen within me,
risen and never
    to decline

فَدَيْتُكِ يَا مَنْ عَزَّ حُسْنًا وَنَخْوَةً
فَلَيْسَ لَهُ بَيْنَ ٱلْحِسَانِ عَدِيلُ

فَرَوْضُكِ مَطْلُولٌ وَوَرْدُكِ يَانِعٌ
وَحُسْنُكِ مَعْشُوقٌ عَلَيْهِ قَبُولُ

وَزَهْرُكِ بَسَّامٌ وَغُصْنُكِ نَاعِمٌ
تَمِيلُ لَهُ ٱلْأَرْوَاحُ حَيْثُ يَمِيلُ

وَظُرْفُكِ فَتَّانٌ وَطَرْفُكِ صَارِمٌ
بِهِ فَارِسُ ٱلْبَلْوَى عَلَيَّ يَصُولُ

I ransom my life
    for you, asking
nothing but beauty
    in return

Your dewy garden
    glistens, your rose
unfolds, and all
    the world adores you

Your flowers gleam
    Your boughs are tender
Spirits bend
    with them as they sway

Your charm lures
    Your glances pierce
Tribulation's rider
    charges me

59

لِطَيْبَةَ ظَبْيٌ ظُبَى صَارِمٍ
تَجَرَّدَ مِنْ طَرْفِهَا ٱلسَّاحِرِ

وَفِي عَرَفَاتٍ عَرَفْتُ ٱلّذِي
تُرِيدُ فَلَمْ أَكُ بِٱلصَّابِرِ

وَلَيْلَةِ جَمْعٍ جَمَعْنَا بِهَا
كَمَا جَاءَ فِي ٱلْمَثَلِ ٱلسَّائِرِ

يَمِينُ ٱلْفَتَاةِ يَمِينٌ فَلَا
تَكُنْ تَطْمَئِنٌّ إِلَى غَادِرِ

مُنًى بِمِنًى نِلْتُهَا لَيْتَهَا [5]
تَدُومُ إِلَى ٱلزَّمَنِ ٱلْآخِرِ

تَوَلَّعْتُ فِي لَعْلَعٍ بِٱلَّتِي
تُرِيكَ سَنَا ٱلْقَمَرِ ٱلزَّاهِرِ

رَمَتْ رَامَةً وَصَبَتْ بِٱلصَّبَا
وَحَجَّرَتِ ٱلْحَجْرَ بِٱلْحَاجِرِ

وَشَامَتْ بُرَيْقًا عَلَى بَارِقٍ
بِأَسْرَعَ مِنْ خَطْرَةِ ٱلْخَاطِرِ

وَغَاضَتْ مِيَاهُ ٱلْغَضَا مِنْ غَضًى
بِأَضْلُعِهِ مِنْ هَوًى سَاحِرِ

I Came to Know

Táyban gazelles entrance with glances,
sword edges flashing bright

At Árafa I saw what she wanted
and lost all patience there

We joined her late one night in Jem
as foretold down the generations

A maiden's oath is but a promise
Don't trust in one who'll desert you

The wishes I was granted in Mína— [5]
would they'd lasted till the end of time!

In Lá'la' I was set aflame
by one who shows the full moon rising

In Râma she searched, at Sába she burned,
in Hājir she broke the seal

In Bāriq she saw the signs of lightning
flash quicker than thought in the mind

The waters of Gháda were parched
by desire aflame within me

وَبَانَتْ بِبَانِ ٱلنَّقَى فَٱنْتَقَتْ [10]
لَآلِئَ مَكْنُونَهِ ٱلْفَاخِرِ

وَآضَتْ بِذَاتِ ٱلْأَضَى ٱلْقَهْقَرَى
حِذَارًا مِنْ ٱلْأَسَدِ ٱلْخَادِرِ

بِذِي سَلَمٍ أَسْلَمَتْ مُهْجَتِي
إِلَى لَحْظِهَا ٱلْفَاتِكِ ٱلْفَاتِرِ

حَمَت بِٱلْحِمَى وَلَوَتْ بِٱللِّوَى
كَعَطْفَةِ جَارِحِهَا ٱلْكَاسِرِ

وَفِي عَالِجٍ عَالَجَتْ أَمْرَهَا
لِتُفْلَتَ مِنْ مِخْلَبِ ٱلطَّائِرِ

خَوَرْنَقُهَا خَارِقٌ لِلسَّمَا [15]
ءِ يَسْمُو ٱعْتِلَاءً عَلَى ٱلنَّاظِرِ

At White Dune's moringa she departed [10]
then gathered her choicest hidden pearls

At Dhāt al-Áda she turned back,
wary of a lion in wait

In Dhū Sálam she submitted my soul
to her lethal gaze

At Híma stood watch and in Líwa swayed
through the predator's crush

In peril at ʻĀlij, she slipped
through the raptor's claws

Her Khawárnaq tower soars [15]
beyond the heavens

60

أَلْـمِـمْ بِمَـنْـزِلِ أَحْـبَـابٍ لَهُـمْ ذِمَـمُ
سَحَّتْ عَلَيْهِ سَحَابٌ صَوْبُهَا دِيَمُ

وَٱسْتَنْشِقِ ٱلرِّيحَ مِنْ تِلْقَاءِ أَرْضِهِمِ
شَوْقًا لِتُخْبِرَكَ ٱلْأَرْوَاحُ أَيْـنَ هُمُ

أَظُنُّهُـمْ خَيَّمُوا بِٱلْبَانِ مِـنْ إِضَـمٍ
حَيْثُ ٱلْعَرَارُ وَحَيْثُ ٱلشِّيحُ وَٱلْكَتَمُ

Artemisia and Arâr

Pass by the lovers' station
    where covenants are kept
    Let it be blessed
by quenching rains

Breathe in the spirits
    that hail from their lands
    and long to know
where your loves have gone

Their tents perhaps pitched
    near Ídam's moringa
    on grounds dappled
with artemisia and arâr

61

أَلَا يَا بَانَةَ ٱلْوَادِي
بِشَاطِي نَهْرِ بَغْدَادِ

شَجَانِي فِيكِ نَيَّاحٌ
طَرُوبٌ فَوْقَ مَيَّادِ

يُذَكِّرُنِي تَرَنُّمُهُ
تَرَنُّمَ رَبَّةِ ٱلنَّادِي

إِذَا سَوَّتْ مِثَالِثَهَا
فَلَا تَذْكُرْ أَخَا ٱلْهَادِي

[5] وَإِنْ جَادَتْ بِنَغْمَتِهَا
فَمَنْ أَنْجَشَةُ ٱلْحَادِي

بِذِي ٱلْخَضِمَاتِ مِنْ سَلْمَى
يَمِينًا ثُمَّ سِنْدَادِ

لَقَدْ أَصْبَحْتُ مَشْغُوفًا
بِمَنْ سَكَنَتْ بِأَجْيَادِ

غَلِطْنَا إِنَّمَا سَكَنَتْ
سُوَيْدَا خِلْبِ أَكْبَادِي

لَقَدْ تَاهَ ٱلْجَمَالُ بِهَا
وَفَاحَ ٱلْمِسْكُ وَٱلْجَادِي

Tigris Song

O moringa of the flood-bed
at the Tigris's banks

The cry of a dove on a swaying bough
saddens my heart

Her song's like the song
of the assembly's queen

At the sound of her oud, you'll
forget the music of al-Rashīd

And when she sings, the chants [5]
of Ánjash fade

In Khadimāt, Sálma's direction,
and in Sindād, I swear,

I'm gone for a girl
in Ajyâdī

No, she dwells within
my liver's black bile

In a rush of saffron and musk
beauty falls bewildered

NOTES TO THE POEMS

Poem 1. This poem, and with it the *Tarjumān* as a whole, begins with the poet asking where his beloved and her company might be in their journey away from him. That motif establishes the *Tarjumān*'s first-order poetics in which the lover is voiced as male, and the beloved primarily (although not exclusively) as female. The poet may refer to the beloved in the singular or the plural. Thus, the plural "if they knew" refers to a specific group, the women of the tribe who, accompanied by male camel-drivers or guides, would travel together, shielded from the elements and from the gaze within their howdahs. "They" can then refer to the ensemble or to the beloved specifically. In many *Tarjumān* poems, the lover has his own ensemble with the companions who are asked to share the poet's grief.

Verse 4 introduces the bewilderment that inflects poems throughout the *Tarjumān*. Lovers, referred to grandly as the "lords of love" (*arbāb al-hawā*), are ensnared and bewildered by that which they should master. In the *Tarjumān*, bewilderment comes in many forms and goes by many names, as the poet and even beauty itself find themselves perplexed, speechless, astonished, or lost.

Poem 2. This poem begins with "the moment of departure," when the beloved and the other women of the tribe mount into their elaborately brocaded camel palanquins, before being led away by their camel-guides. The poem then shifts through a range of Qur'anic and cultic allusions, first and foremost to the Queen of Sheba, who is unnamed in the Qur'an but known in the tradition as Bilqīs. She first appears in verse 2, when peacock-like beauties in their howdahs are said to "Take possession / with glances that kill / like Bilqīs of Sheba / on her throne of pearl." The Qur'anic story of Bilqīs (Q 27:15–44) culminates with Bilqīs having submitted (*aslamtu*) along with the prophet Sulaymān to the one God. Bilqīs continues to hover over the central verses of the poem before reemerging explicitly at the end.

Idrīs is a prophet mentioned twice in the Qur'an (Q 19:56–57; 21:85–86); he was associated in tradition with the biblical Enoch and the Greek Hermes, especially within the Arabic traditions surrounding Hermes Trismegistus. In hadith and biographical accounts of Muḥammad's heavenly ascent, Idrīs appears as the prophet of the fourth heaven, which was viewed as the sphere of the sun.

In verse 4, the poet compares this goddess-like figure to the Qur'anic 'Īsā, who is able to bring the dead to life. He then associates her with the tablets of the Torah. From there the transformations pick up speed. She appears as a bishop; as the daughter of the Rūm or Byzantine Christians; as a being bathed in the light of the *nāmūs*, which is associated in both Christian and Islamic traditions with the Holy Spirit; as an anchorite who retreats to a tomb (specifically a marble mausoleum) in contemplation; and as a personification of wisdom who baffles Muslim sages as well as rabbis, psalmists, and priests. She is a being of such magnetic power that, were she to show an interest in the gospel, the lover and his companions would appear suddenly as church dignitaries.

Verse 10 returns to the moment of separation, with the poet begging the camel-driver not to lead his beloved away. In verse 12, at the point of death, the poet pleads with her to release him. She yields, relents, or submits (*aslamat* in the past tense)—just as Bilqīs had submitted to the one God along with Sulaymān.

The poems ends with a reference to Iblīs, the Lucifer-like figure in the Qur'an who refused the divine command to bow before Adam, was cast from his high station, and became the tempter of humankind. ("May salvation's king": Nicholson reads *malak* [angel] in place of *malik* [king].)

Why would the poet ask for release on the point of death, which throughout the *Tarjumān* can reflect his passing away in union with the beloved? In *Priceless Treasures*, Ibn 'Arabī explains the poet's hesitation as due to his fear of *ḥulūl*, which occurs when the mystic believes he has become one with an incarnate God. He also quotes a hadith according to which the prophet Muḥammad says to God, "I take refuge from you in you" (*a'ūdhu bika minka*).

Poem 3. This poem opens and closes with the poet asking his companions to contact his beloved(s) or those who might know where the beloved's party has gone. The first site of the longed-for contact is Mecca, the evocation of which leads to the scene of the lover's self-sacrifice at the hajj.

Verses 2–4 evoke several core rites: the casting of pebbles at the stone cairns of Minā, near the station of Muḥaṣṣab; the drinking from the waters of Zamzam spring, which in the Qur'anic account was opened miraculously when Hājar and her son Ismāʿīl were about to perish from thirst; "fasts," which refer to the daily acts of fasting (*ṣawm*) obligatory throughout the month of Ramaḍān and are viewed as a voluntary act of piety during periods of the hajj. "Feast" (*ʿīd*) is the term used for the sacrifice and shared consumption of a camel, sheep, or goat in remembrance of Abraham's sacrifice, an event that culminates the pilgrimage experience at the hajj and is carried out on the same day by nonpilgrims across the world. Verse 2, "my hajj": more fully "my hajj and *ʿumra*." *ʿUmra*, the voluntary minor pilgrimage, centers on the circumambulation of the Kaʿba and the running back and forth between the two hills in remembrance of Hājar's search for water. It can be carried out directly after the hajj, or separately throughout the year outside of the hajj season. (On the lover's self-sacrifice during the hajj, see Muṣṭafā Shaybī's commentary on verses attributed to al-Ḥallāj on that same theme, in the course of which Shaybī offers several examples from later poets. Kāmil Muṣṭafā Shaybī, *Sharḥ dīwān al-Ḥallāj* [Paris: Manshūrāt Asmār, 2005], 366–37.)

After the hajj verses, the poet resumes his journey by proxy, calling on the driver of the camel-train to travel through various desert sites in search of the beloved and her party. (Whose camel train: the beloved's or the poets, or in the poet's mind at least, both.) In the event that the driver's shouted greetings are not returned, the poet begs him to call out the names of the beloveds of the past: "Daʿd and Rabáb, / Záynab and Hind, / Lúbna, then Sálma." Lubnā was the beloved of the poet Qays ibn Durayd, and their tale is told in the *Great Book of Songs*. (The phrase *wa zamzami* at the end of the verse is not a reference to Zamzam spring but is an imperative verb meaning to "ring forth.")

Hálba (Ḥalba, v. 10) is a district on the southwestern side of the Tigris River in Baghdad. Its mention here, along with other references to sites in or near Baghdad (as in poems 54, 56, and 61), has enhanced interest in the possibility that Niẓām may have been living in the Baghdad area after her time in Mecca.

Poems 4–6. These poems begin a pattern within the *Tarjumān* with short lyrical interludes alternating with longer and more complex poems. **Poem 4** opens in *jinās* mode with the *s/l/m* and *ḥ/l/l* consonants echoing one another throughout the verse: ***salāmun ʿalā salmā wa man ḥalla bi-l-ḥimā wa ḥuqqa li-mithlī an yusallima***: "Peace [be to] Sálma / and Peace to those / who halt at al-Híma / It's right I greet you." Tucked within these phonetic fireworks is what may be a rejoinder to Qurrat al-ʿAyn who, in the preface devoted to her, had rebuked Ibn ʿArabī by declaring that it was not fitting "for one like you (*mithlak*) to speak in such a way." Here the poet responds that it is right for one like me (*mithlī*) to greet you. The poem ends with the voice of the beloved breaking in to respond to the lover's complaint. She does so by emphasizing the paradox of *shawq* that recurs at other critical moments in the *Tarjumān*: "*Each moment he / beholds me anew / in his heart*, she said / *What more can he ask?*"

Poem 5 opens with the binary relationship between the Arabian uplands of Najd and the region of Tihām (more fully, Tihāma), the coastal plain along the Red Sea. The poet intensifies the theme by following the mention of Najd and Tihāma with two Arabic verbs based on the *n/j/d* and *t/h/m* roots. *Anjada*: "to ascend in travel" or "to travel to the highlands of Najd." *Athama* denotes the descending movement of travel or, more specifically, travel to the lowland, coastal region of Tihāma.

Poem 6 begins by extending the theme of patience that concluded the previous poem. Verse 1 takes shape around the double meaning of the Arabic verb *bāna*, one of many classical Arabic words that carry opposite meanings. *Bāna* can mean either "to appear, become present" or "to depart, become absent." In either case, the beloveds who are gone live still or once lived (the time frame is indefinite) within the grieving lover. Verse 2 extends the verbal play on *bāna* by mentioning the moringa (*bān*), a mention intensified by its placement in verse-end rhyming position. The final verse takes on a particular poignancy, given that those who are gone may represent not only the beloved and her party but all the friends and loved ones of the poet's past.

Poem 7. The poet returns to the hajj motifs found in poem 3 but in a new key, with huri-like figures opening and closing the poem. The various hajj rites unfold verse-by-verse through the body of the poem: the touching of the black stone in the Kaʿba wall during the ritual circumambulation; the march from ʿArafa (which can also be spelled ʿArafat) to Minā; the casting of pebbles at Minā's three cairns; the "standing" at ʿArafa for most of a day;

and partaking of waters from the Zamzam spring. Here the poet, rather than offering himself for sacrifice, risks perishing at the sight of unveiled beauty. By this point in the *Tarjumān*, a pattern has been established, with the lover encountering death or dying at the center of many of poems. If he has in fact perished, that leaves his continuing voice in verses that follow as a sort of ghostly presence or else, as some poems will later suggest, as part of a continual process of dying and being brought back to life. If he resists gazing at these personifications of beauty, he has, at the very least, fallen deep into lovesickness.

Two poems from ʿUmar ibn abī Rabīʿa offer a possible subtext for poems 3 and 7 in the *Tarjumān*: ʿUmar ibn Abī Rabīʿa, *Dīwān* (Beirut: Dār Bayrūt li-ṭ-ṭibāʿas wa-n-nashr, 1984), 399 and 422.

Poem 8: This deceptively simple poem begins with a mournful nasib in pre-Islamic style. The poet gestures toward the *aṭlāl*, then points to his own tears shed in memory of his beloved and all those associated with the remembered or imagined time of intimacy and belonging. He then tells of his reaction to the beloved's departure. As verse 4 transitions into verse 5, there is a shift in time as the poet turns to address the beloved directly.

The words "aflame / with ceaseless sorrow" lead naturally to the references to fire in verse 6, but the continuity in fire imagery is accompanied by a shift in address with the introduction of a new character, the fire-striker (*mūqida n-nār*), who in the premodern context would bring up images of a person striking flint or rubbing sticks together. The fire-striker should take it easy, the poet tells him, for right "here" (that is, here with the poet or, as Ibn ʿArabī glosses the verse in his commentary, "here in my heart") is passion's fire. The fire-striker need only take an ember from it to start a fire of his own. Here, the love-poet launches a twofold boast. As a lover, he brings his own fire, a fire from which any less passionate lover might borrow a flame. As a poet, his words burn with poetic fire, from which other poets might borrow a flame.

The Arabic *iqtabasa* means "to take an ember" but carries wider meanings as well: "to borrow from"; "to emulate"; "to study under" (in the sense of a student studying under the master of a particular discipline); "to quote"; and in literary-critical discourse, "to embed words or phrases from the Qur'an within a literary text." In classical Arabic poetry, an analogy to prophetic revelation could serve to intensify the poetic boast, and in this poem Ibn ʿArabī provides a subtle example. The second half of verse 6 evokes the Qur'anic story of Mūsā and the fire. "Here is passion's fire / Just take an ember" (*hādhihi nāru al-ṣabābati sha'nakum an taqtabisu*). In Q 20:9, Mūsā tells his journey companions to stay behind while he investigates a fire that he has discerned in the distance. Perhaps, he says, the fire he discerns may provide an ember (*qabas*) for his group or may offer guidance (*al-hudā*). (See also Q 27:8; Q 28:29.) When Mūsā approaches the fire, the divine voice addresses him, revealing the identity of the one God and commissioning him with the message he will deliver to Pharaoh. By the twelfth century, the analogy between Mūsā's fire and the fire within the lover's heart had become a core motif within Arabic love poetry.

The fire in the lover's heart introduced here recurs in other poems in the *Tarjumān*, with each occurrence resonating with earlier instances and foreshadowing later ones. That fire (erotic, poetic, prophetic, and mystical) passes its embers from one poem to another within the *Tarjumān* even as it borrows embers from the Qur'an and earlier poets.

For more on the motif of Mūsā's fire and the lover, see Emil Homerin, "A Distant Fire: Ibn al-Shahrazūrī's Mystical Ode and Arabic Sufi Verse," *Journal of Sufi Studies*, 4:1 (2015): 27–58.

Poem 9. This poem opens with the interpermeation of the natural and the human that will recur in other poems in the *Tarjumān*. It concludes in verse 5 with an image of monumental splendor as figures of beauty pose poetically like the graces in Renaissance art. In the case of the *Tarjumān*, however, these beauties are described through allusions to Qur'anic verses on the huris of paradise who appear as the archetypes of beauty and acceptance (Q 37:48–49). Verse 5 also echoes the opening and closing of poem 7 even as it foreshadows the central section of poem 12.

Poem 10. These two verses form an apparently simple repartee. In verse 1, the beloved rebukes the poet. The lover's response, "You're seeing yourself / in the mirror / of humankind," is rooted in a play on the word *insān*—a word that can mean "a human being," "humankind" in general, or "pupil of the eye." Poets and Sufis had long played on the metaphorical aspects of the mirror reflection. When you see yourself in the mirror, the self you see in the mirror is looking at you.

The unnamed lady is said to see her own reflection in the mirror of a human being *insān*. *Insān* is always gender nonspecific. It is also a word with deep Qur'anic resonance, as in Q 82.6 when the divine voice asks its human creation, "O human being, what has led you away from your generous lord," suggesting that *insān* can designate the human condition.

The mystical possibilities of this couplet will be drawn out further in poem 11. A bridge is provided by the word "garden." In his commentary to poem 10, Ibn ʿArabī writes that the vision of the divine beloved in his heart/eye is nothing other than the vision of the afterlife garden of the blessed as well as the garden of Eden. In poem 11, the poet declares his own amazement at "a garden among the flames" and proceeds to proclaim that his heart has become receptive of every form. For a discussion of the complete human being and the mirror image in the mystical thought of Ibn ʿArabī, see Michael Sells, *Mystical Languages of Unsaying* (Chicago: University of Chicago Press, 1994), chapter 3 ("Identity Shift and Meaning Event"), 63–89.

Poem 11. This poem, the keystone of the *Tarjumān*, takes us through a series of quietly spectacular transformations and reversals. In the first three verses, the poet engages in a dialogue with mournful doves of the moringa and the persica (*arāk*), a tree or large shrub that in the nasib came to be associated with the smile of the beloved. In verse 4, spirits howl and mourn in the branches of a third tree, the gháda (*ghadā*), which was valued for its shade and for use as cooking coals. In the *Tarjumān*, it is associated with the fire in the lover's heart and, in the commentary and other writings of Ibn ʿArabī, with the burning bush from which God addressed Mūsā (Q 20:11–14; 27:8–10; 28:30–31). As the spirits rustle and bend the branches, they bring the poet through the experience of "passing away" (*fanā'*).

At this point, the poet echoes poems 3 and 7 and foreshadows later poems by situating himself within the hajj. Two stations are mentioned: Jem (*al-jamʿ*, "the union," "the assembly") is an epithet for Muzdalifa, a site on the hajj route toward Minā where the vast numbers of pilgrims who have been traveling in staggered groups come together. Muhássab (*al-muḥaṣṣab*) is a site just nearby where the pilgrims gather the pebbles that they will cast at the three cairns (since reinforced as large pillars) of Minā. Equally significant are the two sites not necessarily associated with the hajj: Naʿmān and Tamarisk, which both mark times spent with or near the beloved. The verse elicits a homology between the hajj, in which pilgrims ritually approach the divine beloved, and the lover's pilgrim-like effort to follow the beloved along her journey away from him back to the lost time of union.

The hajj experience and the identity of the poet shift in verse 5, as the poet now speaks not of lovers and pilgrims performing the hajj but of his heart as the Kaʿba around which spirits or beloveds circle. Who are they who circle his heart? The most immediate possible antecedent of "they" is "the spirits." The image here recalls the Qur'anic depictions of the celestial temple around which angels circle and into which they disappear. But the verses that follow suggest that it is huri-like beauties who circle his heart. No longer is the poet as lover wandering Arabia in search of the lost beloved. No longer is he a pilgrim at the hajj. Rather, his heart has become the Kaʿba, the goal and still center of all movement. Here the poem enacts the Sufi idea, mentioned throughout Ibn ʿArabī's writings, that the greatest Kaʿba is the heart of the human being at the threshold of mystical union. The next two verses evoke the lover's complaint about the deceptiveness of the beloved's promise. Then, as is if in continuation of the same thought but in a reversal of it, the poet expresses wonder at the gazelle (a figure somewhere between a metaphor and an epithet for the beloved), who engages in the sign language and subtle communication that had long been a motif in ghazal poetry. (For a classic example, see ʿUmar ibn abī Rabīʿ, *Dīwān*, 344–45.)

Verses 10–13 form one of the most anthologized passages in Arabic poetry and especially in Sufi literature, though much is lost when those verses are shorn of the rest of poem. The verses begin with a play on the gazelle figure and the fire within the poet's heart, a play that will anchor other poems in the *Tarjumān*: "A pasture between / breastbone and spine / Marvel, a garden / among the flames." See also poem 20, verses 6–7: "My father's life, / my own! for / a gazelle browsing / within my ribs / What burns for her / there is light / and only light / can quell this fire."

Beginning the next verse, with "My heart can take on / any form," the poet proceeds to recall the sacred texts and sites of veneration that his heart can take on. He then declares the religion of love (*dīn al-ḥubb*)—even as he recalls beliefs and practices that sounded through poem 2, albeit in a different key.

The poem concludes with an homage to the lover/beloved pairs of the past. Bishr and Hind, like Qays and Laylā, are poet/beloved pairs from the early ghazal tradition whose stories were elaborated in the *Great Book of Songs*. Ghaylān (Ghaylān Ibn ʿUqba, d. ca. 735 CE), popularly known as Dhū al-Rumma, was considered the last representative of the early Arabic Bedouin ode. His odes consisted almost exclusively of the nasib and *raḥīl* (journey-quest). Rather than returning from the isolation of the solitary journey to celebrate the tribe or to present a missive to the ruler, however, this poet-lover journeys ceaselessly after the beloved Mayya and back to the times spent with her. (For an introduction to and translation of one of Dhū al-Rumma's odes, see Michael Sells, *Desert Tracings: Six Classic Arabian Odes* [Middletown, CT: Wesleyan University Press, 1989], 68–76.)

These classic lover-pairs serve as the poet's model (*uswa*), exemplars of the worldly and unworldly love celebrated in the *Tarjumān*. A couplet of Qays (Majnūn Laylā) in which he compares himself to an Udhrī lover-poet named ʿUrwa is particularly relevant to the dynamism of poem 11, with its emphasis on continual death and rebirth as the protean heart of the lover or mystic takes on ever new forms: "I marvel that ʿUrwa the ʿUdhrī / became a legend for generations / He died, comfortably, one time / while I die anew each day" (*Dīwān Majnūn Laylā*, edited by Yūsuf Farḥat [Beirut: Dar li-kitāb al-ʿArabī, 1994], 221).

As a whole, poem 11 consists of several movements. The dove scene (verses 1–3) establishes an intense emotional register. In verses 4–5, the poet "passes away" amid the moaning of spirits in the *ghaḍā* branches and, in a ghostly fashion, suffers torments after he has expired and anticipates new ordeals along the hajj stations (verse 6). The evocation of the hajj sets the stage for the radical transformation of verse 7, where the poet no longer speaks about the Kaʿba but *as* the Kaʿba. With verse 8 the lover's complaint about the beloved(s) turns to wonderment. He announces that his heart has become receptive of every form, unfolds the various forms it takes, and professes a "religion of love" modeled by the legendary lovers of the past.

Readers of other editions and translations of this poem will note the absence of two verses in this translation. The verses appear neither in the historic manuscripts of the *Tarjumān* nor in the version of poem 11 in *Sessions of the Righteous*. They do appear in *Priceless Treasures*, but without comment other than the statement that the meaning of the verses needed no explanation.

In other editions and translations, the verses follow the reference in verse 7 to spirits or beloveds circling the poet's heart. The poet states that these beings circled his heart just as the "Best of Creation" (an epithet for the prophet Muḥammad) circled the Ka'ba—a construction of mere stones that the intellect would consider unworthy of veneration. Yet the Prophet was *nātiq,* which means rational or capable of speech, the Arabic term used by philosophers who defined the human being as a rational/ speaking animal. The verses read: "As the Best of Creation / circled the Ká'ba / which reason and its proofs / would deem unworthy / And kissed stones there / he! a voice of reason / and what is the House [an epithet for the Ká'ba] / compared to human being?"

كَمَا طَافَ خَيرُ آلْخَلْقِ بِلْكَعْبَةِ
الَّتِي يَقُولُ دَلِيلُ آلْعَقْلِ فِيهَا بِنُقْصَانِ

وَقَبَّلَ أَحْجَارًا بِهَا وَهْوَ نَاطِقٌ
وَأَيْنَ مَقَامِ آلْبَيْتِ مِنْ قَدْرِ إِنْسَانِ

Poem 12. This poem takes up themes and images from poem 2, but in a different key. At its heart is an interplay between human and nonhuman realms of creation as well as in the tension between a transcendent reality and the manifestation of that transcendent reality within the world, and more specifically within the marble or porcelain figures mentioned in the first verse. It then extends that tension to the three-in-one being proclaimed in various Christian theologies, a triplicity mirrored in the poet's personae as gazelle-minder, astrologer, and monk. Statues: *al-dumā*, referring to the statues or figurines that Ibn 'Arabī associated with Christian veneration in greater Syria.

For the use of *dumya* / *dumā* in the poetry of medieval Islamic Spain, see Henri Pérès, *La poésie andalouse en arabe classique au XIe siècle; ses aspects généraux, ses principaux thèmes et sa valeur documentaire* (Paris: Maisonneuve, 1953), 178, 181, 334–43. And for *al-dumā* in early ghazal poetry, see 'Umar ibn Abī Rabī'a, *Dīwān*, 293–94.

Poem 13. The first four verses of this poem return to the mournful colloquy between the poet and dove or doves, and in this case enact that colloquy through an embedded dialogue. In verse 5, the poet recalls his experience at ʿĀlij, the immense sand desert known today as the Nefūd, just north of the medieval pilgrimage route from Mecca and Medina to Iraq. The rest of the poem proceeds in classical nasib style. Verse 8 recalls the trauma of the day of separation (*yawm al-bayn*). Verses 9–10 recall the beloved's party's journey away from the poet, a scene that extends the poet's memory into the realm of imagination, given that the poet-lover would not have been traveling with that caravan and could not, strictly speaking, remember it. Verse 11 presents desert travelers tightening the saddles and loosening the reins at the start of the journey or else, once the journey is underway, increasing the camels' pace. The reference could be to the journey of the beloved's party or to the journey undertaken by the poet and his companions to rejoin the beloved, a journey that, within the nasib world of the poem, is unending. In verse 10, the poet finds the "death's cords" before him. By this point in the *Tarjumān*, the lover's encounter with death has emerged as a pattern, evoked most often in a single verse at a moment of particular emotional intensity within a given poem.

Poem 14. This poem is rooted in protocols of hadith transmission, which came to be used for a variety of orally transmitted reports, whether or not they constituted hadiths in the formal sense. Such reports consisted of two parts: the chain of transmitters that, by Ibn ʿArabī's time, could span more than six centuries, and the speech that was being reported, ideally in the form of verbatim quotation. Reports of the verses and sayings for the first generations of Muslim love poets were gathered, along with chains of transmission, into immense works such as the *Great Book of Songs*, even as love poets had begun presenting interiorized hadith conversations—a conceit that Ibn ʿArabī developed and employed with particular intensity. In this poem, the lover receives a message down through a chain of transmitters who comprise personified states of consciousness or emotion. Here, the lover sends a return message *back in time*, through the transmitters, to the original speaker (a procedure that does not, of course, occur in the formal hadith presenting the words or actions of the prophet Muḥammad). In some cases, as with this poem, I have employed italics to indicate the message or *matn* of the original speaker and, where it seems appropriate, the return message of the lover.

Verse 3, "brought us / the word": the term here for bringing a word or a report is *muʿanʿan*. That term could refer to a report that is passed on from generation to generation through a chain of transmitters or to a tale as passed on by a tell-all or gossip. Verse 5, "*The one you seek / is within your ribs, / turned in each breath / from side to side*": a subtext here is a hadith stating that "the heart of the person of faith is between two fingers of God." On that hadith, see Morris, *The Reflective Heart*, 52, 65. In *The Meccan Openings,* Ibn ʿArabī quotes another couplet on the same topic (*Fut.*, vol. 5, ch. 178, pp. 593–94).

Poem 15. This poem proceeds in a hyperbolic register. After a brief mention of the beloved and her party leaving the poet, the verses barrel along a track of expressive flashes. The poet evokes the erotically charged memory of the cheek of the beloved, gendered as male. He breaks into complaint and calls for a friend to help him in his trials. He begs for a glimpse of the beloved and receives a kind rejection. He casts another look back to the beloved's departure, then curses the cawing crows that portended it and that are transformed in his mind into the camels that carried her off. The poem concludes with the lover recalling and reliving a separation that for him always has occurred and always is occurring.

Poem 16. This poem begins with a remembrance of the day of departure. The poet then recalls or imagines the beloved journeying toward Yemen and then, in a sudden switch, turning back toward Khawarnaq and Sadīr, semilegendary palaces in the border regions between Arabia and Iraq that were associated with the vanished grandeur of past civilizations. For verses 5–6, I have employed the colloquial "damn it" for the Arabic *thubūran*. The word might be more formally translated as "ruination," "destruction," or "perish" (as in "perish the day"). Verse 6 is a direct paraphrase of Q 25:14 concerning the final day of judgment. When wrongdoers find themselves consigned to their place of punishment, they cry *thubūran* and the divine voice answers, "Do not, today, cry out *thubūran* just once; cry it over and over."

The tone shifts as the poet addresses a dove, moving into a deep lament at the dove's cry. In this he echoes the dove-poet dynamic that opened poem 11. When the poet complains that the dove's cry has increased his own sadness, we might ask if he is not also addressing himself, given that he was the one who was crying out his anguish in the previous verses. The dove in this poem and elsewhere in the *Tarjumān* appears as multivalent and may also intimate an association with the beloved, as the poet imagines his beloved weeping as he does. The lamentation culminates in the poet's announcement that "death hovers in a dove's cry" and his asking for a brief remission, a request that recalls the plea for release in poem 2.

The poem moves on to address the Eastwind, the star shepherd, and the lightning gazer, three figures at the heart of the nasib tradition. The star shepherd represents the desert poet who, beset by cares, passes a sleepless night "grazing the stars," that is, watching them as they move across the night firmament until they slip over the horizon or fade into the light of dawn—just as a herder watches his flock as it sets out to graze by day and returns at dusk.

For a classic exploration of this motif, see Stetkevych, *Zephyrs of Najd*, chapter 4: "Meadows in the Sky," 134–67. ʿAbd al-ʿAziz Sayyid al-Ahl offers a brief discussion of several verses from poem 16; see *Muḥyī al-Dīn Ibn ʿArabī: min shiʿrihi* (Beirut: Dār al-ʿIlm: 1970), 246–47.

Poem 17. Verse 6, "my liver's caul": Arabic poetry redounds with words for "heart" but also mentions other organs of the body as seats of love and passion, including the liver or, as in this case, the caul or membrane surrounding the liver. Elsewhere in the *Tarjumān*, the liver can be associated more explicitly with black bile and melancholy—not surprisingly, given the influence of ancient Greek medical treatises on Arabic thought and literature. (For "caul" as the membrane around the heart or liver, see the King James translation of Hosea 13:8, "the caul of the heart," and Exodus 29:13, "the caul that is above the liver.")

Poem 18. This poem opens with the poet standing before the *aṭlāl*, asking the ruins or area around them to speak. In this case, the poet seems to be calling on others to question the now-deserted meadows, though he may in fact be calling on himself as well. In the nasib tradition the *aṭlāl* remain mute before the poet's questioning, yet a response (from somewhere, perhaps from the poet himself) is given. The poem proceeds in three projective movements: the address to the meadows and the response that the beloved's party has gone off seeking al-Udháyb; the delegation of the Eastwind to serve as a scout and her subsequent report; and finally the sending forth of companions to track down the beloved and her party.

Poem 19. This poem proceeds from *aṭlāl* lament to recollections of the young women who will come to represent the beloved's party. Wherever they alight (or alighted, the remembered past and timeless present become indistinguishable), the drought-stricken land burgeons with life, and when they leave, it bears "the tombs of those who loved them." Like the spirit, which in Ibn ʿArabī's mystical thought brings everything it touches to life and flower, the beloved and her party revive the land when they alight and leave it barren again when they depart. The ending reverses the tomb theme of poem 16. In poem 16, it was not the lovers who are confined to tombs in the wake of the beloved's departure but those who failed to love in the first place.

Poem 20. This poem includes the most sustained allusions to the Niẓām figure within the *Tarjumān*. The poet begins in a frenetic mode (verses 1–5), with each verse taking up one motif that recurs, often in expanded form, elsewhere in the *Tarjumān*. These motifs include lovesickness, for which the only cure is the name of the beloved who caused the ailment; the mournful cry of the dove; the lover's exclamations over a girl's beauty and charms; the figuring of the beloved in terms of rising and setting heavenly bodies (in this case the sun); and the poet's address to the *aṭlāl* and his recollection of beauties that once filled the place.

The movement from motif to motif slows somewhat at verses 7–8 with the image of the gazelle and the fire within the poet's breast, then comes to a halt in verses 9–15. In these verses, the poet calls on his companions to help him grieve at the ruins of the beloved's campsite, although he acknowledges that ultimately he must face his loss alone. He perseverates at this point, repeating his pleas to the companions as if he were frozen in place before the *aṭlāl*. The reanimation of the poet occurs as he urges his companions to console him with names of various beloveds, tales of intimate goings-on at the stations of Ḥājir and Zarūd, and verses recounting the fate of star-crossed lovers such as Bishr and Hind, Qays and Laylā, and Ghaylān and Mayya. As he recites the names of these muses, poet-lovers, and sites of love from a now-mythic past, he begins to revive.

With verse 17, the poem shifts to the Niẓām figure and into a new lyrical register. The poet longs for a girl who is a master of the rhetorical arts ("for a young girl, / harmony in verse, / in prose, in oration!"), more fully, "a young girl who is master of prose, poetry, pulpit, and elucidation": *dhāti nathrin wa **niẓāmin** wa minbarin* [*pulpit*] *wa bayyāni*). The word for poetry (*niẓām*) offers yet another instance in which Niẓām is embedded within the poetry rather than named by the poet as a beloved. In his Niẓām preface, Ibn ʿArabī had extolled her as a girl (*ṭafla*, the same word used in this poem) who not only embodied beauty in all its forms but also mastered all forms of verbal eloquence, had called her a master (*shaykha*), and suggested that she might have been his own master.

That the verse alludes to the Niẓām figure mentioned in the preface is confirmed in the following verse, which extols the beloved as a daughter of Persian kings and of Iṣfahān—the city of Niẓām's father and aunt. The unnamed, obliquely referenced beloved is then associated with Iraq, an association that resonates with other poems in the *Tarjumān* expressing longing for a beloved in Baghdad or places near to it. The conjuration of Niẓām brings into play the East/West polarity of Arabia-Persia and, with a slight tilt, Yemen-Iraq. (At the time, the designation Iraq referred primarily to the region of Baghdad rather than any particular polity.) The poet uses a courteous address appropriate for formal circles ("my lords" or "gentlemen") to challenge the logic that contradictions can never meet. He then announces a mystical communion in which he and the beloved share wine without having to pass the cup back and forth and share a song of rapture without sound (verses 21–22).

In this poem, the precise alignment of the opposites that by logic cannot meet shifts from verse to verse. In the final verse, the poet rebukes an unnamed poet for claiming that Suhayl and the Pleiades, two signal points of the night sky, could never come together, given that one rises toward Syria while the other is setting over Yemen. (The verses in question are ascribed to ʿUmar ibn ʿabī al-Rabīʿa [*Dīwān*, 438].)

Poem 21. In verse 1, the poet urges the wadi to respond to "the lady / of this hallowed ground": *rabba al-ḥimā*. *Rabba* is the feminine of *rabb*, "lord," the plural of which, *arbāb*, appeared in the concluding verse of poem 1: "The lords of love." *Al-ḥimā*, translated here as hallowed ground, can be interpreted as a common noun, as in this translation, or as a place-name. In pre-Islamic poetry, the word referred to a tribe's sacred pasture grounds. Its sacral character shows forth clearly in poetry and lore: if someone from a rival tribe transgressed upon a *ḥimā*, it was a cause for war.

In the nasib, the *ḥimā* epitomizes a site of beauty and bounty, and the abode of the beloved. The poet urges the wadi garden to provide shade for the "lady of the *ḥimā*" until her assembly, which includes desert travelers setting up their tents by the wadi, can gather around her. That assembly appears as pastoral counterpart to the audience that might have assembled around a diva in Baghdad. It also foreshadows the gathering (*nādī*) assembled around its mistress or lady (*rabba*) in poem 61. Only when the lady of the *ḥimā* is fully accommodated and her assembly has gathered around her will it attain the shade, dew, and rain that it needs. Here as elsewhere in the *Tarjumān*, the verdant meadow or garden is tied intrinsically to the presence of the beloved.

Poem 22. This exquisite lyric exemplifies the sensuous visionary imagery of the *Tarjumān*. The imagery of verse 6 echoes within and beyond the *Tarjumān*'s interior frame. The first part of the verse, "she extends you a hand / soft as undyed silk," may recall the opening of the Qurrat al-ʿAyn preface: as Ibn ʿArabī finished reciting the four verses that had come to his mind near the Kaʿba, he felt a jolt between his shoulders "from a hand softer than undyed silk."

Poem 23. This poem consists of a slow ascent (verses 1–5) followed by a rapidly accelerating movement that concludes with the poet's self-portrait in a time out of time. It opens with a group of riders posed at dawn after a long night journey. They gaze at something appearing in the early dawn light. The scene and the specific word for "appear" (*lāḥa*) indicate an apparition as much as an appearance. The vision occurs at the liminal moment when an object first emerges into visibility, prompting the observer to wonder whether he really sees something or not, whether what he sees is real or imaginary, and what it in fact truly is. The features of what is seen gradually emerge into clarity as a prominent object on a mountain peak, and then into further definition as a monumental structure like the fabled castle of ʿAqūq. The poetic lens then moves in to a close-up of the inscription carved, like an ancient graffito perhaps, into the structure's brick or rock walls. As the tale carved there unfolds, the poetic pace accelerates, propelled by parallel constructions, the poem's anapestic *mutaqārib* meter, and increased alignment between metrical feet and syntactical units.

Poem 24. With this poem, Ibn ʿArabī plumbs a particularly deep vein of nasib sensibility. The poem proceeds at a steady, solemn pace into and through a passage of grief. It begins with the lover asking an unnamed addressee to stay and grieve by the ruins at the station of Laʿlaʿ. By leaving the addressee unnamed, he evokes the possibility that he may be addressing himself. Verse 2 continues the address but ends by suggesting the poet has indeed been addressing himself. In verse 3, the poet grieves for the times spent near "her moringa," thereby tying together the ruins, the moringa, the station of La'la', and the beloved. There follows the dervish's verse that inspired the poem as the poet complains that the lightning (a sign of rain for the desert traveler and, in the lightning of the beloved's smile, a sign of promised intimacy) has been unfaithful only to him. The station of La'la', the ruins, the moringa, the lightning, and the formerly "luxuriant land" seem to respond as one with the beloved:

> We used, she said,
> to come there together
> in my branches' shadows
> in that lush land
>
> My lightning, once
> a smile's flash,
> is now a blaze
> of barren stone

In verse 8, the poet shifts to speaking in the third person about his interlocutor:

> I forgave her
> as I heard her speak,
> grieving as I grieved
> with wounded heart

Over the final three verses, the dialogue shifts as the poet asks the deserted meadow where the beloved and her party might be. The meadow no longer responds as one with the grieving beloved but instead informs the poet of the beloved's itinerary.

Poem 25. This poem takes up the most informal of all classical meters, *rajaz*. The first part of the poem consists of exclamations, chains of images, and rapid shifts in address. In verses 4–6, the beloved is gendered as male, then suddenly, in verse 7, as female.

Verses 11–13 praise the beloved with parallel evocations of Qur'anic themes. Verse 11, "Had Iblīs seen . . . he'd have fallen down in prayer": the

Qur'an relates that when the creator announced his intention to create the human being, Adam, who would serve as his regent (*khalīfa*) on earth, the angels protested, asking why he would create one who will "spill blood and corrupt the world." Adam is shown to know something, "the names," that the angels do not. The angels take the position of ritual prayer (*sujūd*) before Adam. When Iblīs refuses, he is cast from the heavens (Q 2:30–34; 15:28–31; 32:7–9; 38:71–75). In this poem, the beloved outshines Adam: a glimpse of her beauty would have compelled even the proud Iblīs to fall into *sujūd*. Verse 12 evokes the Idrīs–Enoch–Hermes figure, the legendary inventor of writing. Verse 13 returns to the Qur'anic story of Bilqīs and Sulaymān that formed the poetic frame for poem 2.

Poem 26. Like poem 14, this poem enmeshes itself within the language of hadith transmission and images of the lost, verdant meadows of the nasib. "The Garden of Eden": literally "The Garden of Safe Abode" (*jannat al-ma'wā*) beheld in Muḥammad's prophetic vision (Q 53:15). In the hadith and prophetic biographies, Muḥammad encounters *jannat al-ma'wā* near the culmination of his heavenly ascent. *Jannat al-ma'wā* could be viewed as the garden of the future paradise as well as a retrieval of the Garden of Eden. Arabic poets had long boasted of the ancient vintage of their wine: a vintage of ancient Persia or of Enoch, Noah, or Adam, or even, as in the opening verse from Ibn al-Fāriḍ's famous wine ode, a vintage of a time that preceded the creation of the grapevine. For the association of wine with musk, see the Qur'anic reference to the wine of paradise (Q 83:26) as "wine sealed with musk."

Poem 27. The poem begins with the expression "old house" (*al-bayt al-'atīq*), which can serve as an epithet for the Ka'ba. The poet's reference to it as "high above" may reflect the manner in which the Ka'ba temple looms over the pilgrims. Yet the verse may also allude to the Qur'anic "Frequented House" (*al-bayt al-ma'mūr*, Q 52:7), the celestial counterpart to the Ka'ba, around which a different set of seventy thousand angels perform ritual prayers each day according to hadith in the highly regarded compilations of al-Bukhārī and Muslim bin al-Ḥajjāj.

Sessions of the Righteous (*MAb* 1:290) introduces this poem with these words: "I was circling the Ka'ba one night when I was overcome with a particularly sweet feeling. And I said, complaining of the thirst I suffered during my desert journey, 'Old house high above . . .'"

Poem 28. This poem takes the short, dimeter form of the informal *rajaz* meter. Due to the short verse length, I have translated it into couplets, with some minor adjustments, starting at verse 15, to fit the English cadence. The verse number indications (15, 20) reflect the verse numbering in the Arabic text.

Poem 29. This poem begins with a sixteen-verse reverie, a dance of erotic images, and the vision of an endless cascade of acceptance, with the Qur'anic visions of huris as a subtext. At its midpoint (verse 16), the mood turns as the poet plunges into a short version of the classical ode's harrowing journey-quest (*raḥīl*). The poem culminates with an eerie set of verses in which a fearsomely attractive figure, gendered masculine, appears as a moon during the ritual circling associated with Ka'ba, which we've encountered in poems 3, 7, and 12. In poem 29, the Ka'ba is not mentioned and the circling is performed as the poet and the moon figure circle each other, with the former continually effacing his footprints with the train of his robe. Such circling resonates strongly with the first chapter of *Meccan Openings* in which Ibn 'Arabī encounters a mystical youth who is at once a manifestation of the Holy Spirit, a personification of the Ka'ba, and the agent of mystical initiation. The scene also resonates with one of the core rituals of Sufism, when a group chants a *dhikr* (repeated mantra-like words or short phrases from the Qur'an or other revered sources) while moving in a circular motion. In some sessions, two individuals from the circling group come to the center, lock hands together, and spin in the opposite direction of the circling group. The faces of the two spinning in the center stand out to each other with clarity as the chanting devotees appear as a blurry whirl. Verse 21, "I folded toward him / in desire and fear" (*fa-ṭawwaytu min ḥadharin 'alayhi sharāsifan*): the eeriness of the final verses is intensified by the use of an Arabic word (*shursūf*, pl. *sharāsif*) that can mean either "rib cage" (as in I bowed from below the rib rage or I held him to my rib cage) or "ill-luck" and that, with a single shift of vocalization (*shursūf*, pl. *sharāsif*), would mean "shroud." Verse 22 begins with "he [a full moon] appeared in the circling": *qamarun ta'arḍa fī-ṭ-ṭawāf*. The same words appear in the second verse of a poem by Ibn 'Arabī included in *Sessions of the Righteous* (*MAb* 1:411–14).

Poem 30. In this, the longest poem of the *Tarjumān*, the poetic voice wanders through various modalities and moods of ghazal verse. The poem also features a number of Qur'anic allusions. The first occurs in verse 8 with "Sabā's [Sheba's] lost tribes" (Q 34:15–31). Some have suggested that Sūra 34 reflects a Yemen or land of Sabā in decline, presumably well after the time of Bilqīs, perhaps after the collapse of the great Ma'rib dam, the ruins of which are visible today. "Sabā's lost tribes": *aydī sabā*, literally "the hands of Sabā," a metaphor that could mean "the power of Sabā" or "the forces of Sabā." In verses 10–14, the poet laments his loss and asks each of the winds in turn to report a hadith that will speak to his condition. Verses 19–21 move through differing perspectives of nature/human empathy and mutual mirroring. The natural (evening clouds, sunset glow, rain, narcissi, and roses) and the human (tears, cheeks) are intertwined. The nature-human convergence here resonates strongly with the endings of poem 12 and poem 28.

After an interlude of ghazal flirtation that reaches a point of poetic self-parody, the poet presents himself through two Qur'anic characters. The first is the mysterious al-Sāmirī (verse 32), who appears in the Qur'anic story of Mūsā, the Israelites, and the golden calf (Q 20:85–97). When Mūsā comes down from the mountain and confronts his people worshiping the calf, they excuse themselves by pointing to al-Sāmirī as the responsible party. After they melted down the jewelry that they had taken from Egypt and molded it into the shape of a calf, al-Sāmirī sprinkled it with dust taken from the footprint of "the messenger" (*rasūl*), causing it to low. That messenger is usually taken to be the spirit (*rūḥ*) or Jibrīl. Ibn ʿArabī associates the messenger in this story with the spirit as a life force. A core theme throughout his writings holds that wherever the spirit passes, life surges.

Another Qur'anic character is evoked in verses 33–34, where the poet declares that he will pursue the beloved's party, no matter where they travel, like Dhū al-Qarnayn ("the two-horned"). In Q 18:83–98, Dhū al-Qarnayn is depicted traveling to the eastern and western ends of the earth along heavenly "cords" (*asbāb*). In Islamic lore, Dhū al-Qarnayn was associated with Iskandar (Alexander the Great), the name I have employed in the translation.

On the Qur'anic portrayal of Dhū al-Qarnayn, see Kevin van Bladel, "Heavenly Cords and Prophetic Authority in the Quran and Its Late Antique Context," *Bulletin of the School of Oriental and African Studies* 70, no. 2 (2007): 223–46; and *idem*, "The Alexander Legend in the Qur'an," in *The Qur'an in Its Historical Context*, edited by Gabriel Said Reynolds

(London: Routledge, 2008), 83–102. For a brilliant exploration of the "the trace" or "footprint" in the Moses/Mūsa accounts in rabbinic literature and Islamic traditions, see David Halperin, *Faces of the Chariot* (Tübingen: J. C. B. Mohr [Paul Siebeck], 1988): 14–190, 476–83.

Poem 31. This elegant ghazal recalls poem 22 in register and pace but in longer, more sustained form.

Poems 32–38. An interior suite of short poems. In **poem 32**, the poet hearkens back to the times of his youth when he traveled from Najd to Tihām and lit a campfire for his beloved. The lover's memories are sparked by words heard between Karkh (the western part of Baghdad) and Ḥadītha, which lies on the Euphrates some 150 miles northwest of Baghdad. "Fifty years": commentators have pointed out that Ibn ʿArabī would have been about fifty years old at the time he composed the *Tarjumān*. In the context of the Niẓām romance, Karkh, like Ḥalba and Dār al-Falak, is associated by some readers with the residence of Niẓām. In verse 4, the poet recalls building a fire from "flametree and markh"—two desert plants, *ʿafār* and *markh*, valued as kindling. **Poem 33**. The entire poem is devoted to the dove-poet colloquy, with its own distinctive emphasis and tone. **Poem 34**. This short, apparently simple poem features reverberating patterns, etymological excavations, puns, and elaborate alliterations. The sophisticated employment of *jinās* results in a light touch of wit and a pictorial impression of poignant simplicity. **Poem 35**. Tanʿīm is a site outside of Mecca. Women pilgrims who were menstruating would wait there until their menses had passed before proceeding to the Kaʿba and performing the hajj. "I'm here for you now" (*labbayka*) is the ritual phrase pronounced by pilgrims at various points during the hajj.

Poem 36. Verse 4, "Flashed over Híma": there is a particularly intriguing text puzzle regarding this verse. The manuscripts consulted for this book (described in appendix 1) read *al-ḥimā*, as do *Diwān al-Maʿārif* and *Sessions of the Righteous* (*MAb* 2:261), yet the manuscripts and printed editions of *Priceless Treasures* read *al-ghaḍā*, which is the word Ibn ʿArabī proceeds to interpret in his commentary.

In *Sessions of the Righteous*, the poem is followed by the same commentary found in *Priceless Treasures*: this is the only instance of Ibn ʿArabī providing a commentary on a poem in *Sessions* identical to that found in

Precious Treasures. In *Sessions*, the poem is introduced by "Among my poems on the *laṭā'if al-'irfāniyya fī al-ishārāt* (mystic subtleties within the allusions) is the following . . ."

This poem extends the themes of poem 32 and the poet's reflection on his fifty years. It concludes with a play on the first verse of a poem by Ibn Dumayna (d. ca. 800). Ibn 'Arabī included Ibn Dumayna's entire six-verse poem along with his own commentary on it in *Sessions of the Righteous*, where he followed it with Ibn Sīna's famous "fall of the soul" poem, before proceeding to present a group of ten *Tarjumān* poems. *Sessions of the Righteous* (*MAb* 1:286–93) thereby provides a window onto poetic intertextuality in thirteenth-century Arabic poetry and into Ibn 'Arabī's own poetic sensibility.

Poem 37. This poem distills a recurring theme of the *Tarjumān*, that of the lover's message, into five exquisitely wrought verses. The poet commissions his companion-messengers to travel through the Arabian imaginary's archetypal sites (verses 1–3) in order to proclaim his devastated condition and make inquiries on his behalf (verses 4–5). The messenger's trajectory begins near al-Ḥimā ("Preserve," "Sanctuary"), hearkening back to the vernal tribal grounds of the pre-Islamic poets. The first goal is the highland plateau of Najd that for the poets is the land of fragrant east winds, fresh springs, the fellowship of lovers and seekers, and intimations of the beloved's presence. In Najd, the poet adds, the messengers will encounter a solitary waymark, literally "that waymark" (*dhāka al-'alam*), an expression in which the demonstrative adjective "that" connotes uniqueness or special significance. For the poets, an *'alam* could refer to a mound of stones or cairn set up along a desert route, a natural feature such as a mountain peak, a ruined fortress, or other another constructed or natural feature that served to guide the traveler in the unforgiving vastness of the desert. The word evokes the desert topography and those who venture through it but, as noted in reference to poem 23, can elicit deeper questions regarding perception and knowledge, appearance and reality; issues that, for the traveler attempting to find the path through the desert maze, constitute a matter of life and death.

In this poem, that certain special waymark is the one that would guide the messengers toward a place and time of proximity to the beloved and her party. On that path they will pass by Twisting Sands (*al-liwā*), a feature or site that took a prominent place in the nasib from the time of the pre-Islamic poet Imru' al-Qays, who associated it with the place where (or near to where) the beloved set off on her journey away from the lover. After Twisting Sands comes the shade of the lote (*al-ḍāl*), the tree that could mark the *locus amoenis* of the lover's union with the beloved in that primordial time before the separation, and Salam (also known as Dhū al-Salam, "the place of *salam* trees"), yet another station in the travels of the beloved.

Then, finally, comes the traveler's goal: Minā, site of the most intense rites of the hajj pilgrimage, including the great sacrifice that marks the holiest day of the Muslim calendar—the place that holds the poet's heart. Minā is at the heart of a vast concourse of pilgrims. There the messengers are to listen to the reports brought by travelers from near and far, to pass on to them news of the lover's condition, and, most importantly, to inquire. The poet uses an emphatic sequence of three verbs to indicate the act of inquiry and does so in a manner that leaves the proposed inquiry both open-ended and urgent, rendered here at "why . . . why?" (One might also interpret the questions as "how, where, why?") In the nasib context, that question may be posed to the companions of the beloved, to the sweet fragrances, lightning flashes, Eastwind, or to the ruins of the beloved's campsite, the *aṭlāl*, that since pre-Islamic times have answered the poet's question with silence.

Poem 38. This poem starts out as an homage to Baghdad as the home of both the poet's imam and of a beautiful Persian girl. Verse 4 is built upon the wordplay between two radicals. The first, *ḥ/y/y*, forms the basis for words such as "life," "greet," and "tribe," all three of which are semantically interrelated: to greet someone is to wish that person long or healthy life, and a tribe—or, in later usage, neighborhood—is the locus of life. The first hemistich of the verse, translated literally, reads: "She greets and thereby brings back to life the one she slew with her gaze." The second hemistich of the fourth Arabic verse (the final quatrain in the English) is built upon three different forms of the radical *ḥ/s/n*: *ḥusn* (beauty); *ḥusnā* (an action carried out in a generous way or one that turns out happily or "for the best" or simply a happy outcome); and *iḥsān*, a word with a particularly deep ethical and religious valence. Arabic commentators and lexicographers viewed *iḥsān* as an extension of the beautiful into the realm of the ethical and social spheres. A famous hadith characterizes *iḥsān* as: "to worship God as though you see him, and even if you cannot see him, know that he sees you." More widely, the virtue of *iḥsān* can entail making every act, however humble, an act of worship.

Poem 39. This poem opens with huri-like figures teasing the poet at the Kaʿba, an echo of poem 7. It then unfolds as an extended elaboration of the light/night and sun/moon binary that recurs throughout the *Tarjumān*, often breaking into longer poems in the form of one to three verse segments. The poem unfolds as a dance of images, each of which extends the core light/night contrast into a new set of oppositions and reconciliations, particularly through the contrast between the splendor of the beloved's unveiled countenance and the sheltering dark of her hair.

Poem 40. This homage to a girl is also a meditation on time and place. The girl is said to be fourteen years old. She appears as the full moon, which occurs on the fourteenth day of the month according to the Islamic lunar calendar. Yet this moon-girl does not undergo growth or decline, the twin aspects of the "natural" moon as it moves through time. The phases of the moon take on particular importance during the month of Ramadan, which begins with the spotting of the new moon. The month falls into two fourteen-day segments, the first in which the moon waxes, and the second in which it wanes. By stating that the moon-girl in question neither moves through constellations nor goes through phases, the poet places her beyond the natural cycles of time and place. Thus, she "knows no doubling, odd to even" (*fa mā tushaffiʿu l-witra*) but remains singular. It is timelessly "full." To double the odd (oneness) to the even (twoness) would be to fall into the world of time. For a Qur'anic subtext, see Q 36:40: "And the moon—we have determined mansions for it through which it [travels] and returns, the night does not outstrip the day, and each [of the heavenly bodies] is gliding along in its own sphere." See also Q 89:1–6, where the divine voice swears by essential polarities and patterns of the cosmos: "By the dawn / By the nights ten / By the odd and the even / By the night as it eases away / Is there not in that an oath for the thoughtful mind?" (Qur'anic exegetes have interpreted the ten nights as the ten nights of the hajj.) The girl-moon thereby transcends the polarities and patterns within the created world and within the act of creation.

Ibn ʿArabī also notes in his commentary that fourteen is considered a perfect number in that it combines the perfect number four with ten

(1+2+3+4). See also *Meccan Openings* (*Fut.*, vol. 2, ch. 69, pp. 416–17), especially the opening of the eleventh verse of the poem presented there.

Poem 41. In this poem, the call of a bird in a moringa tree (which in this case could be either the mournful coo of a dove or the ominous caw of a crow) incites the lover's journey that will take up the rest of the poem. The poem is composed in the anapestic *mutaqārib* meter, with uniform feet of three syllables patterned as ˘ ˘ ¯ or ˘ ¯ ¯ . That meter contributes to the poem's galloping forward momentum, a momentum that is further enhanced by the manner in which the two halves of each verse create a syntactical call-and-response effect, especially in poem's middle section. I have adjusted the default uppercase protocol for the beginning of stanzas to reflect the way the poetic voice in this poem charges across the verses. Like poem 12, this poem concludes with a declaration regarding the nature-human symbiosis: the softness of a lover's cheek is not like the softness of a fresh bough, but vice versa. The attributes of nature are patterned on the human: "Blush red's the garden rose."

Poem 42. Here the poetic voice approaches full delirium. The first three verses are based upon intense employment of *jinās*. Verse 1 juxtaposes *mahāt* (doe oryx) with *mahā* (onyx or sunstone), echoing earlier *Tarjumān* representations of the gazelle and oryx as luminous beings analogous to the sun. The second verse entwines itself around the Arabic radical *s/h/ā*, which yields *suhā*, the faint star that was considered to be most difficult to spot and became a test case for stargazers, as well as the verb *sahā*, "to neglect" or "fail to perceive." The third verse culminates with the theme of the sacrificial offering, with complex *jinās* play on the letters *s/r/b* and *l/h/ā*:

sir bihī	***bi-sirbihī***	***li-sirbihī***
lead him away	with his heart	for (taking the place of) his herd
fa-l-luhā	***taftaḥu***	***bi l-ḥamdi l-lahā***
for oblations	open	with praise the throats (open throats in praise)

The final two verses tie together love-madness, hadith traditions regarding allowable forms of exchange, and the power of invocation. They do so with a play on the Arabic syllable "*hā*," which serves as an end rhyme throughout the poem. Yet the penultimate verse begins with the poet stating that this poem has no proper end-rhyme construction. The poet declares that his only aim (*qaṣḍ*, the word from which the word for the classical ode, *qaṣīda*, is derived) is the letter or syllable *hā*, which can feature as part of a word or as an independent pronoun. His claim is partially unpacked in the next verse, which begins, literally translated, "my goal is the expression 'her' (*hā*) for the sake of 'her.'" The full implication of this appeal unfolds in the final hemistich, which would read, word for word, "the only trade or exchange I love is *hā wa hā* ("her and her," "it and it," or "this and this"). In his note to this poem, Nicholson suspected that *hā wa hā* was "a formula used in completing a bargain." Here the expression may reflect a principle in Islamic rulings on trade. Indeed, hadiths outlining what commodity trades were permissible employ a nearly identical expression. The trade in certain commodities, such as gold, silver, wheat, and barley, was subject to stringent rules. It was licit to trade gold bullion for gold jewelry, for example, but not for silver jewelry. Gold could only be traded in the form of *hā' wa hā'*: "this item for that item of the same species, immediately and without delay." (For one party to delay handing over an item would raise the question of usury in Islamic legal considerations.) The letter *hamza* in *hā'* would have been dropped in the poem in accord with the rules of poetic license.

The poet addresses the beloved saying, "you so full with / beauty—I've nothing." He has nothing to give. She needs nothing. He then declares his solution: he will trade "her" for "her." In the jurisprudence of the religion of love, the poet's permissible terms of exchange (gold for gold, etc.) align with the magic of invocation: by calling "her," he brings her into his presence.

For the relevant hadith traditions, see Volkan Yildiran Stodolsky, *A New Historical Model and Periodization for the Perception of the Sunnah of the Prophet and His Companions*, PhD diss., University of Chicago, 2012, 109–17, 235. On the question of proper rhyme (*qāfiya*) in regard to this poem, Ibn ʿArabī states in his commentary that some grammarians consider the kind of end rhyme employed in this poem as lacking the proper preceding syllable but that others take a different position. See *Priceless Treasures*: *Dīwān Dhakhā'ir al-Aʿlāq* [*sic*], edited by Muḥammad ʿAlam al-Dīn al-Shuqayrī (al-Haram [Egypt]: al-ʿAyn lil-Dirāsāt wa-al-Buḥūth al-Insāniyya wa-al-Ijtimāʿiyya, 1995), 454.

Poem 43. This poem begins with the poet's plea to the camel drivers who are leading the beloved and her party away. It proceeds through a haze of memories concerning the day of separation, recalled or imagined trajectories of the beloved, and the lover's complaint at being abandoned and neglected. "Splitting bittergourd" in verse 6 recalls the *muʿallaqa* (Hanging Ode) of the pre-Islamic poet Imru' al-Qays, in which the lover describes his shock and pain at the lover's departure with the same words—a phrase interpreted by commentators as evoking burning eyes and tears. Bittergourd or bitter apple (*ḥanẓal*) is the fruit of an earth-hugging vine known for its astringency. The poem concludes with two verses on patience, echoing the final verse of poem 5.

Poem 44. Divine ineffability plays a central role in Islamic theology and within Sufi thought particularly. The divine reality, being infinite, cannot be described in human language, although the names and attributes given to it in the Qur'an, viewed as the word of God, are affirmed. This poem centers on the ineffability of the beloved, who eludes the grasp of those who would delimit her or tie her down.

Verse 10: the manuscripts indicate considerable confusion over two words in this verse, which are based on the radical *r/w/ḥ* (which yields meanings of spirit, wind, and refreshment) and *n/q/l* (which yields meanings of move, transport, transmit, and translate).

Poem 45. While poem 44 evoked the ineffability of the beloved, poem 45 evokes the infinity of *shawq*. The lover longs to be with the beloved, but, when with her, his fear of separation comes between them. In other poems, the infinity of *shawq* reflects the motif that at the point of union with the beloved, the lover has lost all consciousness of self. When self-consciousness returns with the lover realizing he is one with the beloved, he falls back into separation. Ibn ʿArabī addresses this aspect of the lover's dilemma in the chapter on love theory in the *Meccan Openings* (*Fut.* 5: 593–94; Gloton, *Traité d'Amour*, 57–58). In the classical ghazal tradition, the union of lover and beloved is, by definition, ephemeral at best. In the thought of Ibn ʿArabī (as noted in reference poem 11), the mystic is ever perishing out of love for the divine beloved, becoming one with the beloved, then thrown back into separation at the beloved's appearance in a new form, and then joyfully reuniting with the beloved in that new manifestation. This poem, composed in the rollicking *rajaz* meter and with numerous puns and interior rhymes, provides a change of pace and tone at this point in the *Tarjumān.*

Poem 46. A dialogue between the poet and the Eastwind serves as the emotive heart of this poem. I have used italics to clarify the dialogue without resorting to quotation marks, which in Arabic love poetry—as in the hadith and the Qur'an—can result in embedded chains of double quotes and single quotes: "I asked the Eastwind about them / And who are you to want / to know? she answered / *At Twin Flash I left / the pilgrims, and at the relays of Ghimād and Ghamīm, close by / It's said no land can hold them* / But they will never elude / the cavalries of my longing . . ." Here and in other cases, however, the exact moment when the speech of one party ends and the other begins can be open to more than one interpretation.

Poem 47. This short poem begins with the poet-dove scene encountered in earlier poems. In this case, a Qur'anic passage serves as the subtext for the complaint. The divine speaker states (Q 33:72), "We offered the trust (*al-amāna*) to the heavens and the earth and the mountains, but they each shrank from it in fear. The human being accepted it, but proved to be unjust and foolhardy." In the poem, love is in effect the trust that the world could not bear to accept. In his commentary on this poem, Ibn ʿArabī quotes the twelfth-century garland poet of Seville, al-Aʿmā al-Tuṭīlī: "His laugh flashed pearl. The full moon shone as he removed his veil. / Time could not hold him, but my heart took him in" (*ḍāḥikun ʿan juman / sāfirun ʿan badrī / ḍāqa ʿanhu z-zamān / wa ḥawāhu ṣadrī*). A subtext for Ibn ʿArabī's commentary is a *hadīth qudsī* (divine saying): "My heaven and earth could not hold me, but the heart of my believing servant does." On this hadith in the work of Ibn ʿArabī, see William Chittick, *The Sufi Path of Knowledge: Ibn al-ʿArabī's Metaphysics of Imagination* (Albany: State University of New York Press, 1989), 107. See also Hermann, vol. 2, pp. 258–59; and A. R. Nykl, *Hispano-Arabic Poetry, and Its Relations with the Old Provençal Troubadours* (Baltimore: J. H. Furst, 1946). For the Arabic text of the Tuṭīlī's twenty-one-verse *muwashshaḥa* along with a translation, see James T. Monroe, *Hispano-Arabic Poetry: A Student Anthology* (Berkeley: University of California Press, 1974), 252–55. For the theme of accepting the trust that the cosmos itself has refused, see also Hafiz's

"The sky couldn't bear the burden of His trust, so they cast lots and drew the name of crazy me," translated by Elizabeth Gray, *The Green Sea of Heaven: Fifty Ghazals from the Diwan of Hafiz*, ghazal 29, verse 3, pp. 98–99.

The final two verses of the poem return to the imagery of circling (*ṭawāf*), echoing the mutual-circling verses in poem 29.

Poems 48–50. Here we encounter another suite of short poems. **Poem 48**, a work of consummate lyricism, needs no commentary. **Poem 49** opens with three verses oscillating between the lover's complaints about and praise of the beloved. In verse 4, the body of the poet becomes the *aṭlāl* or ruins in which there is a garden, a garden that elsewhere in the *Tarjumān* springs into blossom when the beloved and her party are present. This garden, however, is the haunt of a dove and of the lover, each mourning their own loss. The dove motif recalls similar passages in poems 11, 13, 16, 20, 33, and 47, and anticipates those in 56 and 61, although each of those passages takes on a distinctive inner dynamic and specific placement within each poem in which it appears. The final verse, in which the poet complains of a beloved who seems to take pleasure in his torment, returns the poem to the ghazal discourse with which it began. **Poem 50** recalls the pre-Islamic nasib motif of the phantom (*ṭayf* or *khayāl*) of the beloved, which makes a night visitation to the lover. For a translation and study of a pre-Islamic ode centered on the phantom theme, see John Seybold, "The Earliest Demon Lover: The Ṭayf al-Khayāl in al-Mufaḍḍaliyāt," in Suzanne Pinckney Stetkevych, ed., *Reorientations: Arabic and Persian Poetry* (Bloomington: Indiana University Press, 1994): 180–89.

Poem 51. This short poem opens with a reference to a nightwalker (*ṭāriq*), a word with baleful associations in Arabic poetry. As the poem continues, it becomes clear that it is the lover who is walking through the night. There follows a procession of place-names deeply resonant within the Arabic poetic tradition. As elsewhere, I have used both transliteration and translations to weave such names into the acoustics of the English text and to hint at some of their associations. In the poem's final verse, the poet declares a kingdom for the beloved and a kingdom for the lover, a declaration that, in poems to follow, will be complicated by more tangled reflections on mastery and subjection in love.

Poem 52. This poem embodies a phenomenon central to the classical Arabic nasib: the lover laments his distance from the beloved yet "recalls" her journey away from him even though he could not have witnessed it. Alternatively, he presents himself as speaking during the departure, predicting the trajectory she would follow after her departure. Here, as in verses 3–4 of poem 19, Ibn ʿArabī radicalizes the phenomenon to the point of schizophrenia. The poet presents one part of himself as standing with his companions at the site of departure or at one of the beloved's abandoned stations, and depicts the other part as clinging to, trailing, and haunting the beloved's party at every stage of their journey, "howling on their trail."

Poem 53. Visual and acoustic metaphors combine in this three-verse poem. The doubled letter is a core element of Arabic phonology and orthography. In Arabic, consonant doubling is a fundamental phonemic marker. To ignore it is to babble incomprehensibly. Printed copies of the Qur'an always include a small mark (*tashdīd*) above the consonant in question, and copyists or editors sometimes added the *tashdīd* to poetic texts. The conceit underlying this poem is based on the default writing system, in which the doubled letter remains unmarked. Arabic readers are expected to know when to read a single consonant and when to read it as doubled. In the latter case, the letter is pronounced as doubled as if two identical letters had been merged into a single sign. The letter is in this sense "heard but unseen."

With "I'm shadow, and he is light," the poem moves to a more cross-linguistic, two-in-one image. For the motif of the largely invisible yet audible lover in a poem by the Andalusian lyric master Ibn Zaydūn (d. 1070), see Michael Sells, "Love," in María Rosa Menocal, Raymond P. Scheindlin, and Michael A. Sells, eds., *Cambridge History of Arabic Literature: The Literature of al-Andalus* (New York: Cambridge University Press, 2000), 128–29; Ibn Zaydūn, *Dīwān* (Beirut: Dār Sādir, 1967), 74.

Poem 54. Love's dialectic of mastery and subjection drives this poem. The poem may not fit the specific subgenre of Arabic riddle poem, yet it is layered with riddle-like employment of *jinās*, complicated still further by plays on the visual aspects of Arabic script involving the diacritical dot. Those who neglect to dot the "i" when writing English, or who have struggled to read the handwriting of those who neglect it, will appreciate the importance of the dot. Arabic has numerous letters that can be distinguished one from the other only by such dots, and given the human fallibility of copyists and the fragility of a dot on a centuries-old sheet of paper, diacritics play a major role in variant readings for a word. The final verses of this poem are strewn (riddled in fact) with plays on two Arabic consonants, the *dāl* (د) (equivalent to English "d" and the *dhāl* (ذ) [dh], which is pronounced as the "th" in "thou"), particularly in words based on the *d/l/l* root and the *dh/l/l* root. Most *d/l/l*-based words carry meanings of intimacy and closeness while *dh/l/l* words signify subjection, humbleness, lowliness. The following two verses, attributed to Ibn ʿArabī by the historian al-Maqqarī, suggest a reward in store for anyone who discerns the proper reading: "Between *tadhallul* (subjection) and *tadallul* (intimacy) is a dot / wherein the scholar loses his way / It is the dot of the universe. Traverse it / and you'll gain wisdom and the elixir of life."

بَيْنَ التَّذَلُّلِ وَالتَّدَلُّلِ نُقْطَةٌ
فِيهَا يَتِيهُ ٱلْعَالِمُ النِّحْرِيرُ

هِيَ نُقْطَةُ ٱلْأَكْوَانِ إِنْ جَاوَزْتَهَا
كُنْتَ ٱلْحَكِيمَ وَعِلْمُكَ ٱلْإِكْسِيرُ

"Dar al-Falak" (literally, "The House of the Heavenly Sphere"), mentioned in verses 1 and 6, is likely a reference to the convent in Baghdad founded by the caliph Nāṣir li-ad-Dīn in 1180, and, as mentioned, the references to it in this poem have enhanced the enigma regarding the relationship between Ibn ʿArabī and Niẓām. See Muḥyiddīn Ibn ʿArabī, *Deuter der Sehnsüchte (Turjuman al-Ashwaq)*, 2 vols., trans. Wolfgang Hermann (Zürich: Edition Shershir, 2013–16), 2:284; Addas, *Red Sulfur* 210–11; Ḥājj Yūsuf, *Shams al-maghrib*, 250–255. For the two "dot" verses attributed to Ibn ʿArabī by al-Maqqarī, see *Nafh al-ṭīb*, 2:165.

Poem 55. Although this poem is anchored firmly within the ghazal imaginary, it also evokes such themes as *fanāʾ* (the "passing away" of the lover out of longing for the beloved) and *wajd* (trance, ecstasy, fervor) that are among the core concepts in Sufism and specifically within Ibn ʿArabī's mystical thought. The poem was also included in *Meccan Openings* (*Fut.*, vol. 5, ch. 179, p. 594). There, Ibn ʿArabī introduces it as being "on the topic of the unlimited surge in love that occurs at the moment of vision and *shawq*." He adds the following comment to the poem: "[The poet] alludes to God's manifestation in various forms, in the afterlife and within the world inside the heart of his servant—as is reported in the *ḥadith* of *Saḥiḥ Muslim* [one of two most authoritative hadith collections in Sunni Islam] regarding the transformation through forms. [Such transformation] is in accord with the divine 'essence' (*dhāt*), which transcends all *tashbīh* (likeness) and *takyīf* (location)." The words *dhāt*, *tashbīh*, and *takyīf* are key terms in Ibn 'Arabī's wider mystical philosophy. The gist of Ibn 'Arabī's statement is that God or "the real" (*al-ḥaqq*) is infinite; it eludes confinement within space and time (*takyīf*) or likeness (*tashbīh*) to a finite object or being. Nor can it be excluded from the world or any aspect of the world. It is at once transcendent to the world and immanent within it, and most fully immanent within the heart of the faithful servant. The manifestation of the beloved is constantly changing its form and manifesting itself anew. The mystic's goal is to achieve constant transformation along with the manifestations of the beloved. This entails the self's passing away in each moment in order to be receptive of the new manifestation, the joy of receiving that manifestation and joining the beloved within it, and the sorrow of losing it as the beloved takes on a new manifestation.

Poem 56. This homage to Baghdad begins by praising the city over Sindād, one of several legendary sites of ancient vanished grandeur. Legend placed Sindād near the town of al-Ḥīra and provided it with the epithet "Dhū al-Shurufāt" (the castle with grand cornices or battlements). Verse 3, "branches are stirred / by the wind and bend, / lovers joined / together at last," echoes verse 4 of poem 11: "Spirits moan / in the Gháda branches, / bending them over / as I pass away." In his commentary on poem 11, Ibn 'Arabī notes that the word *arwāḥ* can mean either spirits or winds.

Verse 4, "Násir, Mansúr, best of the caliphs": a likely reference to the caliph Nāṣir li-Dīn Allāh, who ruled 1180–1225. Ibn 'Arabī had a strong attachment to the person and memory of Nāṣir, as is evident from the poems of the *Tarjumān* and from the encomium to him in *Sessions of the Righteous* (*MAb* 1: 87–88). Nāṣir integrated many of the thriving Sufi networks of the time into a society of chevaliers (*futuwwā*), who, in addition to other works of gallantry, served to reinforce the caliphate's military campaigns against the Byzantine Greeks, the Franks, and regional rivals. (Neither Nāṣir, the Byzantines, the Franks, nor Nāṣir's nominal subordinates—the Seljuks in Anatolia and the Ayyubids in Egypt and the Levant—anticipated that within a little more than two decades, Hulugu's Mongol army would sack Baghdad and abolish the five-century-old Abbasid caliphate.)

The likely subtext for the opening of the poem is a verse attributed to the early Arabic poet al-Aswad b. Yaʿfūr in one of the earliest collections of Arabic poetry, the *Mufaḍḍaliyyāt*. The verse recalls "the peoples of al-Khawarnaq and al-Sadīr and Bāriq / and the castle of Dhū al-Shurufāt." All four of the sites mentioned feature in the *Tarjumān*. Another version of al-Aswad's poem refers to Sindād by the epithet Dhū al-Kaʿbāt (the Castle of the Kaʿbas). Both versions appear in the most famous classical biography of Muḥammad, *The Sīra* [Life] *of the Messenger of God*, by Ibn Hishām (d. 833). See *The Life of Muhammad*, trans. A. Guillaume (New York: Oxford University Press, 1955), 39, 705.

Poem 57. The expression "dream stuff" in verse 6 is a quotation from Sūra 12 of the Qur'an, which relates the story of Yūsuf (Joseph). In the Qur'anic narrative, the Egyptian potentate (al-ʿAzīz) asks those in his circle to interpret a dream or vision in which he saw seven fat cows being devoured by seven lean ones, and seven fresh heads of grain along with others that were dry. Those in his circle reply that what he saw was "dream stuff" (*aḍghāthu aḥlām*: clumps of dreams, often translated as "confused dreams") and explain that they are not skilled in dream interpretation. Later, Joseph goes on to interpret the meaning of what the potentate saw as foretelling seven years of plenty followed by seven years of scarcity (Q 12:43–49).

Poem 58. Verse 3, "a voice within" (*lisān al-ḥāl*): literally "the tongue or language of condition (*ḥāl*)." In Arabic poetry, the *ḥāl* (pl. *aḥwāl*) denotes a powerful state of mind and emotion that comes upon the lover. In Sufi discourse, it indicates the states of being, emotion, or consciousness that "come upon" mystics in their quest for the divine beloved. Such states can oscillate between extremes: union and separation, intimacy and alienation, exhilaration and panic, centeredness and disintegration, expansiveness and contraction, intoxication and sobriety, airy lightness and paralyzing heaviness. In the *Treatise on Sufism* of al-Qushayrī (d. 986), which

Ibn ʿArabī had read and acknowledged as a major influence, a full chapter unpacks more than two dozen *aḥwāl* with verses of Arabic love poetry serving to exemplify many of them. For an introduction to and translation of Qushayrī's chapter on the *aḥwāl,* see Michael Sells, *Early Islamic Mysticism* (New York: Paulist Press Classics of Western Spirituality, 1996), 97–150. In the verse at hand, the *ḥāl* emerges as yet another transmitter in the chain of transmitters bearing the beloved's words or whereabouts to the poet. From another perspective, the entire chain of transmitters given in poem 14 can be considered a classic enumeration of the conditions through which the lover passes.

Poem 59. This poem serves as bookend to poem 2, the collection's first long poem, and it contains nearly the same number of verses (fifteen as opposed to the thirteen of poem 2). Poem 2 ended with the poet on the verge of death, pleading with a Bilqīs-like figure to release him from her grip. She yields or submits (*aslamat*) to the lover's prayer for release. Here a similarly powerful female figure navigates a series of threats and then submits (*aslamat*) the lover "to her lethal gaze." In his commentary to poem 2, Ibn ʿArabī states that his prayer to be released from the Bilqīs figure's spell was uttered in order to avoid the error of *ḥulūl,* in which the mystic at the point of *fanā'* misinterprets his experience as a union through divine incarnation. In this poem, it is the Bilqīs figure who submits the poet's soul to her gaze, suggesting perhaps that the poet's earlier hesitation may have been overcome by the conviction that the *fanā'* in question would not result in the error of *ḥulūl.*

Poem 60. In this evocation of the days of love and youth, the poet addresses an unspecified, singular "you" that can indicate the poet, the beloved or the sympathetic third party (one of the poet's friends), or the listener who is placed rhetorically within the clan of love and longing. In verse 3, the Arabic lists three desert plants here, artemisia, *katam,* and *ʿarār.* Both *katam* and *ʿarār* denote small shrubs prized as firewood. I have left out the *katam* to preserve the English cadence.

Poem 61. This final poem centers on a musical theme. It begins by celebrating a figure who fits the profile of the *jāriya*-diva, the young woman who dazzles the court with her voice and musicianship. This young woman, rather than enchanting the court of a caliph, enchants her audience by making them forget the splendorous courts of the caliph Harūn al-Rashīd, referred to in the poem as Hādī's brother. (Rashīd's brother Hādī himself was known as an accomplished musician.) She also drives from memory the chants of Anjasha, the prophet Muḥammad's camel driver, who was said to put the camels into a trance through his chanting. Verse 4, "oud": literally, "her triple strand" (*mithālithahā*), which would likely refer to a type of oud string that was triple-twisted.

In the poem and the *Tarjumān*'s final verses, the poet declares he has fallen for a girl in Ajyād (a height near Mecca), then immediately and emphatically corrects himself, stating that she lives instead deep in the *suwād* (black) of his liver. As mentioned above in reference to poem 17, the term evoked the black humor (*melancholia*) of Greek medicine. At the same time, blackness here, as throughout the *Tarjumān*, indicates the deep interior of something, a place of intimacy, the repository of the secret or mystery (*sirr*), the innermost core of the heart. In that deep space, the beloved resides. In his chapter on love in *Meccan Openings*, Ibn ʿArabī quotes two unattributed verses expressing the contradictory realities faced by the lover-mystic: the lover complains that the beloved is somewhere far away, when that same beloved lives deep within. In the *Meccan Openings* poem, the loved ones are found within the black (that is, the pupil) of the lover's eye and beneath his ribs (*Fut.* vol. 5, ch. 178, pp. 593–94). The lover looks without, but they are in the dark center of his perception. He sighs for those who dwell near (or within) his lungs.

How strange that I yearn for them and longing
    ask about them while they're with me
My eyes weep for them but they're there
    in their blackness. I sigh and they line my ribs

وَمِـنْ عَـجَـبٍ أَنِّي أَحِـنُّ إِلَيْـهِـمُ
وَأَسْـــأَلُ شَـوْقًـا عَـنْـهُـمُ وَهُـمُ مَعِي
وَتَبْكِيهُـمُ عَيْنِي وَهُـمْ فِي سَوَادِهَا
وَتَشْتَاقُهُمْ نَفْسِي وَهُـمْ بَيْنَ أَضْلُعِي

A similar dynamic occurs near the end of Ibn ʿArabī's Niẓām preface: "She dwells among the noble; and she camps among the brave—and in the black pupil of the eye, and deep within the heart."

The poem ends with the declaration that, with the appearance of the beloved, beauty itself wanders in bewilderment (*tāhat*), just as, we might recall, the lords of love found themselves ensnared and bewildered in the love of which they were the lords.

Appendix 1

NIẒĀM PREFACE

Prologue

Praise be God, the glorious, the one who acts, the beautiful, the lover of beauty;[1] who created the world in the most complete form and adorned it; and in making it, apportioned out degrees of wisdom about the beyond; who alluded to the place of his secret and determined it; and unfolded it before his intimates and made it clear;[2] who bathed the earth in beauty and passed his entranced lovers away in the contemplation of that beauty.

May God bless Muḥammad bin ʿAbdullāh who manifests his most beautiful form who was sent forth with the complete sharia and exemplary life; destined for the highest station and endowed with universal wholeness. God's blessings and peace upon him, his family, and companions.

Mecca, 598

Now: when I arrived in Mecca in the year 598 (1202 CE), I found a large number of notables, scholars, and intellectuals—men and women of Persian background—who had settled there. There was no one, however noble, who was as attentive to the state of their soul and immersed in the moment as the learned shaykh and imam of the shrine of Abraham (blessings upon him): that immigrant to the sacred land, Makīn al-Dīn bin Rustam of Isfahan, may God rest his soul, and his learned and elderly sister, the Shaykha of the Ḥijāz, Fakhr al-Nisāʾ bint Rustam.[3]

I heard the shaykh recite from al-Tirmidhī's hadith collection and other works in the company of his circle of distinguished scholars.[4] He held his symposia in a garden, and he was, God rest his soul, a kind and captivating companion, delightful conversation partner, generous host, and dear friend. His advanced age left him free to express exactly what was on his mind.

As for his sister, Fakhr al-Nisāʾ, "Pride of Women"—she should rather be named "Pride of All Scholars" (men and women alike). She was known for her impeccable hadith scholarship. So I wrote to her asking permission to receive her hadith reports from her in person. "My expectation in such matters has passed," she responded. "My time has come. Urgent demands preoccupy me now, and I am unable to grant the sessions you request. Death seems to be charging in on me, and my advanced age turns me to contrition." When her words reached me, I replied, "My condition and yours in hadith are one / To know and to act accordingly is our only aim."

She had her brother compose for me a general diploma granting me permission to pass on all of her hadith transmissions and had him deliver it to me in person. In addition to the general diploma, he also wrote out for me in his own hand all of his own hadith narrations. In response I composed the following verses for him.

> I heard al-Tirmidhī in the voice of Makīn,
> imām of the people in the Balad al-Amīn[5]

Niẓām

Now, this shaykh (God bless him) had a daughter—a lissome maiden who would bind the gaze, dazzle a gathering with her speech, and astonish anyone engaging her in conversation. Her name was Niẓām, and she was known as Sun Splendor.[6]

She was the shaykha of the two holy shrines for woman scholars, worshippers, itinerants, and renunciates in Mecca and Medina.[7] She was, without exaggeration, the very quintessence of culture throughout the sacred land. Her gaze cast a deep spell. Her Iraqi wit scintillated. When she elaborated, she was thorough; when she spoke succinctly, she left her rivals in silence.[8] When she spoke with artistic formality, she remained lucidly clear. In power of expression, she surpassed Qass bin Saʿda; in generosity she put Maʿn bin Zāʾida to shame; in loyalty she would have left faithful Samawʾal to stop in his tracks, leap bareback onto the steed of treason, and ride off in shame.[9]

Were it not for my concern for small-minded, suspicious souls, I would expand further on the character and virtues with which God had endowed her so generously. She is a rain-graced meadow, a sun among scholars, the prodigy of her time, the jewel of her generation; in generosity unstinting, in aspiration sublime. She was her own father's teacher. She's the mistress of every assembly she graces with her presence. She dwells among the noble, and she camps among the brave—and in the black pupil of the eye, and deep within the heart. Tihāma glows in her presence; gardens burst into life when she is near, the hills bloom. Knowing and acting in her are one. Her touch is an angel's, her resolve a king's.

Whenever I was with her, I remained aware of her noble character and ever mindful of her aunt and father, my dear friends. In this volume,[10] I have made for her a priceless necklace from the nasibs and decorous ghazals that I composed.[11] Yet I have expressed only a part of what I have discovered over the course of our long acquaintance, intimate company, and shared affection; from the subtlety of her thought and the purity of her station. For she is the request and the fulfillment, she, the virgin most pure.[12] Yet from these treasures and lockets (*al-dhakhā'ir wa al-a'lāq*),[13] I have harmonized verses from the surges of longing of an impassioned soul.

So I have given voice to an afflicted soul and signaled the relationship we had, hearkening back to those long-passed times and that blessed company. Each name that I mention in this volume refers to her, each yearned-for abode is her abode, and throughout this work I employ our accustomed style to allude to divine influences, inspirations, and correspondences.[14] For, *the end for us is better than the beginning.*[15] In regard to her knowledge (God grace her with favor), to which I refer, *none can better inform you than one who is ever aware.*[16]

May God protect readers of this volume—as well as those of my larger poetic *dīwān*—from unseemly thoughts regarding men of upright character and celestial concerns. Amen.

> In the name of the almighty, other than whom there is no lord.
> *And God speaks the truth and shows the way.* (Q 33:4)

Appendix 2

QURRAT AL-ʿAYN PREFACE

Here, by the grace of God, is the story of what happened to me when I was circling the Kaʿba. I was in a particularly sweet state of mind when I was overcome with a condition [*ḥāl*] that I had felt before. So as not to disturb anyone, I withdrew from the area covered with paving-stones to the sands along the periphery of the shrine, and continued my circling there. Some verses came to my mind, and I recited them for myself and to anyone who might have been listening:

> I wish I knew if they knew
> whose heart they've taken
>
> Or my heart knew which
> high-ridge track they follow
>
> Do you see them safe
> or perishing?
>
> The lords of love are in love
> ensnared, bewildered

No sooner had I spoken than I felt a jolt from a hand softer than undyed silk. When I turned around, I found before me a Rūmī maiden. Never had I encountered so radiant a face, so sweet a voice, such modesty; such refined thought, elegant allusions; such spirit in conversation. There was none like her in wit, learning, beauty, and intuition.

"What was it you were saying just now, master?" she asked.

"I wish I knew if they knew / whose heart they've taken," I said.

"How very strange that you, the sage (*ʿārif*) of your time, would say something like that!" she objected. "Is not everything that is taken known to the one who takes it? Is it possible to have something and not know it? On the other hand, it is certainly fitting for one without knowledge (*ma'rifa*) to exclaim 'would that I know'![1] The true path requires *a sincere tongue*.[2] How could one like you fall short in such a way? What was it you said next, master?" she asked.

"Or my heart knew which / high-ridge track they follow," I said.

"Master," she said, "the high-ridge track leads between two layers of the heart. Knowledge of it is forbidden. How is it that one like you wishes for that which cannot be attained? The path requires *a sincere tongue*. How is that one like you would fall short in such a way? And what was it you said next?"

"Do you see them safe / or perishing?" I said.

"They are safe indeed," she said. "What you should be asking is whether *you* are safe or perishing. And what did you say after that?"

"The lords of love in love / are ensnared, bewildered," I said.

"Amazing!" she exclaimed. "How can one pierced through the heart by love have any trace of self left to be bewildered? Love consumes. It numbs the senses, drives away intellect, astonishes thoughts, and sends the one in love off with the others who are gone. Where is there place for bewilderment, and who is left to be bewildered? The path requires a sincere tongue. It is unbecoming for one like you to fall short in this regard."[3]

"Cousin," I said, "may I ask your name?"[4]

"Comfort for the eye," she answered.

"*For me*," I said.[5]

Then she bid me farewell and departed. Later on, I came to know her, frequented her company, and beheld in her subtleties of mystical knowings (may God find favor with her!) that no one could possibly describe.[6]

Appendix 3

APOLOGIA

If I mention a ruin, a station, meadows, or the like; or say "her," "o you," "oh," or "would it not be"; or speak of him, her, or the two of them; or mention men or women in the plural; or fate taking me upland to Najd or down to Tihām; a cloud weeping or a flower that smiles; my words to camel drivers bound for Hājir's moringa or Híma's doves; full moons veiled in palanquins that pass into the distance; suns or maidens like stars; lightning, thunder, or the easterly breeze; winds from the north or winds from the south; a track, ravine, dune, mountain, phantom, or sands; a friend, journey, garden, hill, thicket, or holy land; maidens with breasts like rising suns or white marble figurines—; all these and whatever is like them (understand this!) contain lights and secrets brought by heavenly riders.

My heart and the hearts of those like me bear the mark of knowledge—holy witness that these words are true. So, turn your attention from the surface and look within—that you may know.

Appendix 4

IBN ʿARABĪ'S POEM ON AL-ZAHRĀ'

At the gate to Madīnat al-Zahrā', I recited the following verses, imagining the ruins of the caliphal palace there as an abode of birds and wild animals. Once it was a wonder of al-Andalus, hard by Cordoba. Let the wise remember and the oblivious take heed!

Empty chambers glimmer
with sunset, desolate

At every side, birds wail,
then pause, then renew their cry

To one who stood alone
in anguish, I asked why

Why are you grieving so?
For time now passed, he said,
never to return

دِيَـارًا بِـأَكْنَـافِ ٱلْـمَغِيـبِ تُلَـمِّعُ
وَمَـا أَنْ بِهَـا مِـنْ سَـاكِنٍ وَهِـىَ بَلْقَعُ

يَنُوحُ عَلَيْهَا ٱلطَّيْرُ مِنْ كُلِّ جَانِبٍ
فَيَصْمُتُ أَحْيَانًا وَحِينًا يَرْجِعُ

فَخَاطَبْتُ مِنْهَا طَائِرًا مُتَفَرِّدًا
لَـهُ شَجَنٌ فِي ٱلْقَلْبِ وَهْـوَ مُـرَوَّعُ

فَقُلْتُ عَلَى مَاذَا تَنُوحُ وَتَشْتَكِي
فَقَالَ عَلَى دَهْرٍ مَضَى لَيْسَ يَرْجِعُ

(Ibn ʿArabī, *Sessions of the Righteous* [*MAb* 2:259–60]; Maqqarī, *Nafḥ al-Ṭīb* [1:123])

Appendix 5

CHRONOLOGY OF IBN ʿARABĪ'S LIFE AND TIMES

1165	Birth of Ibn ʿArabī in Murcia, Spain, on the 17th of Ramadan 565 H.
1171	Saladin abolishes the three-hundred-year Fatimid Caliphate, establishing the Ayyubid Dynasty. Death of ʿAbd al-Qādir al-Jilānī.
1171–72	Ibn ʿArabī's family settles in Seville, northern capital of the al-Muwaḥḥid (Almohad) Empire, which was based in the North African city of Marrakesh.
1180	Ibn ʿArabī meets the philosopher and jurist Ibn Rushd (Averroes) in Córdoba.
1181	Ibn ʿArabī embarks on the mystical path. Birth of Ibn al-Fāriḍ.
1187	Saladin retakes Jerusalem.
1195	Ibn ʿArabī in Tunis, frequents the Sufi shaykh ʿAbd al-ʿAzīz al-Mahdawī.
1195–97	Ibn ʿArabī in Fez, experiences a series of mystical visions.
1188–89	Ibn ʿArabī in Andalusia, farewell tour of his native land.
1199	Attends funeral of Ibn Rushd in Córdoba.
1201	Death of Ibn al-Jawzī, the Hanbalite preacher and author whose writings on the hajj were particularly appreciated by Ibn ʿArabī.
1201–02	Ibn ʿArabī in Marrakesh, then in Tunis, where he spends several months with al-Mahdawī.
1202	Travels to Cairo, visits tomb of Abraham in Hebron, al-Aqṣa mosque in Jerusalem, and Muḥammad's tomb in Medina, before arriving in Mecca in July or August.
1202–04	Ibn ʿArabī in Mecca, where he frequents the symposia of the scholar and pious devotee Ẓāhir bin Rustam of Isfāhān, re-

ceives hadith transmissions through his sister, Fakhr al-Nisā', and encounters his daughter, Niẓām.

1204	Death of Maimonides. Crusaders plunder Constantinople.
1207	Birth of Jalāl ad-Dīn Rūmī.
1209	Death of the Persian mystic Ruzbehān Baqlī in Shiraz.
1211	Seljuk Turkish prince Kaykaus assumes rule over the Sultanate of Rūm in Anatolia, where Ibn 'Arabī, Jalāl al-Dīn Rūmī, and other mystics would find hospitality and support.
1212	Ibn 'Arabī in Baghdad, corresponds with Kaykaus. Birth of the poet and mystic Abū al-Ḥasan al-Shushtarī in Guadix (Wadi Ash) near Granada.
1214	Ibn 'Arabī composes *Tarjumān al-Ashwāq*.
1215	Ibn 'Adīm reads portions of the *Tarjumān* commentary to an assembly of Aleppan notables.
1215	Ibn 'Arabī back in Anatolia, at Sivas and Malatya (Melitene), where he completes the *Tarjumān* commentary.
1223	Ibn 'Arabī settles in Damascus where he receives the support of the Ayyubid ruler.
1225	Death of Abbasid caliph Nāṣir li-Dīn Allāh, whose decades-long rule witnessed an explosive growth in organized Sufi networks.
1229	Death of Farīd al-Dīn 'Aṭṭār. Rūmī's family settles in the Anatolian cultural center of Konya.
1232–37	Rūmī in Aleppo and Damascus. No historical evidence he met Ibn 'Arabī.
1235	Death of Ibn al-Fāriḍ in Cairo. Ibn 'Arabī composes *The Ringstones of Wisdom*.
1236	Córdoba falls to the Reconquista.
1237	Ibn 'Arabī completes his *Great Dīwān*.
1238	Ibn 'Arabī completes the second edition of the *Meccan Openings*.
ca. 1238	Reputed birth of Yunus Emre, master of love poetry and mystical poetry in Turkish.
1240	Death of Ibn 'Arabī in Damascus, the 22nd of Rābī' al-Thāni, 638 H; November 10, 1240 CE.

Appendix 6

ESTABLISHING THE TEXT: MANUSCRIPTS, EDITIONS, AND METHOD

The manuscript evidence for Ibn ʿArabī's writings is exceptionally strong. By the time he arrived in Damascus in 1221 CE, Ibn ʿArabī was accompanied by a faithful and expanding group of followers. They produced copies of his texts and recited them in his presence, often in the presence of others. During an occasion known as a "hearing" (*samāʿ*), Ibn ʿArabī would listen to a copy of his text as it was read aloud. He would then make any needed corrections before approving the copy. Those present at the hearing would sign the new copy under Ibn ʿArabī's own handwritten, signed attestation of approval. In some cases, there would be more than one hearing for a given copy before the author would grant the final attestation of approval. These sessions served simultaneously as both editing and publishing workshops and as advanced seminars. Original copies, with Ibn ʿArabī's signed approval, are called "autographs." Copies signed by those who were present at a hearing are themselves called "hearings." Remarkably, Ibn ʿArabī left a number of "holograph manuscripts," that is, manuscripts that were composed entirely in the hand of the author—including most of his voluminous *Meccan Openings* and a significant part of his *Great Dīwān*.

Although there are no known surviving holograph or autograph manuscripts of the *Tarjumān*, there can be little doubt that Ibn ʿArabī authored it. The *Tarjumān* poems are found in both *Sessions of the Righteous* and *Dīwān al-maʿārif*; they are consistent with the style of dozens of other nasib and ghazal poems in *Dīwān al-maʿārif*; several are quoted or referenced in *Meccan Openings*; and the *Priceless Treasures* commentary fits in with Ibn ʿArabī's wider mystical-philosophical oeuvre, both in terms of content and, crucially, in terms of Ibn ʿArabī's distinctive mode of literary expression. Over the past fifty years, scholars have identified and cataloged dozens of manuscripts for both works. A number of those manuscripts are of high historical significance and quality.

Historically significant manuscripts include information on the "original" from which the copy was transmitted down through centuries by copyists, often with the name of the final copyist and the date of that copy. In each stage of the transmission process, the copyist was expected to check his copy against the original or the copy from which he was working, often under the supervision of an acknowledged expert on the work and its transmission—in much the way modern, responsible editions are given careful proofreading, copyediting, and page-proof checks. Although copyists, as they would point out in their final comments, were humble, all-too-fallible humans, a robust set of manuscripts from different transmission families allows the *Tarjumān*'s modern editor considerable clarity in establishing the Arabic text, especially in view of the major advance in scholarship on Ibn 'Arabī's manuscripts that has occurred over the past decade. For recent work on the manuscripts of Ibn 'Arabī, see Osman Yahya, *Histoire et Classification de l'Oeuvre d'Ibn 'Arabī* (Damascus, 1964) ; Jane Clark and Stephen Hirtenstein, "Establishing Ibn 'Arabī's Heritage," *JMIAS* 52 (2012): 1–32; Jane Clark, "Mystical Perception and Beauty: Ibn 'Arabī's Preface to *Tarjumān al-ashwāq*," *JMIAS* 55 (2014): 33–62; and Stephen Hirtenstein, "In the Master's Hand: A Preliminary Study of Ibn 'Arabī's Holographs and Autographs," *JMIAS* 60 (2016): 65–106.

Below are the sources used for the establishment of this edition, beginning with the manuscript I have used as the base, and following with the other sources by order of their historical pedigree and copyist accuracy. This edition adopts the formally correct forms for broken plurals in preference to the manuscript base and printed editions based on it in which *yā'* replaced hamza, possibly under the influence of pronunciation in areas of Turkish and Persian influence, neither of which languages includes a *hamza* equivalent.

Although the sixty-one poems of the *Tarjumān* included in the first printed edition by Nicholson in 1911 are almost certainly authentic, and there is little ambiguity in the sequencing of *verses* within each poem, my current work finds that the sequencing of the last ten poems *within* the *Tarjumān* is not standard within the most reliable manuscripts. Ibn 'Arabī may have transmitted the *Tarjumān* poems in different sequences at different times, just as he may have produced various prefatory and commentary material at different periods. The influence of the Nicholson edition on subsequent printings and translations has established the modern expectation for how the *Tarjumān* poems are sequenced; and although the more historic and higher-quality manuscripts consulted for this edition offer a variety of sequences for the last part of the collection, I have seen no reason to complicate matters by departing from Nicholson's ordering of the poems.

Manuscripts Consulted

RP Rāghib Pāsha 1453, 181b–202b

The manuscript, which is itself undated, bears a copy of a verification by Ibn ʿArabī dated 614/1217. It begins with the prologue and versified apologia, followed by the *jāriya* preface, including poem 1. There follows the full text of poems 2–61, which is followed in turn with the epilogue. The text is composed in a clear script, with consistent accuracy and extensive vocalization, and is in excellent physical condition. The final poems are presented in the following order: 50, 54, 55, 57, 58, 59, 60, 61, 51, 52, 53. This document offers a window into the transmission process at the time of Ibn ʿArabī and over the following centuries.

After the final verse, the text reads:

> The author [Ibn ʿArabī] of this book declares: "All the verses that I composed (*naẓamtu*) for this volume were completed with the help of God in a state of ritual purity during the ʿUmra visit as I mentioned earlier [in the months of Rajab, Shaʿbān, and Ramaḍān in the year 611 [Nov 1214–Feb 1215 CE]—with the exception of the verses that begin with "I wish I knew if they knew whose heart they have taken" [poem 1], for that incident took place in the year 604 [1207–1208 CE]. Praise be to God and blessings and peace upon Muḥammad and his family. The text was completed on the fifth day of the month of Rajab the Bounteous (*al-ashabb*) in the year 614 [Oct–Nov 1217 CE] in the city of Malatya [Melitene] in the lands of the Greeks [Yunān, lands formerly held by the Byzantine Roman Empire]—may God have mercy on its writer (*kātib*), his parents, and on all of the community of Muḥammad, peace upon him."

There follows a colophon that states:

> Muḥammad bin ʿAlī bin Muḥammad bin al-ʿArabī al-Ṭāʾī declares, "This volume, *Tarjumān al-Ashwāq*, which I authored (*min inshāʾī*), was recited before me by the most learned imam and scholar ʿImād al-Dīn [J]abr bin ʿAlī bin ʿAlī al-Barmakī (may he find God's favor), as I listened personally, during a single session (*majlis*). I approved for him a general permission (*ijāza*) to pass on my narrations (*riwāyātī*) and my written works (*muṣannafātī*) according to the usual stipulations among practitioners in this area (*ahl hādhā al-shaʾn*); and I was pleased to bestow upon him that *ijāza* on the 3rd day of the month of Rajab the Unique (*al-fard*) in the year 614 [Oct 6, 1217 CE]—praise be to God and with blessings and peace on Muḥammad and his family."

It appears from the wording of the colophon that the session with Barmakī would have occurred on 5 Rajab, two days after Ibn ʿArabī bestowed the general *ijāza* upon him.

M Manissa 6596, 78a–91a
This manuscript is undated but bears a note saying that it was taken from the personal copy of the work held by Ibn ʿArabī's most important companion and literary heir, Ṣadr al-Dīn al-Qunawī. It is composed in clear script, although without the elegance of *RP*, and confirms *RP* in the vast majority of cases where variants of particular words exist. It breaks off abruptly after verse 5 of poem 31.

F Fātiḥ 5322, 1181–1511
The copy is dated 934 H. It begins with the *Dhakhāʾir* introduction (and 611 *naẓamtu*), followed by the versified apologia and the Qurrat al-ʿAyn preface, and then proceeds with a full copy of *al-Dhakhāʾir*. The title page states that it was originally written in 622 H in the month of Jumādā al-Ākhira by Ibn ʿArabī's companion Ayyūb Badr al-Dīn al-Manṣur al-Muqrī (al-Miṣrī al-Jarāʾidī). It also contains a replica of the shaykh's attestation of approval (*ijāza*), which the shaykh would have written in his own hand on the original manuscript. (For an account of Ibn ʿArabī's transmission circles, see Addas, *Red Sulfur*, 245–70; on Ayyūb Badr al-Dīn in particular, *idem*, 265–68).

EM-a Evkaf Musezi 1713, 252–366
This copy is dated 873 H. The copyist states that it was copied from a manuscript that had been read out before Ibn ʿArabī. It begins with a

piece of the prologue, apologia, and Qurrat al-ʿAyn preface, followed by *Dhakhāʾir*, followed by the rest of the prologue. The *Dhakhāʾir* text is complete, but as with RP, the final poems are sequenced in a manner that differs from that of Nicholson's edition. The sequence in EM-a is as follows: 1–47, 49, 51, 54, 55, 57, 58, 48, 52, 50, 53, 56, 59, 60, 61. The title page states the copy was based on the original written by the same companion of Ibn ʿArabī, Ayyūb Badr al-Dīn al-Manṣūr al-Miṣrī al-Jarāʾidī, mentioned above. A colophon on the final page dates the copy to 873 H and affirms that the copy had been collated with the text that had been recited (apparently by Ayyūb Badr al-Dīn) before Ibn ʿArabī and which had received his signed approval.

EM-b Evkaf Müzesï 1713, 367–69
This text begins right after *EM-a*. It consists solely of the Niẓām preface and is dated 888 H.

P Paris, Bibliothèque nationale de France (Arabe BN 2583)
This copy of *Dīwān al-Maʿārif* places the sixty-one poems of the *Tarjumān*, in the standard sequence, at the end of the *Dīwān* (ff. 250–73), along with the full *Dhakhāʾir* commentary for poems 1–14. The commentary ends with poem 15, verse 3 (f. 267r).

AS-a Ayasofia 1723 1–96
The copyist, Ilyās bin Shaykh ʿAbd al-Salām, dates his copy to 835 H. The manuscript, written in a clear dual-color script (with the poems in red), takes the following sequence: Niẓām preface, part of the epilogue, apologia, Qurrat al-ʿAyn preface, *Dhakhāʾir*, and the part of the epilogue mentioning the two companions (Badr al-Ḥabashī and Ibn Sawdakīn) that asked Ibn ʿArabī to compose the commentary. The sequence of the final poems is: 31, 33–49, 54–55, 57–58, 32, 48, 52, 50, 53, 56, 59–61.

AS-b Ayasofia 1724, 1–127
The undated *AS-b* begins with the introduction to *Dhakhāʾir*, followed by the versified apologia and the Qurrat al-ʿAyn preface. There follows the first part of *Dhakhāʾir*, but the manuscript breaks off abruptly after verse 3 of poem 27. The title page contains an epigraph of several verses that are not found in the *Tarjumān*, including the "*inna al-hawā ʿujmatun*" poem that Ibn ʿArabī included in his *Muḥāḍarat al-Abrār* (vol. 2, p. 476, of the 1968 edition referenced below).

K Kutuhaya 111, 1a–73a
This manuscript of *al-Dhakhā'ir* is transmitted from an original copy made by Khalīl al-Ḥalabī bin al-Ḥājj Aḥmad al-Miṣrī on 18 Muḥarram 640 H in Damascus, in the *ribāṭ* (lodge) of al-Shimshānī (or al-Shimsānī). Despite its historical quality, elegant script, and dual-color arrangement (with the poems in red), the copy is riddled with errors. It takes the following sequence: prologue, Qurrat al-ʿAyn preface, apologia, *al-Dhakhā'ir* (in full), epilogue.

Printed Editions Consulted

Reynold Nicholson 1911 Nicholson used the manuscript Cambridge OR 1462/9 (Cambridge University Library) as the default text for his edition. It was in Nicholson's private collection at that time and dates from 1025 H (1616–17 CE). As Nicholson notes, it contains the text of the poems (in red ink) and the *Dhakhā'ir* commentary. Nicholson also points out "inscriptions on the last page certify that it has been twice diligently collated and corrected." In addition to Cambridge OR 1462/9, Nicholson consulted and represents in his apparatus two other manuscripts: Leiden 875 (2) Warn., which he states contains "only the text of the poems, with a preface and is dated 922 H"; and Leiden 641 Warn., of which he writes that it "is dated 984 H and contains both text and commentary."

Sh The 1995 edition of *Dhakhā'ir* by al-Shuqayrī is based upon five manuscripts. They include a microfilm of a manuscript in Basra that is held at the University of Arab States and four manuscripts held in Cairo's Dār al-Kutub (Adab 6614 dated 969 H; Adab 4393 dated 904 H; Adab Ṭalʿat 4089 dated 1273 H; and Adab Ṭalʿat 4373 dated 1079 H), along with the Nicholson 1911 edition (Muḥammad ʿAlam al-Dīn Shuqayrī, *Dhakhā'ir al-aʿlāq: Sharḥ Tarjumān al-ashwāq* [al-Haram [Egypt]: al-ʿAyn lil-Dirāsāt wa-al-Buḥūth al-Insāniyya wa-al-Ijtimāʿiyya, 1995]). Al-Shuqayrī includes extensive introductory material and is careful to note and cite the hadith traditions alluded to by Ibn ʿArabī in commentary. Shuqayrī also gives one of the manuscripts (Adab Ṭalʿat 4089) the very same origin as that of *K* as described above: from 18 Muḥarram 640 H, written in the *ribāṭ* of al-Shimshānī, although Shuqayrī does not specify the name of the writer. He does state, however, that the copy he has inspected is riddled with errors.

DS The Beirut Dār Ṣādir edition (available in several undated printings), although useful and widely distributed, does not explain its manuscript base.

Manuscript and Printed Editions of *Sessions of the Righteous* (*Kitāb muḥāḍarat al-abrār wa-musāmarat al-akhyār fī al-adībāt wa-al-nawādir wa-al-aḥbār*)

As mentioned, the large part of the *Tarjumān*, including almost all of its long poems, appears in *MAb*, which contains 34 of the 61 poems comprising 319 of the *Tarjumān*'s 576 verses. In addition to *MAb* (discussed above), I have studied the following:

MAb1 *TSM* Topkapi Sarayi Müzesï III: Ahmed Kïtapliği 2415. This manuscript of *Muḥāḍarāt al-Abrār* is written in clear script. It is not reliable for the prose sections of the text, but the poems, including those from the *Tarjumān*, are more accurately represented.

MAb2 The Cairo 1888 al-Maktaba al-ʿUthmāniyya edition. No editor named.

MAb3 The Cairo 1906 printed at Maktaba al-Saʿāda in Cairo by Mustafā al-Sayyid Aḥmad Tāj al-Kutubī in Ṭanṭa and his son Ibrāhīm Tāj.

MAb4 The Beirut 1968 Dār al-Yaqẓa al-ʿArabīyya printed edition.

MAb5 The Beirut 2007 Dār al-Kutub al-ʿIlmiyya edition, edited by Muḥammad ʿAbd al-Karīm al-Namarī, which is nearly identical to Beirut 1968, with the exception of the translator's introduction and the pagination.

The *Tarjumān* poems in *MAb*, in order of appearance, are as follows (with page numbers coinciding with those in *MAb4*):

1. Poem 8 [*MAb* 1:260–61]
2. Poem 36 [*MAb* 1:261]
3. Poem 44 [*MAb* 1:282–83]
4. Poem 21 [*MAb* 1:288–89, which is missing verse 5]
5. Poem 25 [*MAb* 1:289–90]
6. Poem 12 [*MAb* 1:290]
7. Poem 27 [*MAb* 1:290, introduced by "I was circling the Kaʿba one night when I was overcome with a very sweet mood, and I said in

complaint of the thirst I suffered during my desert journey, 'Old shrine high above . . .'" (*ṭuftu laylan bi-l-bayti fa adrakanī t-taʿabu, fa qultu atʿabu nafsī ʿalā l-badīhati min ghayr rawiyyatin: yā ayyuhā l-baytu l-ʿatīqu . . .*)]
8. Poem 13 [*MAb* 1:291]
9. Poem 28 [*MAb* 1:291–92]
10. Poem 5 [*MAb* 1:292–93]
11. Poem 9 [*MAb* 1:293]
12. Poem 34 [*MAb* 1:293]
13. Poem 15 [*MAb* 1:318]
14. Poem 11 [*MAb* 1:319–20, without the two suspect verses]
15. Poem 33 [*MAb* 1:320]
16. Poem 14 [*MAb* 1:338–39]
17. Poem 10 [*MAb* 1:345]
18. Poem 30 [*MAb* 1:345–47]
19. Poem 7 [*MAb* 1:349]
20. Poem 17 [*MAb* 1:360]
21. Poem 32 [*MAb* 1:360]
22. Poem 6 [*MAb* 1:360–61]
23. Poem 29 [*MAb* 1:368–69, with a variant reading for verses 17–19]
24. Poem 35 [*MAb* 1:369]
25. Poem 18 [*MAb* 1:370]
26. Poem 16 [*MAb* 1:386–87]
27. Poem 1 with the Qurrat al-ʿAyn story [*MAb* 2:56–58]
28. Poem 2 [*MAb* 2:58–59]
29. Poem 3 [*MAb* 2:59, which is introduced by these words: "I once had a wife who was the solace of my eyes (Qurrat al-ʿAyn), but time and circumstances came between us. I recalled her and her residence at Ḥilla (or Ḥalba), near Baghdad."]
30. Poem 4 [*MAb* 2:59]
31. Poem 41 [*MAb* 2:372–73]
32. Poem 20 [*MAb* 2:386–87, introduced by "And among our poems on Niẓām (*wa lanā fī n-niẓāmiyyāt*) is . . ."]
33. Poem 55 [*MAb* 2:438]
34. Poem 57 [*MAb* 2:468]

The *Tarjumān* poems represented in *MAb*, according to Nicholson's *Tarjumān* sequence: 1–18; 20–21; 25; 27–30; 32–36; 41; 44–45; 55; 57.

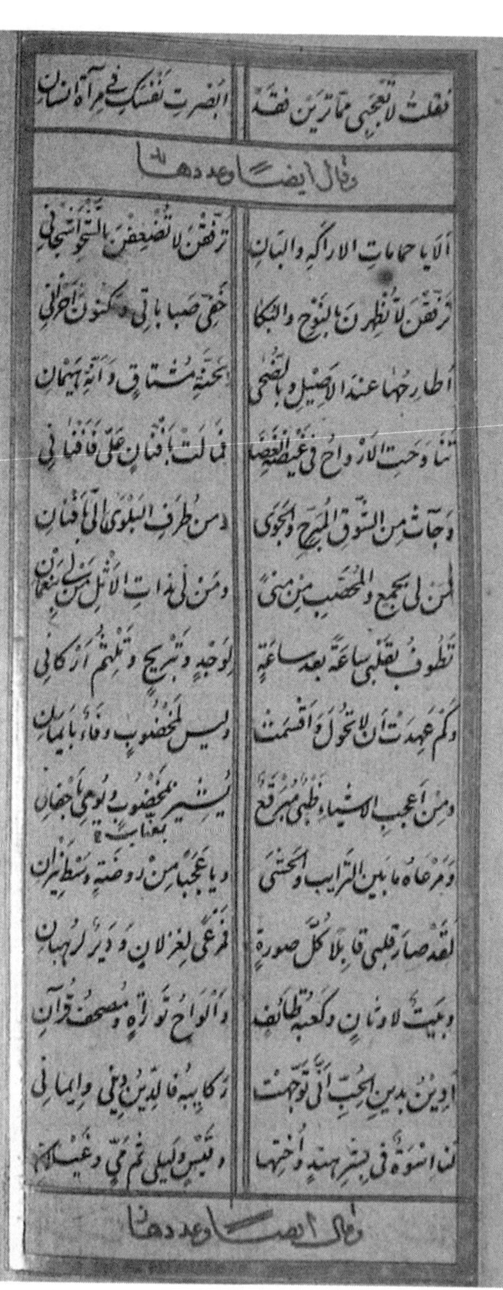

فقلت لا تعجبي مما ترين فقد / ابصرت نفسك في مرآة انسان

وقال ايضا

الا يا حمامات الاراكة والبان / ترفقن لا تضعفن بالشجو اشجاني

ترفقن لا تظهرن بالنوح والبكا / خفي صبابتي ومكنون احزاني

اطارحها عند الاصيل وبالضحى / بحنة مشتاق وانة هيمان

تناوحت الارواح في غيضة الغضا / فمالت بافنان علي فافناني

وجاءت من الشوق المبرح والجوى / ومن طرف البلوى الي بافنان

فمن لي بجمع والمحصب من منى / ومن لي بذات الاثل من لي بنعمان

تطوف بقلبي ساعة بعد ساعة / لوجد وتبريح وتلثم اركاني

وكم عهدت ان لا تحول واقسمت / وليس لمخضوب وفاء بايمان

ومن اعجب الاشياء ظبي مبرقع / يشير لمخضوب ويومي باجفان بعناب

ومرعاه ما بين الترائب والحشا / ويا عجبا من روضة وسط نيران

لقد صار قلبي قابلا كل صورة / فمرعى لغزلان ودير لرهبان

وبيت لاوثان وكعبة طائف / والواح توراة ومصحف قرآن

ادين بدين الحب انى توجهت / ركائبه فالدين ديني وايماني

لنا اسوة في بشر هند واختها / وقيس وليلى ثم مي وغيلان

وقال ايضا

Poem 11 of Tarjumān al-Ashwāq (MS Ragıp Paşa #1453, Süleymaniye Library, Istanbul).

Appendix 7

ANNOTATED CHRONOLOGY OF *TARJUMĀN* TRANSLATIONS

Reynold A. Nicholson, *The Tarjumán Al-Ashwáq: A Collection of Mystical Odes*. London: Royal Asiatic Society, 1911. Includes a complete Arabic text and translation along with a translation of most of the prefatory material and selected portions of the commentary.

Vicente Cantarino, *Casidas de amor profundo y místico*. México: Porrúa, 1977. In this anthology, devoted to poems by Ibn Zaydūn and Ibn ʿArabī, the translator includes all 61 poems of the *Tarjumān*, along with an overview of their poetics, including metrics, alliteration and punning, and other features.

Sami-Ali, *Le Chant de l'ardent désir*. Arles: Actes Sud, 1989. This work consists of selections of poems and passages of poems from throughout the *Tarjumān*.

Maurice Gloton, *L'interprète des Désirs = Turjumān Al-Ashwāq*. Paris: Albin Michel, 1996. Includes full translations of all the poems and prefatory material as well as a nearly complete translation of the commentary. Gloton's work broke new ground with the commentary and remained the only translation of it until the German-language translation by Wolfgang Hermann discussed below.

Michael Sells, *Stations of Desire: Love Elegies from Ibn ʿArabi and New Poems*. Jerusalem: Ibis Editions, 2000. This volume includes translations of *Tarjumān* poems 1–19, 21, 24–25, 48, and 50.

———, *Bewildered: Love Poems from Ibn ʿArabī's Translation of Desires*. Paris: The Post-Apollo Press, 2018. This volume includes translations of *Tarjumān* poems 1, 6–9, 11–13, 19–20, 22–23, 31–33, 36–37, 39, 41, 45–47, 49, 51, 55, 57, 59–61. [Note: The translations of *Stations of Desire* and *Bewildered* were based on harmonizing the selected poems into styles adjusted according to the interior exigencies of the given selection and in consideration of the intended readership; even as this present volume adopts a different style for the same reason.]

Carlos Varona Narvión, *El Intérprete de los Deseos = (Taryuman Al-Aswaq), Traducción y Comentarios.* Murcia: Editora Regional de Murcia, 2002. This is a complete translation of the poems and prefatory material, along with commentary selections (which are for the most part the same passages selected by Nicholson for translation), as well the translator's overview of the poetics, mystical resonances, style, and other aspects of the *Tarjumān.*

Georg Bossong, *Das Wunder von al-Andalus: Die schönsten Gedichte aus dem Maurischen Spanien.* Munich: C. H. Beck, 2005. In a rich selection of Arabic and Hebrew poetry from al-Andalus, the translator includes *Tarjumān* poems 1, 2, 3, 5, 9, 14, 26, 27, 57, and 49 along with Ibn 'Arabī's elegy for the palace of al-Zahrā' outside of Córdoba from *Sessions of the Righteous* (see appendix 4) as well as notes on rhyme, meter, and previous translations.

Mahmud Kanık, *Arzuların tercümanı.* İstanbul: Iz Yayinlari, 2006. A translation into modern Turkish.

R. Rossi Testa, *L'interprete delle passioni.* Milano: Apogeo, 2008. A translation of the *Tarjumān* poems as well as the excerpts of Ibn 'Arabī's commentary that had been translated by Nicholson into English.

Hamza Tanyas, *Arzuların tercümanı.* İstanbul: Kaknus, 2010. A translation into modern Turkish.

Alma Giese, *Urwolke und Welt: Mystische Texte des Größten Meisters.* Munich: C. H. Beck, 2015. This work includes a section (pp. 226–303) of translations of selected poems from the *Tarjumān* along with full translations of Ibn 'Arabī's commentaries on them. The poems selected are 6, 9, 10, 12, 13, 17, 24, 26, 27, 33, 35, 41, 44, 45, 53, 54, and 49.

Wolfgang Hermann, Ibn 'Arabi, Muhyiddin. *Deuter der Sehnsüchte (Turjuman al-Ashwaq): Band 1 (Gedichte 1–20).* Trans. Wolfang Hermann. Zurich: Edition Shershir, 2013.

———, *Deuter der Sehnsüchte (Turjuman al-Ashwaq): Band 2 (Gedichte 21–61).* Zurich: Edition Shershir, 2013. Hermann's two volumes include fine translations of all the poems, prefatory material, and commentary, with extensive notes on the vocabulary, idiom, philological, and lyrical contexts for the poems. They also identify subtexts within the Qur'an, hadith, and early Arabic poetry, and provides extensive transliterations of key terms used within the poems and commentary.

A major contribution to the understanding of Ibn ʿArabī and the essential work on Ibn ʿArabī's *Priceless Treasures.*
Stefan Weidner, *Der Übersetzer der Sehnsüchte Liebesgedichte aus dem arabischen Mittelalter.* Salzburg: Jung u. Jung, 2016. Weidner translates the poems of the *Tarjumān* as well as the prefaces to them. His translation adopts a variable approach to the Arabic verses, which can entail moving between couplets, triplets, and quatrains within a single poem.
Ensemble Ibn Báya, Cofradía Shustari, Omar Metioui, and Eduardo Paniagua, *Ibn ʿArabī (Murcia 1165–Damasco 1240), El Intérprete de los deseos (Taryumán al-Ashwáq): Poems from the Tarjumān Selected by Pablo Beneito, with Translations into Spanish, English, and French by Carlos Varona, Reynold Nicholson, Henri Gloton, and Pablo Beneito.* Madrid: Pneuma, 2002.

GLOSSARY

Note: Each word below is indicated first in anglicized form with stress accent markers meant to allow the word to fit into the English verse soundscape, and then by the word in formal transliteration. In Arabic usage, place-names usually contain the definite article, in contrast to English usage. Thus, the full Arabic name for *ʻaqūq*, in the second entry below, is *al-ʻaqūq*, and so on for the majority of the Arabic place-names listed.

Ajyādi (*ajyād*, with grammatical suffix kept in the anglicized form of the word as it appears in the poems, for the sake of euphony). A height near Mecca overlooking the Kaʻba.

Aqūq (*ʻaqūq*), Khawárnaq (*khawarnaq*), Sadīr (*sadīr*), and Sindād (*sindād*). Ancient castles in the regions between northeast Arabia and Iraq, the ruins of which exemplified the lost grandeur of the past.

Árafa (*ʻarafa or ʻarafat*). The plain and adjoining mount near Mecca where Muḥammad gave his last sermon and where hajj pilgrims stand through the afternoon in remembrance of that event. At this time, the pilgrims also chant *labbayka,* "here I am for you," the expression each person will utter at the final judgment.

Ālij (*ʻālij*). The vast dunescape in north-central Arabia, known more commonly today as the Nefūd.

Bilqīs (*bilqīs*). The name given by tradition to the Queen of Sheba, whose story appears in Q 27:15–44.

Bishr (*bishr*). The ghazal poet known for his love of Hind, a love that led him to be known as "Bishr Hind." The romance of Bishr and Hind was included in Isfahānī's *Great Book of Songs.*

Dhū al-Qarnayn ("the two-horned one"). Dhū al-Qarnayn, who appears in the Qur'an with mythic capabilities, was identified in Islamic lore with Alexander the Great (Iskandar, Iskander) or, alternatively, with King Cyrus of Persia. He is able to travel across the world from West to East on the cords (*asbāb*) of the heavenly firmament. He also constructs a great dam to wall off Gog and Magog (*yajūj* and *majūj*), the apocalyptic peoples or tribes who, once unleashed, will bring on the end-times.

Gháda (*ghaḍā*). A thick-trunked tree of the Arabian desert, valued for the shelter it provided and prized for use as cooking coals. In his commentary, Ibn ʿArabī associates the tree with fire, and more specifically with the fire in the lover's heart, and with the "burning tree" from which the divine voice addressed Mūsā.

Hadītha (*ḥadītha*). A city in Iraq on the Euphrates River.

Hājir (*ḥājir*). A relay station in Arabia associated in the *Tarjumān* with the notions of "interdiction" and "prohibition." There were at least two different stations by that name on classical pilgrimage routes from Iraq to Mecca and Medina. One was southeast of al-Ḥīra in Iraq, toward the beginning of the Iraq-to-Mecca pilgrimage route. Ibn Jubayr includes it in his pilgrimage account, and Ibn ʿArabī would have passed through it on his way to or from Mecca. The second, on the same route, is far to the southwest, a bit south of the central expanse of the ʿĀlij desert, near the present-day city of Hāʾil. The consonantal root of *ḥājir*, *ḥ/j/r*, is associated not only with the meanings mentioned above but also with words for "stone." The semicircular wall near the Kaʿba is known as *al-ḥijr*. Al-Ḥijr is also a name for the city of Madāʾin Ṣāliḥ, the ancient Nabataean site in central Arabia. The site was associated in Islamic tradition with the city of Thamūd, destroyed when its people refused to follow the guidance of their prophet Ṣāliḥ and instead committed a sacrilegious slaughter of the camel mare of God.

Halba (*ḥalba*). A neighborhood in Baghdad.

Híma, al-Híma (*ḥimā*). A *ḥimā* is a sacred tribal pasture in Bedouin Arabia, marked with boundary stones, the transgression of which by another tribe would lead to war. In Ibn ʿArabī's poems, *al-ḥimā* could be taken as a common noun, "the sanctuary" or "the private pastureland," or as a place-name, as I have done by capitalizing it in the translation.

Ídam (*iḍam*). A name attributed to more than one site in Arabia that in the poetry of Ibn ʿArabī and Ibn al-Fāriḍ is associated with yearning for a past sense of belonging.

Idrīs (*idrīs*). An ancient Qurʾanic prophet who was associated in later tradition with Enoch and in some significant instances with Hermes

Trismegistus, a god of wisdom at the heart of the late antique hermetic tradition. In the Arabic tradition, including the classical accounts of Muḥammad's heavenly ascent (*miʿrāj*) as well as philosophical and Sufi writings, Idrīs is associated with the fourth heavenly sphere, that of the sun. In Islamic lore, Idrīs became an exemplar of learning and wisdom, credited, among other things, with the invention of writing.

Iskandar. See Dhū al-Qarnayn.

Jem (*jamʿ*). A site near Mecca, known more commonly as Muzdalifa, at which pilgrims reassemble for a time during their rigorous journey from ʿArafāt back to Minā. The literal meaning of the word is "assembling, coming together."

Karkh (*karkh*). The name given to a section of Baghdad on the west side of the Tigris River.

Kathīb, Sand Hill (*kathīb*, sandy hill). As with many other such words, *al-kathīb* could be rendered as a common noun (the sandy hill) or a place-name (Sand Hill).

Khawárnaq (*khawarnaq*). See Aqūq.

Láʿlaʿ or Láʿlaʿi (*laʿlaʿ*). Stone-Flash, one of many toponyms built upon natural features, along the lines of American place-names such as Flint-Rock, Rock-Creek, or Flint-Creek.

Láyla (*laylā*). The beloved in the poetry attributed to Qays ibn Mulawwiḥ, the Bedouin poet said to have lived at or shortly after the time of the prophet Muḥammad. In the poems attributed to him, and in the romances about him (in Arabic, Persian, Ottoman, and other languages), Qays is said to have gone mad and ultimately perished for love of Laylā. He became known as Majnūn Laylā (Mad for Laylā). The epithet *majnūn* (mad) also carried the etymological sense of "jinned," that is, possessed by the *jinn* (genies). The ghazals attributed to Majnūn, which address his beloved Laylā, were gathered into the *Great Book of Songs* along with tales of their star-crossed romance.

Lote, lote tree (*ḍāl*). A tree steeped in Arabian mythopoesis. It is associated with the times spent with the beloved and with a similar tree mentioned in the Qur'an as *al-sidr* (*sidr al-muntahā*), the *sidr* of the furthest boundary, that was associated with Muḥammad's prophetic vision (Q 53:14) and, through hadith traditions, with the highest reach of the heavens. The *sidr* (Zisiphus lotus) is most often translated as "lote tree." Zisiphus lotus is also said to have been the baleful tree of the Island of the Lotus Eaters in the Odyssey, but neither the Qur'anic *sidr* nor the *ḍāl* of classical nasibs bore fruit with narcotic-like properties. It has also been translated as Christ-thorn tree (though the Qur'an has no discussion of Jesus's crown of thorns). Preservationist web pages from the Arabian peninsula feature pictures of the tree, often in praise of its medicinal properties. Botanical specialists have suggested that it corresponds to a particularly striking species of acacia with yellow puff flowers native to the Red Sea regions, acacia vechellia seyal *(ṭalḥ)*.

Ma'zimáyn (*al-ma'zimān*, in the nominative form). An area near Mecca, between 'Arafa and Muzdalifa, at the boundary of the sanctuary area around Mecca and its immediate environs.

Markh (*markh*, leptadenia pyrotechnica, broom brush). A desert shrub that, as the name suggests, was valued for its use as kindling.

Máyya (*mayya*). The beloved in the poems of Ghaylān Ibn 'Uqba, d. ca. 735 CE, also known as Dhū al-Rumma, who flourished in the Umayyad period and whose poetry may have served as a model for Ibn 'Arabī's more classically elegiac poems.

Medina, Sweet Medina (*madīna*, *ṭayba*, *yathrib*). The site of Islam's first polity and of the home and grave of the prophet Muḥammad.

Mína (*minā*). The station of the hajj where pilgrims cast stones at three cairns (more recently large concrete pillars) representing evil tendencies or Satan; and where sheep, goats, or camels are sacrificed in memory of Abraham's offering, made in place of his son. The ritual is carried out on the day known as the Holy Day or Eid of the Sacrifice ('Īd al-Aḍḥā).

Moringa (*bān*, moringa peregrina). A tree native to the Red Sea and Arabian regions. It has wispy boughs and fragrant flowers that were visually striking within the Arabian steppe and dunescape. It was associated with the beauty of the beloved as well as times spent with the beloved in its shade.

Najd (*najd*). The highland plateau of north-central Arabia. It is associated with the world of love poetry, Majnūn Laylā, and the vivifying Eastwind. Najd is frequently contrasted to Tihāma, the lowland area that extends from Mecca or nearby Jidda southward along the Red Sea toward Yemen.

Nāmūs (*nāmūs*). The word can refer to a great spirit and is thought to be etymologically related to the Greek *nomos*. In Arabic Christian traditions it refers to the spirit that descended upon the disciples at Pentecost. Although the term does not occur in the Qur'an, in Islamic traditions it was associated with the Qur'anic holy spirit (*al-rūḥ al-qudus*).

Náqa (*naqā*, white sands). The name of a site or sites in the Arabian peninsula that appears in nasib poetry as a station on the beloved's journey.

Násir (*nāṣir*). Abbasid caliph Nāṣir li-Dīn Allāh, who ruled in Baghdad from 1180 to 1225 CE.

Pebble-Ground (*muḥaṣṣab*). The area around Muzdalifa where hajj pilgrims collect the pebbles to cast later in Minā.

Persica (*arāk*, *arāka*, salvadora persica). A small tree or shrub with a fragrant scent and small, reddish berries that are edible. The plant appears in the *Tarjumān* along with the moringa as a marker of beauty, lushness, and longing. Its root was used as a natural toothbrush (miswak) by the prophet Muḥammad, and such tooth twigs are still sold in souks today.

Râma (*rāma*). The name of a site or sites in Arabia, one of which was a way station on the pilgrimage road between Medina and al-Ḥīra. The word can be etymologically associated with the Arabic word for "seeking."

Sadīr (*sadīr*). See Aqūq.

Salʿ or Splitrock (*salʿ*). A mountain near Dhū al-Khulayfa overlooking Medina.

Sámiri (*al-sāmirī*). A character who plays a key role in the Qur'anic account of the Israelites and the golden calf by casting dust from the footprint of the messenger (spirit or Jibrīl in Ibn ʿArabī's interpretation) onto the calf, making it low.

Sindād (*sindād*). See Aqūq.

Splitrock (*salʿ*). A mountain overlooking Medina.

Sulaymān (*sulaymān*, Solomon). See Bilqīs.

Tamarisk (*uthayl*, a diminutive form of *athl*). The plural, *uthaylāt*, is translated here as "Tamarisk Stand."

Ṭáyba (*ṭayba*). An epithet for Medina that means "sweet place."

Tháhmad (*thahmad*). A settlement in central Arabia made famous by a verse from the nasib of the pre-Islamic poet Ṭarafa's *muʿallaqa* or "hanging ode."

Tihāma (*tihāma*). See Najd.

ʿUdháyb (*ʿudhayb*). A site known for its abundance of fresh water and verdant surroundings. Ibn Jubayr mentions a verdant site by that name just southwest of the city of al-Ḥīra in Iraq on the pilgrimage route to the holy cities of Arabia.

Yalámlam (*yalamlam*). A site south of Mecca valued for its sweet waters. The sight became one of the four designated entry points (*muqīt*s) for the hajj. There, pilgrims undertake the actions required to place them in a ritually pure state, such as dressing in white tunics and cutting their hair and nails.

Wādilaqīq (*wādī al-ʿaqīq*). There were several Arabian wadis known by this name, one of them located in or near the oasis city of Medina. By the time of Ibn ʿArabī, the toponym Wādī al-ʿAqīq had come to represent, in poetry especially, the lost homeland and past happiness.

Wajrā (*wajrā*). A site associated with gazelles, lush vegetation, and times spent with the beloved—as in the nasib of the celebrated *muʿallaqa* of the poet Labīd.

Zámzam (*zamzam*). The spring near the Kaʿba, which tradition holds was opened by God in response to Hagar's desperate search for water.

Zarūd (*zarūd*). A way station on the pilgrimage road from Iraq to Mecca, which is located between prongs of the desert extending south of the dunescape of ʿĀlij. Unlike many of the sites mentioned in the *Tarjumān*, Zarūd can be found—with its ancient name intact—on the present-day map of Saudi Arabia.

NOTES

Translator's Introduction

1. His fuller name parses his heritage: Muḥyī al-Dīn abū ʿAbdullāh Muḥammad bin ʿAlī bin Muḥammad bin ʿAlī al-Ṭāʾī al-ʿArabī al-Ḥātimī al-Mursī al-Andalūsī. Muḥyī al-Dīn ("Reviver of the Faith") is his honorific. Such honorifics were taken by Abbasid caliphs and other rulers, and, by the twelfth century, by prominent or aspiring individuals, such as poets, philosophers, theologians, soldiers, and scribes. Other attributes bestowed upon Ibn ʿArabī include al-Shaykh al-Akbar (the equivalent to "doctor maximus" in the western Christian tradition) and al-Kibrīt al-Aḥmar (Red Sulfur), the name for the key element in the alchemical transformation of base metals into gold. Muḥammad is his given name, the equivalent of the first name in modern Western societies. Ibn ʿAlī bin Muḥammad bin ʿAlī (son of ʿAlī, the son of Muḥammad, the son of ʿAlī) is his patronymic. Al-ʿArabī reflects his patrilineal descent back to the Arabian peninsula at the time of the prophet Muḥammad. Al-Ṭāʾī is a tribal designation, "of the tribe of Ṭayyiʾ," a tribe of pre- and early Islamic Yemen, elements of which migrated throughout the Arabian peninsula and beyond. Its most renowned member, Ḥātim al-Ṭāʾī, lived at the time of the Prophet and became a paradigm for truthfulness and eloquence in later literature. Ibn ʿArabī traced his patrilineal descent back directly to Ḥātim, and Ibn ʿArabī's poet-persona in the *Tarjumān* refers to himself as a scion of Yemen. Al-Mursī (the Murcian) and al-Andalusī (the Andalusian) are toponymics indicating the city and region in which he was born. Ibn ʿArabī, alternatively Ibn al-ʿArabī, is his popular name. In the *Tarjumān* the poet-persona identifies himself as pure Arab in contrast to the pure Persian descent of his beloved, a contrast that the poet shapes as West and East. The choice of what to call him—Ibn ʿArabī or Ibn al-ʿArabī—has generated a legacy of controversy and discussion. In his vast political and literary history of al-Andalus, al-Maqqarī (d. 1632) writes that the longer form Ibn al-ʿArabī was common in the Maghrib (the western areas that included al-Andalus as well as present-day Morocco, Algeria, Tunisia, and the northern parts of West Africa), while Ibn ʿArabī became the

preferred form in the Arab East. Shihāb al-Dīn al-Maqqarī, *Nafh al-Ṭīb*, 8 vols., edited by Iḥsan ʿAbbās (Beirut: Dār Ṣādir, 1968), 2:175. In the print era, editions and translations of Ibn ʿArabī's works and works about him vary between the two designations, and that split is now deeply embedded in the bibliographical materials. It also continues to generate earnest debates over which version of the name is correct.

2. Ibn ʿArabī, *Tāj al-rasā'il wa-minhāj al-wasā'il* [The Diadem of Epistles and the Way of Intercessions]. This work has not been translated in full. For a discussion of the work, with translations of some passages, see Denis Gril, "Love Letters to the Kaʿba: A Presentation of Ibn ʿArabī's *Tâj al-rasâ'il*," *JMIAS* 17 (1995): 40–54.
3. Ibn al-ʿArabī, *Kitāb muḥāḍarat al-abrār wa-musāmarat al-akhyār fī al-adībāt wa-al-nawādir wa-al-aḥbār* (Beirut: Dār Ṣādir, 1968). This major work of Ibn ʿArabī has not been translated. The full title might be rendered as "The Book of the Sessions of the Righteous and the Salons of the Select with Attention to the Literary Arts, Curious Tales, and Historical Reports." See the "Notes on the Poems" concerning poems 1, 3, 20, 27, 29, and 55, which indicate the impact, sometimes profound, of *Sessions of the Righteous* for any assessment of Ibn ʿArabī's comments on and recollections of these poems.
4. For a critical edition of *Meccan Openings* (*al-Futuḥat al-Makkiyya*), see *al-Futūḥāt al-makkīyah li-Muḥyī al-Dīn Ibn al-ʿArabī*, 12 vols, edited by ʿAbd al-ʿAzīz Sulṭān al-Manṣūb (Sanaʿ, Yemen: al-Jumhūrīya al-Yamanīya, Wizārat al-Thaqāfa, 2010), hereafter referred to as *Fut.* For a translation of the "Treatise on Love" within that work (ch. 178 of *Meccan Openings*), see Ibn al-ʿArabī, *Traité de l'amour*, trans. Maurice Gloton (Paris: A. Michel, 1986). For the Arabic text of the "Treatise of Love" (*Fī maʿrifa maqām al-maḥabba*: "On Connaissance of Station of Love"), see *Meccan Openings* (*Fut.* 5:582–624). For a translation of chapter 1, which depicts Ibn ʿArabī's encounter with the mystical youth at the Kaʿba, see Ibn al-ʿArabī, *The Youth: The Figurative Made Literal*, book 1, trans. Eric Winkel (Self-published, 2016). Chapter 72 revisits the hajj and Kaʿba themes: see *Ibn al-ʿArabī on the Mysteries of the Pilgrimage: The Futūhāt al-Makkiyya*, trans. Aisha Bewley (Chicago: Kazi, 2009). For translations of *Fuṣūṣ al-Ḥikam*, see Ibn al-ʿArabī, *The Ringstones of Wisdom*, trans. Caner K. Dagli (Chicago: Kazi, 2004), and Ibn al-ʿArabī, *The Bezels of Wisdom*,

trans. R. W. J. Austin (New York: Paulist Press, 1980). (In Ibn ʿArabī's thought, the ringstone and its setting or bezel are molded on each other like the heart of the mystic and the manifestation of the divine manifestation, and are, in terms of form, one. The complexity of the theme in *Fuṣūṣ al-Ḥikam* has resulted in differing translations for the title of the work.)

5. Approximately half of Ibn ʿArabī's *Great Dīwān* was published in Cairo in the nineteenth century and is known as the *Būlāq Dīwān* after the publishing house that produced it. Only in the past two decades have scholars rediscovered what appears to be a copy of *Dīwān al-Maʿārif* in a Parisian manuscript collection. *Dīwān al-Māʿārif* contains more than a thousand of Ibn ʿArabī's poetic compositions, most of which are in the mode of nasib and ghazal. All the *Tarjumān* poems as well as Ibn ʿArabī's commentary on poems 1–13 and the first part of 14 are included at the end of that work. A full evaluation of Ibn ʿArabī's poetic oeuvre will require more time, but the basic genres, purposes, and styles within his greater *Dīwān* are beginning to emerge more clearly. One type of poem, which occurs most impressively in *Ringstones of Wisdom* and *Meccan Openings*, might be called gnomic. It offers a set of verses (often between eight and twenty in length) that combine ghazal and nasib with riddles, puns, and intimations of cosmological, ontological, and mystical insights. Such poems often appear at the beginning of a chapter or section. The body of the chapter serves as an unpacking of the poem, a reading of the poem, and a translation of the poem into a different mode of discourse, not without warnings that the meaning of the poem cannot be grasped through explication alone. In such poems, love and mystical *connaissance* (*shawq* and *maʿrifa*) are inextricably intertwined. Denis McAuley, in *Ibn ʿArabī's Mystical Poetics* (Oxford: Oxford University Press, 2012), has explored several genres of poems in the *Bulāq Dīwān*: (a) poems dedicated to chapters of the Qur'an; (b) response poems in which the poet quotes an earlier poet and composes his own poem that both honors the earlier poem and rivals it; (c) poems, all in the same meter and rhyme, centered on the divine self-manifestation; (d) a set of "ultra-rhyme" poems in which every verse ends with Allah; and (e) poems in the *muʿāsharāt* genre, ten-line poems in which "each poem represents one letter of the alphabet, each verse of the poem in question beginning and ending with that letter," and

in which "Ibn ʿArabī portrays himself as participating in the divine command that moves the heavenly spheres" (McAuley, *Mystical Poetics*, 12). Ibn ʿArabī was also a pioneer of the Sufi garland poem (*muwashshaḥa*), which was perfected by his younger contemporary Abū al-Hasan al-Shushtarī. For a trilingual Arabic–Castilian–English edition and discussion of the garland poems of Ibn ʿArabī, see Federico Corriente and Ed Emery, *Twenty-Seven Muwashshahaat and One Zajal by Ibn al-ʿArabī of Murcia* (1165–1240) (London and Zaragoza: School of Oriental and African Studies, 2004). The French scholar and Ibn ʿArabī biographer Claude Addas called attention to the Paris manuscript of *Dīwān al-Maʿārif*, discussed Ibn ʿArabī's introduction to that work, and challenged the common assumption that Ibn ʿArabī was more of a thinker than a poet. Julian Cook and Stephen Hirtenstein have put forth a reconstruction of Ibn ʿArabī's poetic oeuvre in light of the rediscovery of *Dīwān al-Maʿārif*. See Claude Addas, "A propos du dīwān al-maʿārif d'Ibn ʿArabî," *Studia Islamica* 81 (January 1995): 187–95, https://doi.org/10.2307/1596025; *idem*, "Ship of Stone," in *Journey of the Heart*, edited by Johnny Mercer (Oxford: Muhyiddin Ibn ʿArabī Society, 1996): 5–24; *idem*, "L'œuvre poétique d'Ibn ʿArabî et sa réception," *Studia Islamica* 91 (January 2000): 23–38, https://doi.org/10.2307/1596267; Julian Cook and Stephen Hirtenstein, "The Great Dīwān and Its Offspring," *JMIAS* 52 (2012): 33–91. More recently, Moroccan researcher Abdelillah Benarafa has published the detailed study on *Dīwān al-Maʿārif*, "Al-Shiʿr al-ʿirfānī, dirāsa wa taḥqīq fī 'Dīwān al-maʿārif' in *Al-ʿAwda ilā al-matn al-akbārī*," edited by Rizqī bin ʿAwmar and ʿAbd al-Qādir Bilgīth (Damascus: Dār Ninawa, 2018), 83–138. Benarafa's study indicates that an edition of *Dīwān al-Maʿārif* is in the works.

6. For the life, travels, and writings of Ibn ʿArabī, see the biography of the Murcian shaykh by Claude Addas, *Quest for the Red Sulphur: The Life of Ibn ʿArabī*, trans. Peter Kingsley (Cambridge: Islamic Texts Society, 1993). Addas had published an earlier edition in French, *Ibn ʿArabī, ou La quête du soufre rouge* (Paris: Gallimard, 1989), but the 1993 edition has been expanded considerably. The other major biography in English is by Stephen Hirtenstein, *The Unlimited Mercifier: The Spiritual Life and Thought of Ibn ʿArabī* (Oxford: Anqa, 1999), which includes a vividly related and carefully sourced narrative of the shaykh's life interspersed with meditations on his mystical teachings

and experiences. More recently, the Syrian scholar Muḥammad ʿAlī Ḥājj Yūsuf has offered a detailed biography in Arabic: *Shams al-maghrib* [The Sun of the West]: *Sīrat al-shaykh al-akbar Muḥyī al-Dīn Ibn al-ʿArabī wa-madhhabihi* (Aleppo: Fuṣṣilat li-l-Dirāsāt wa-al-Tarjama wa-al-Nashr, 2006). On contentions over Ibn ʿArabī in the centuries following his death, see Alexander D. Knysh, *Ibn ʿArabī in the Later Islamic Tradition: The Making of a Polemical Image in Medieval Islam* (Albany: SUNY Press, 1999).

7. Although some manuscripts vocalize the poetry or at least add vocalization where a word could be read in more than one way, authors, copyists, and publishers rarely vocalize prose, and the manuscripts of *Tarjumān al-ashwāq* do not vocalize the title. In what follows I will refer to the collection of poetry translated and discussed here simply as "the *Tarjumān*."
8. For an in-depth study of the nasib, see Jaroslav Stetkevych, *The Zephyrs of Najd: The Poetics of Nostalgia in the Classical Arabic Nasib* (Bloomington: Indiana University Press, 1993). Although Stetkevych, who expresses irritation with Ibn ʿArabī's commentary, shows little interest in the *Tarjumān* itself, his study illuminates the depth, range, and sensibility of the nasib tradition that informs and animates it.
9. Some urban poets, most famously Abū Nuwās (d. 814), instead of adapting the *aṭlāl* theme to the urban environment, parodied it along with the Bedouin cultures that they reflected originally. Yet this parody did not always entail a rejection of the nasib: indeed, only a poet who has interiorized the motifs and mastered its full range of possibilities would be able to parody it so artfully. In one of Abū Nuwās's most exquisite poems, the poet-lover-urbanite aficionado of the good life and debauchery finds that at the end of his drunken revelry, the singing girls strike up a verse with nasib sentiment and the eyes of his poet and his fellow drinkers grow misty.
10. A few of the poems in the *Tarjumān* reflect the style of garland poetry, albeit within a classical metrical and end-rhyme format rather than stanzaic. The first part of poem 25 and the first part of poem 46 are cases in point.
11. Although the Arabic word *ghazal* is shared by the various traditions, American poets and readers have had their understanding shaped by the formally very different Persian poetry composed by the likes of Rumi and Hafez, Ottoman poets such as Na'ili (d. 1666), and Urdu

poets including Ghalib (d. 1869) and Iqbal (d. 1937). Recent American engagement with non-Arabic ghazal traditions has been robust. Examples include: *Angels Knocking on the Tavern Door: Thirty Poems by Hafez*, trans. Robert Bly and Leonard Lewison (Harper Perennial, 1989); *Ghazals of Ghalib: Versions from Urdu*, Mirza Asadullah Khan Ghalib, Aijaz Ahmad (editor), W. S. Merwin (contributor), Adrienne Rich (contributor), William Stafford (contributor), David Ray (contributor), Thomas Fitzsimmons (contributor), Mark Strand (contributor), William Hunt (contributor) (Oxford University Press India, 1994); and Robin Magowan, *The Garden of Amazement: Scattered Gems after Saeb* (West Brattleboro, VT: Longhouse, 2015). For several years, Coleman Barks's Rumi translations topped the American best-seller lists for poetry, and they remain immensely popular.

12. It was Ibn ʿArabī along with his contemporary, the Cairene poet Ibn al-Fāriḍ (d. 1235), who became most known for integrating the sites of the pilgrimage into the Arabian love poem. *Sessions of the Righteous* offers critical new insight not only on the poets that shaped Ibn ʿArabī's poetics of love most strongly, but also on prior developments in integrating the world of the pilgrimage into love poetry. Compositions by two poets, Sharīf al-Raḍī and Mihyār al-Daylamī—both of whom were major Shiʿite leaders in Baghdad and both of whom were in charge of the largest annual pilgrimage caravan to Mecca—dominate the poems cited by Ibn ʿArabī in *Sessions*. The quotations of their poems in *Sessions* open a window into the poetic imagination that grew up around the hajj in the years prior to Ibn al-Fāriḍ and Ibn ʿArabī. The following verses from Mihyār al-Daylamī, which make up just one of dozens of examples in *Sessions*, center on three of the most prominent stations of the beloved within the *Tarjumān*, Ḥājir, Ḥimā, and Laʿlaʿ:

يَا لَيْلَتِي بِحَاجِرٍ
إِنْ عَادَ مَاضٍ فَارْجَعِي

أَرْضَى بِأَخْبَارِ ٱلرِيَا
حِ وَٱلْبُرُوقِ ٱلْلُمَعِ

وَأَيْنَ مِنْ بَرْقِ ٱلْحِمَى
شَائِمَةٌ بِلَعْلَعِ

O night that I passed in Hājir,
 if the past can return, return

I content myself with reports
 from the wind and lightning shimmers

But where in the flash over Himā
 is a sign for La'la'i?

(*Sessions of the Righteous*
[*MAb* 1:191])

The third major contributor to the *Sessions* imaginary was the Ḥanbalite preacher and author of Baghdad, Abū al-Faraj ibn al-Jawzī (d. 1201), two of whose works Ibn 'Arabī cites. Of special importance to the merging of pilgrimage and the lover's quest was Ibn al-Jawzī's work *The Awakener of Dormant Passion for the Noblest Places* (*Muthīr al-gharām al-sākin ilā ashraf al-amākin*). In it, Ibn al-Jawzī uses the full resources of the erotic poetic tradition to reflect and intensify the longing on the part of Muslims to make the hajj and, for those who have made the hajj, to return to Mecca and its environment after they have returned home from their pilgrimage.

13. Northrop Frye, *Anatomy of Criticism* (Princeton: Princeton University Press, 1957): 249–50. Jonathan Culler integrates Frye's remark into his analysis of the "embarrassment of apostrophe" within post-Romantic poetics. See *The Pursuit of Signs: Semiotics, Literature, Deconstruction* (Ithaca, NY: Cornell University Press, 1981): 135–54. He also notes Geoffrey Hartmann's discussion of the almost-always vocative and optative nature of William Blake's poems to the seasons and the ritual character of whatever descriptive element there is. See Culler, *Pursuit*, 139; Geoffrey Hartman, *Beyond Formalism* (New Haven: Yale University Press, 1959), 193. For a related study, with less focus on the Romantics and apostrophes to nonhuman addressees, see William Water, *Poetry's Touch: On Lyric Address* (Ithaca, NY: Cornell University Press, 2003).
14. For the poetic feature of turning in Ibn 'Arabī 's contemporary, Ibn al-Fāriḍ, see 'Abbās Yūsuf Ḥaddād, *al-Anā fī al-shi'r al-Ṣūfī: Ibn al-Fāriḍ unmūdhajan* [The "I" in Sufi Poetry: the Case of Ibn al- Fāriḍ] (al-Lādhiqīyah, Syria: Dār al-Ḥiwār, 2005), 163–76.
15. For one example, see Henry Corbin, *Creative Imagination in the*

Ṣūfism of Ibn ʿArabī, translated by Ralph Manheim (Princeton University Press, 1969), 138–39.

16. Wolfgang Hermann offers a promising suggestion regarding Niẓām and Qurrat al-ʿAyn: if Niẓām was the daughter of the scholar from Isfahān by a Christian wife, then although she was raised as a member of the family and offered the highest educational possibilities, she would still have been, in legal terms, a *jāriya* and a daughter of the Christian Rūm. See Muḥyiddīn Ibn ʿArabī, *Deuter der Sehnsüchte (Turjuman al-Ashwaq)*, 2 vols., trans. Wolfgang Hermann (Zürich: Edition Shershir, 2013–16), 1:11–13.
17. Classical Arabic poetry redounds with words for "young women," who were, by societal definition, unmarried. Many of the terms indicate that the woman was a virgin. Others were less specific. As with the Hebrew word *almah*, ambiguity in this regard could lead to different interpretations—most famously with the millennia-old debate between Jewish and Christian exegetes around the *almah* that Isaiah predicted would bring forth a messiah. Christian exegetes read the word as indicating a young virgin woman (a prefiguration of the Blessed Virgin), and Jewish exegetes insisted that the word did not refer specifically to a virgin—only to a young woman. Ibn ʿArabī referred to the young woman who confronted him at the Kaʿba as a *jāriya*, a word with a semantic ambivalence most comparable to the English maid/maiden/maidservant/handmaiden. The word *jāriya* denoted a young woman slave, and in that role many would have been household servants. Yet their role was by no means limited to such humble circumstances. Educated and artistically talented *jāriya*s became central actors within elite culture as masters of the poetic and musical repertoire. Some became the equivalent of modern "divas," with large and passionate circles of followers, particularly within urban circles and in the courts of rulers. In addition to taking the role of famous vocalists, lute-players, musical arrangers, and poets in their own right, *jāriya*s took on another distinctive role—that of the pious *jāriya* savant. Such *jāriya*-savants had become a feature in Sufi accounts of earlier saints or "friends of God." The most famous, Rābiʿa al-ʿAdawiyya of Baghdad (lived ca. 800), features in numerous such stories, upbraiding and instructing the great Sufi masters of her time. One particularly renowned Rābiʿa story, which is featured in *The Lives of the Saints* by Ibn ʿArabī's contemporary Farīd al-Dīn ʿAṭṭār,

depicts the Kaʿba itself going out to meet Rābiʿa during her pilgrimage, even as the great Sufi sage of the time is left standing, stunned, where the Kaʿba would normally be. *Farīd al-Dīn ʿAṭṭār's Memorial of God's Friends*, translated and introduced by Paul Losensky (NY: Paulist Press Classics of Western Spirituality, 2009), 100–102. In *Sessions of the Righteous*, Ibn ʿArabī transmitted several accounts of *jāriya* divas, but he also included accounts of *jāriya* savants at the Kaʿba, encountering, humbling, and instructing great Sufi masters such as Junayd (d. 910). Some of these accounts bear striking similarity to the story of his encounter with Qurrat al-ʿAyn, which he also included in *Sessions*. For the accounts of *jāriya* savants and *jāriya* divas, see *Sessions of the Righteous*: *MAb* 1:199–204; 1:222–29 which also includes the story of a master female poet who is also a freewoman and therefore (in accordance with the norms of the time) recites her erotic verses from behind a curtain; 1:317–18; 1:338; 1:348 (on a Rūmī princess-savant and the Kaʿba); 1:389. Of particular relevance to the *Tarjumān* prefaces is the story of Ibn ʿArabī's encounter at the Ka`ba with a voice that shouted out and proceeded to interrogate him on the subject of love and mysticism: *Sessions of the Righteous* (*MAb* 1:255–57). For Ibn ʿArabī's encounter with Qurrat al-ʿAyn at the Kaʿba, see *Sessions of the Righteous* (*MAb* 2:255–59). Some *jāriya* savant accounts retold by Ibn ʿArabī appeared in an earlier work by Ibn al-Jawzī, *Safat al-Safwā* (The Select of the Pure). Ibn ʿArabī mentions that work explicitly in the introduction to *Sessions of the Righteous*, though he also notes his reception of these stories through oral transmission, and he often cites at least the last transmitter in the *isnād* by name.

18. In the *Tarjumān* and Ibn ʿArabī's own autobiographical prefaces and commentary, as well as his remarks on the *Tarjumān* poems in *Sessions of the Righteous*, we can see an Islamicate myth unfolding before our eyes. By "myth," I do not mean a story that is false but one that is more than true in purely biographical or historically verifiable terms, and that in literary and imaginative power extends beyond the range of mere facticity.

19. *Priceless Treasures: A Commentary on Tarjumān al-Ashwāq*. Its full title within the manuscript traditions is *Al-Dhakhā'ir wa al-aʿlāq fī sharḥ tarjumān al-ashwāq*, but late nineteenth- and early twentieth-century printed editions changed the title from *Al-Dhakhā'ir wa*

al-aʿlāq (literally, "Precious Items and Lockets") to *Dhakhāʾir al-aʿlāq* ("Precious Items of the Lockets"), which became the de facto title in the years that followed.

20. "My commentary on these verses was prompted by the request of my dear companions, Badr al-Ḥabashī and Ibn Sawdakīn. They had heard a jurist in the city of Aleppo denying that these verses expressed lordly secrets and divine inspirations, claiming instead that the shaykh who composed them wished to veil their intent out of concern for his reputation as a man of religion and righteousness. I authorized a commentary, and the judge Ibn ʿAdīm read it before an assembly of jurists. When my critic heard it, he repented and renounced casting aspersions upon the verse of ghazal and *tashbīb* composed by Sufis and the divine secrets expressed in them." See the Shuqayrī edition of *Priceless Treasures: Dīwān dhakhāʾir al-aʿlāq*, edited by Muḥammad ʿAlam al-Dīn al-Shuqayrī (al-Haram [Egypt]: al-ʿAyn lil-Dirāsāt wa-al-Buḥūth al-Insāniyya wa-al-Ijtimāʿiyya, 1995), 175–76. The manuscript traditions vary in the placement of these remarks. Some attach them to the Qurrat al-ʿAyn preface, some place them at the beginning of the commentary, some attach them to the end of the commentary (appendix 2).
21. For the possibility that Raymond Llull may have played a role in popularizing themes of Sufi love poetry and Sufi commentary in fifteenth-century Spain, see Luce López Baralt, *San Juan de La Cruz y El Islam* (Mexico City: El Colegio de México, 1985): 369–77. For a close comparison between a poem by John of the Cross and poem 30 of the *Tarjumān*, see Georg Bossong, "Sprache, Mystik, Intertextualität bei Ibn ʿArabī und San Juan de la Cruz," in Katherina Maier Troxler and Constantino Maider, eds., *Fictio Poetica: Studi italiani i ispanici in onore di Georges Güntert* (Florence: Franco Cesati, 1998): 141–67. For a recent close study of John's poetry and commentaries, see Bernard McGinn, *The Presence of God: A History of Christian Mysticism*, vol. 6, part 2: *Mysticism in the Golden Age of Spain (1500–1650)* (New York: Crossroads, 2017): 230–45.
22. The saying, known as "the hadith of supererogatory devotions" (*ḥadīth al-nawāfil*), is well attested in such classical hadith compilations as *Saḥīḥ al-Bukhārī*. For sources for the hadith, see William Graham, *Divine Word and Prophetic Word in Early Islam* (Paris: Mouton, 1977), 173–74. Ibn ʿArabī included the hadith in his own

collection of divine sayings, which he collected from the religious scholars of his time through personal chains of oral transmission. See *Divine Sayings: The Mishkāt al-Anwār of Ibn ʿArabī,* Arabic text and English translation by Stephen Hirtenstein and Martin Notcutt (Oxford: Anqa, 2004), p. 88 (translation); p. 51 (Arabic text). For a contextualization of this and other key hadiths in the writings of Ibn ʿArabī, see James Morris, *The Reflective Heart: Discovering Spiritual Intelligence in Ibn ʿArabī's Meccan Illuminations* (Louisville, KY: Fons Vitae, 2005), 163–78.

23. For a discussion of the complete human being and the mirror image in the mystical thought of Ibn ʿArabī, see Michael Sells, *Mystical Languages of Unsaying* (Chicago: University of Chicago Press, 1994), chapter 4 ("Identity Shift and Meaning Event"), 63–89.
24. For a biography of Ibn al-Fāriḍ, see Th. Emil Homerin, *From Arab Poet to Muslim Saint: Ibn Al-Fāriḍ, His Verse, and His Shrine* (Columbia: University of South Carolina Press, 1994).
25. A critical study of the *Tarjumān*'s poetry can be found in Sulaymān ʿAṭṭār, *Al-Khayāl wa-al-shiʿr fī taṣawwuf al-Andalus: Ibn ʿArabī, Abū al-Ḥasan al-Shūshtarī, wa-Ibn Khamīs al-Tilimsānī* (Cairo: Dār al-Maʿārif, 1981).
26. The meters employed in the *Tarjumān* are, by order of frequency: Ṭawīl (19), Kāmil (11), Basīṭ (9), Mutaqārib (6), Ramal (6), Rajaz (5), Khafīf (3), Wāfir (2), Sarīʿ (1). The meter-poem match is as follows:

Ṭawīl	3, 4, 7, 11, 12, 14, 21, 32, 35, 36, 38, 43, 50, 51, 52, 53, 55, 57, 58
Kāmil	8, 9, 13, 18, 22, 24, 26, 27, 29, 34, 56
Basīṭ	2, 6, 10, 17, 39, 46, 49, 60
Mutaqārib	16, 23, 31, 41, 54, 59
Ramal	1, 5, 15, 30, 37, 42
Rajaz	19, 25, 28, 45, 48
Khafīf	20, 40, 44
Wāfir	33, 61
Sarīʿ	47

Poem 30 has also been ascribed the closely related Madīd meter, and poem 61 to the Hazaj meter. See, for example, *Dīwān Dhakhāʾir al-Aʿlāq* (Priceless Treasures), edited by Muḥammad ʿAlam al-Dīn al-Shuqayrī (al-Haram [Egypt]: al-ʿAyn lil-Dirāsāt wa-al-Buḥūth al-Insāniyya wa-al-Ijtimāʿiyya, 1995), which provides the meter identification as the beginning of each poem.

27. For a translation that attempts to re-create the Arabic meters within English, see *The Seven Golden Odes of Pagan Arabia Known Also as the Moallakat*, translated from the original Arabic by Lady Anne Blunt, done into English verse by Wilfrid Scawen Blunt (London, 1903).
28. For examples of the intensive use of *jinās* in the *Tarjumān*, see the notes to poems 4 and 42.
29. For a personal chronicle of the arduous pilgrimage journey to Mecca by an Andalusī acquaintance of Ibn ʿArabī, see Ibn Jubayr, *The Travels of Ibn Jubayr: A Medieval Spanish Muslim Visits Makkah, Madinah, Egypt, Cities of the Middle East and Sicily*, trans. Roland Broadhurst (New Delhi: Goodword Books, 2001). Ibn Jubayr traveled the same pilgrimage route from Iraq to Medina and Mecca as Ibn ʿArabī. See in particular his depictions of stations on the pilgrimage route mentioned within the *Tarjumān*: page 213 on Ḥājir, 214 on Zarūd, 215 on al-ʿUdhayb, and 218 on al-Bāriq.
30. *Sessions of the Righteous* (*MAb* 2:476). The poem also appears in *Dīwān al-Maʿārif*, though with a different introductory comment: "The spirit is Greek (*yunānī*) and the thought-flash (*al-khāṭir*) is Arab." See Benarafa, "Al-Shiʿr al-ʿirfānī," 116.

Appendix 1: Niẓām Preface

1. This preface begins with the kind of formal Islamic prologue that was standard for books and treatises. Such prologues had two parts, one offering praise to God and the second offering praise to the prophet Muḥammad. Yet such prologues were more than pious formalities. The manner in which the author praised God and the Prophet previewed the subject matter of the book in question. Thus, in the preface to the *Tarjumān*, Ibn ʿArabī praises God as both the beautiful and the lover of beauty, then praises the beauty of the world that reflects the beauty of its creator, and, finally, refers to lovers as being annihilated in contemplation of that beauty. The second part of the prologue asks blessings for Muḥammad, who manifested the beauty of God most perfectly, with special attention to the beauty of his exemplary life.

2. "Intimates": *'ārifin* (literally, those who know someone or something in a personal, intimate, or experiential way).
3. Ibn 'Arabī gives the fuller name of the shaykh as Makīn al-Dīn Abū Shujā' Ẓāhir bin Rustam bin Abī al-Rajā al-Isbahānī." "Isbahān" was a common alternative spelling for Isfahān. "God rest his soul" (the idiomatic English equivalent of *raḥimahu allāh ta'ālā*). By adding this expression after the name, Ibn 'Arabī indicates that Makīn al-Dīn was deceased at the time he composed this preface. Ibn 'Arabī repeats the expression a few lines later after mentioning Makīn al-Dīn again, a repetition I have omitted for stylistic reasons.
4. Abū 'Isā al-Tirmidhī (d. 892) was the author of one of the six major Sunni hadith collections, *al-Jāmi' al-ṣaḥīḥ*. He is not to be confused with al-Ḥakīm al-Tirmidhī (d. 869), a Sufi author whose works played a major role in Ibn 'Arabī's writings on saintship.
5. "*Al-balad al-amīn*" is a Qur'anic epithet for Mecca and its environs.
6. "Sun Splendor": literally, "Essence of the Sun and Splendor" (*'Ayn al-Shams wa al-Bahā'*)
7. "The scholars, worshippers, itinerants, and renunciates": *'ālimāt, 'ābidāt, sā'iḥāt, zāhidāt.*
8. "Stunned into silence": *a'jazat.* This word evokes the doctrine of the inimitability of the Qur'an with the suggestion that Niẓām's speech, like God's word in the Qur'an, reduces to silence anyone who would try to imitate it.
9. Qass bin Sa'da was known as a Christian priest and orator praised by the prophet Muḥammad. Some of the oratorical locutions attributed to Ibn Sa'da show strong stylistic similarities to early Meccan suras of the Qur'an. Ma'n bin Zā'ida was a noted Muslim warrior during the Abbasid period. Samaw'al was a Jewish Arabic poet of the pre-Islamic era renowned for his loyalty. Ibn 'Arabī's choice of a Christian, Muslim, and Jew as those exceeded by Niẓām would seem to echo themes in poems 2 and 11 and, as Hermann suggests (vol. 1, 42n24), was likely intentional.
10. "In this volume": *fī hādha al-juz'*. Ibn 'Arabī may be referring here to the *Tarjumān* as "one volume" of his poetic oeuvre or "Greater Dīwān."
11. "Fitting": *lā'iq.* This particular Arabic word appears here as well as in the Qurrat al-'Ayn preface. Here the poet defends his verses as having

been expressed in a fitting manner. In the Qurrat al-ʿAyn preface, the young woman concludes each of her criticisms by asking if the verse in question was a fitting thing for a shaykh like Ibn ʿArabī to compose.

12. "The virgin most pure": *al-baytūl al-aʿdhrāʾ*. Literally, "virgin, virgin": the second word for virgin, *aʿdhrāʾ*, is employed in the hadith collections to refer to the virgin Maryam, the mother of Jesus.
13. "Treasures and Lockets": *al-dhakhāʾir wa al-aʿlāq*, the exact phrase that would form the title for Ibn ʿArabī's commentary. Elsewhere I use the shortened form *Priceless Treasures* to refer to the commentary itself as a text.
14. Throughout this section of the preface, Ibn ʿArabī has referred to himself using a conventional, formal plural. Most translators have taken "our custom" to refer to the manner in which Sufis or pious renunciates composed, quoted, employed or interpreted amatory verses, but it could also be translated as "my custom" and thereby refer to Ibn ʿArabī's own accustomed practices in regard to ghazal and nasib.
15. *The end for us is better than the beginning*: a near-verbatim quote from Q 93:4, "And the end for you is better than the beginning."
16. Q 35:14.

Appendix 2: Qurrat al-ʿAyn Preface

1. The *jāriya* criticizes Ibn ʿArabī for questioning whether or not the loved one knew whose heart they had possessed, pointing out that anyone who has something knows what it is they have. The critique is based upon the Arabic word family *ʿ/r/f*, which indicates a particular kind of knowing, a personal, experiential knowing (similar to the French *connaître*) that contrasts with *ʿ/l/m*, which designates a more objective kind of knowledge (as with the French *savoir*). The lover and mystic have knowledge (*maʿrifa, ʿirfān*) in this personal sense. So of course they know whose heart they have possessed, she explains. On the other hand, Ibn ʿArabī's exclamation "Would I knew" is indeed an appropriate expression of his own lack of *maʿrifa*.
2. "A sincere tongue": *lisānu sidqin*, a Qur'anic phrase. In Q 19:50, the divine speaker states that he has bestowed a sincere tongue on Ibrāhīm, Iṣḥāq, and Yaʿqūb (Abraham, Isaac, and Jacob). In Q 26:84, Abraham prays to be made a paradigm of sincere speech for posterity.
3. Although Ibn ʿArabī has introduced the *jāriya* as an exemplar of

modesty, wit, and tact, she proceeds through her rebuke of each of the four verses with brutal frankness.

4. Ibn ʿArabī employs the word "cousin" (*bint al-khāla*) as a form of polite address to a young woman who has no family ties to him.
5. "Comfort of the Eye": *qurrat al-ʿayn*. The expression could also be rendered "balm of the eye," "cooling of the eye," "solace of the eye," "joy of the eye." It conveys a combination of joy and relief that cannot always be reduced to one or another of the possible English renditions. The expression or equivalents to it appear several times in the Qur'an. In Q 25:74, there is reference to those who pray, "lord, grant us wives and children who will be a comfort for our eyes." In a more universal context (Q 32:17), the divine voice states that "no soul knows how much contentment of the eye (*qurrat al-ʿayn*) is secretly stored up as a reward for what it does." See also Q 33:51: "That is likely to comfort your eye, and you will grieve no more." When the virgin Maryam seeks refuge from her birth pangs near a palm tree, a voice calls to her telling her that a spring has been opened up and the palm tree is bearing dates, and calls her to "eat, drink, and let your eye be cooled" (Q 19:26).

   Most important for this preface are the Qur'anic passages regarding the infant Mūsā. After Musa's mother places him in an ark and sets him loose on the waters, he is discovered by members of Pharaoh's household. At that point (Q 28:9), Pharaoh's wife tells her spouse not to kill the infant, "for he will be a comfort for the eyes—for me and for you" (*qurrat al-ʿayn lī wa laka*). In the end, Mūsā is returned to his distraught mother. At that point, the divine speaker addresses Mūsā: "We returned you to your mother that her eye might be comforted and she grieve no more" (Q 20:40). When Ibn ʿArabī responds to Qurrat al-ʿAyn by saying "for me," his response can be read a kind of proposal or flirtation, but it is also a quote from the Qur'an that would, if read according to the implicit analogy it evokes, place Qurrat al-ʿAyn in the position of Mūsā and Ibn ʿArabī in the position of Pharaoh's wife.
6. "Subtleties of mystical knowings": *laṭāʾif al-maʿārif*. I have used "knowings" here as a substantive in a manner parallel to Julian of Norwich's "showings." The two terms differ in important senses, of course, but both use a substantive gerund to shake loose aspects of intimacy that more common English terms lack.

The Lockert Library of Poetry in Translation

George Seferis: Collected Poems, 1924–1955, translated, edited, and introduced by Edmund Keeley and Philip Sherrard

Collected Poems of Lucio Piccolo, translated and edited by Brian Swann and Ruth Feldman

C. P. Cavafy: Collected Poems, translated by Edmund Kelley and Philip Sherrard and edited by George Savidis

Benny Andersen: Selected Poems, translated by Alexander Taylor

Selected Poetry of Andrea Zanzotto, edited and translated by Ruth Feldman and Brian Swann

Poems of René Char, translated and annotated by Mary Ann Caws and Jonathan Griffin†

Selected Poems of Tudor Arghezi, translated by Michael Impey and Brian Swann

"The Survivor" and Other Poems, by Tadeusz Różewicz, translated and introduced by Magnus J. Krynski and Robert A. Maguire

"Harsh World" and Other Poems, by Angel González, translated by Donald D. Walsh

Ritsos in Parentheses, translated and introduced by Edmund Keeley

Salamander: Selected Poems of Robert Marteau, translated by Anne Winters

Angelos Sikelianos: Selected Poems, translated and introduced by Edmund Keeley and Philip Sherrard†

Dante's "Rime," translated by Patrick S. Diehl

Selected Later Poems of Marie Luise Kaschnitz, translated by Lisel Mueller

Osip Mandelstam's "Stone," translated and introduced by Robert Tracy†

The Dawn Is Always New: Selected Poetry of Rocco Scotellaro, translated by Ruth Feldman and Brian Swann

Sounds, Feelings, Thoughts: Seventy Poems by Wisława Szymborska, translated and introduced by Magnus J. Krynski and Robert A. Maguire

George Seferis: Collected Poems, 1924–1955, Expanded Edition [bilingual], translated, edited, and introduced by Edmund Keeley and Philip Sherrard

The Man I Pretend to Be: "The Colloquies" and Selected Poems of Guido Gozzano, translated and edited by Michael Palma, with an introductory essay by Eugenio Montale

† Out of print

D'Après Tout: Poems by Jean Follain, translated by Heather McHugh†
Songs of Something Else: Selected Poems of Gunnar Ekelöf, translated by Leonard Nathan and James Larson
The Little Treasury of One Hundred People, One Poem Each, compiled by Fujiwara No Sadaie and translated by Tom Galt†
The Ellipse: Selected Poems of Leonardo Sinisgalli, translated by W. S. Di Pietro†
The Difficult Days by Roberto Sosa, translated by Jim Lindsey
Hymns and Fragments by Friedrich Hölderin, translated and introduced by Richard Sieburth
The Silence Afterwards: Selected Poems of Rolf Jacobsen, translated and edited by Roger Greenwald†
Rilke: Between Roots, selected poems rendered from the German by Rika Lesser†
In the Storm of Roses: Selected Poems, by Ingeborg Bachmann, translated, edited, and introduced by Mark Anderson†
Birds and Other Relations: Selected Poetry of Dezső Tandori, translated by Bruce Berlind
Brocade River Poems: Selected Works of the Tang Dynasty Courtesan Xue Tao, translated and introduced by Jeanne Larsen
The True Subject: Selected Poems of Faiz Ahmed Faiz, translated by Naomi Lazard
My Name on the Wind: Selected Poems of Diego Valeri, translated by Michael Palma
Aeschylus: The Suppliants, translated by Peter Burian
Foamy Sky: The Major Poems of Miklós Radnóti, selected and translated by Zsuzsanna Ozsváth and Frederick Turner†
C. P. Cavafy: Collected Poems, Revised Edition, translated and introduced by Edmund Keeley and Philip Sherrard, edited by George Savidis
La Fontaine's Bawdy: Of Libertines, Louts, and Lechers, translated by Norman R. Shapiro†
A Child Is Not a Knife: Selected Poems of Göran Sonnevi, translated and edited by Rika Lesser
George Seferis: Collected Poems, Revised Edition [English only], translated, edited, and introduced by Edmund Keeley and Philip Sherrard
Selected Poems of Shmuel HaNagid, translated by Peter Cole
The Late Poems of Meng Chiao, translated by David Hinton
Leopardi: Selected Poems, translated and introduced by Eamon Grennan
The Complete Odes and Satires of Horace, translated with introduction and notes by Sidney Alexander
Through Naked Branches: Selected Poems of Tarjei Vesaas, translated and edited by Roger Greenwald†

Selected Poems of Solomon Ibn Gabirol, translated by Peter Cole
Puerilities: Erotic Epigrams of "The Greek Anthology," translated by Daryl Hine
Night Journey by María Negroni, translated by Anne Twitty
The Poetess Counts to 100 and Bows Out: Selected Poems by Ana Enriqueta Terán, translated by Marcel Smith
Nothing Is Lost: Selected Poems by Edvard Kocbek, translated by Michael Scammell and Veno Taufer, and introduced by Michael Scammell, with a foreword by Charles Simic
The Complete Elegies of Sextus Propertius, translated with introduction and notes by Vincent Katz
Knowing the East, by Paul Claudel, translated with introduction and notes by James Lawler
In Hora Mortis/Under the Iron of the Moon: Poems, by Thomas Bernhard, translated by James Reidel
Enough to Say It's Far: Selected Poems of Pak Chaesam, translated by David R. McCann and Jiwon Shin
The Greener Meadow: Selected Poems by Luciano Erba, translated by Peter Robinson
The Dream of the Poem: Hebrew Poetry from Muslim and Christian Spain, 950–1492, translated, edited, and introduced by Peter Cole
The Collected Lyric Poems of Luís de Camões, translated by Landeg White
C. P. Cavafy: Collected Poems, Bilingual Edition, translated by Edmund Keeley and Philip Sherrard, edited by George Savidis, with a new preface by Robert Pinsky
Poems Under Saturn: Poèmes saturniens, by Paul Verlaine, translated and with an introduction by Karl Kirchwey
Final Matters: Selected Poems, 2004–2010, by Szilárd Borbély, translated by Ottilie Mulzet
Selected Poems of Giovanni Pascoli, translated by Taije Silverman with Marina Della Putta Johnston
After Callimachus: Poems, by Stephanie Burt, with a foreword by Mark Payne
Dear Ms. Schubert: Poems by Ewa Lipska, translated by Robin Davidson and Ewa Elżbieta Nowakowska, with a foreword by Adam Zagajewski
The Translator of Desires by Muhyiddin Ibn 'Arabi, translated by Michael Sells